Who Wrote the Bible?

Who Wrote the Bible?

A Book for the People

Washington Gladden

WAKING LION PRESS

ISBN 1-60096-514-8

Published by Waking Lion Press, an imprint of The Editorium

The Editorium, LLC
West Valley City, UT 84128-3917
wakinglionpress.com
wakinglion@editorium.com

Contents

Chapter 1

A Look into the Hebrew Bible

The aim of this volume is to put into compact and popular form, for the benefit of intelligent readers, the principal facts upon which scholars are now generally agreed concerning the literary history of the Bible. The doctrines taught in the Bible will not be discussed; its claims to a supernatural origin will not be the principal matter of inquiry; the book will concern itself chiefly with those purely natural and human agencies which have been employed in writing, transcribing, editing, preserving, transmitting, translating, and publishing the Bible.

The writer of this book has no difficulty in believing that the Bible contains supernatural elements. He is ready to affirm that other than natural forces have been employed in producing it. It is to these superhuman elements in it that reference and appeal are most frequently made. But the Bible has a natural history also. It is a book among books. It is a phenomenon among phenomena. Its origin and growth in this world can be studied as those of any other natural object can be studied. The old apple-tree growing in my garden is the witness to me of some transcendent truths, the shrine of mysteries that I cannot unravel. What the life is that was hidden in the seed from which it sprang, and that has shaped all its growth, coordinating the forces of nature, and producing this individual form and this particular variety of fruit,—this I do not know. There are questions here that no man of science can answer. Life in the seed of the apple as well as in the soul of man is a mystery. But there are some things about the apple-tree that may be known. I may know—if any one has been curious enough to keep the record—when the seed was planted, when the shoot first appeared above the ground, how many branches it had when it was five years old, how high it was when it was ten years old, when this limb and that twig were added, when the first blossom appeared, when that branch was grafted and those others were trimmed off. All this knowledge I may have gained; and in setting forth these facts, or such as these, concerning the natural history of the tree, I do not assume that I am telling all about the life that is in it. In like manner we may study the origin and growth of the Bible without attempting to decide the deeper questions concerning the inspiration of its writers and the meaning of the truths they reveal.

That the Bible has a natural as well as a supernatural history is everywhere assumed upon its pages. It was written as other books are written, and it was preserved and transmitted as other books are preserved and transmitted. It did not come into being in any such marvelous way as that in which Joseph Smith's "Book of Mormon," for example, is said to have been produced. The story is, that an angel appeared to Smith and told him where he would find this book; that he went to the spot designated, and found in a stone box a volume six inches thick, com-

posed of thin gold plates, eight inches by seven, held together by three gold rings; that these plates were covered
with writing in the "Reformed Egyptian" tongue, and
that with this book were "the Urim and the Thummim,"
a pair of supernatural spectacles, by means of which he
was able to read *and translate* this "Reformed Egyptian"
language. This is the sort of story which has been believed, in this nineteenth century, by tens of thousands
of Mormon votaries. Concerning the books of the Bible
no such astonishing stories are told. Nevertheless some
good people seem inclined to think that if such stories
are not told, they might well be; they imagine that the
Bible must have originated in a manner purely miraculous; and though they know very little about its origin,
they conceive of it as a book that was written in heaven
in the English tongue, divided there into chapters and
verses, with head lines and reference marks, printed in
small pica, bound in calf, and sent down to earth by angels in its present form. What I desire to show is, that
the work of putting the Bible into its present form was
not done in heaven, but on earth; that it was not done by
angels, but by men; that it was not done all at once, but a
little at a time, the work of preparing and perfecting it extending over several centuries, and employing the labors
of many men in different lands and long-divided generations. And this history of the Bible as a book, and of the
natural and human agencies employed in producing it,
will prove, I trust, of much interest to those who care to
study it.

Mr. Huxley has written a delightful treatise on "A
Piece of Chalk," and another on "The Crayfish;" a French
writer has produced an entertaining volume entitled

"The Story of a Stick;" the books of the Bible, considered from a scientific or bibliographical point of view, should repay our study not less richly than such simple, natural objects.

A great amount of study has been expended of late on the Scriptures, and the conclusions reached by this study are of immense importance. What is called the Higher Criticism has been busy scanning these old writings, and trying to find out all about them. What is the Higher Criticism? It is the attempt to learn from the Scriptures themselves the truth about their origin. It consists in a careful study of the language of the books, of the manners and customs referred to in them, of the historical facts mentioned by them; it compares part with part, and book with book, to discover agreements, if they exist, and discrepancies, that they may be reconciled. This Higher Criticism has subjected these old writings to such an analysis and inspection as no other writings have ever undergone. Some of this work has undoubtedly been destructive. It has started out with the assumption that these books are in no respect different from other sacred books; that they are no more a revelation from God than the Zendavesta or the Nibelungen Lied is a revelation from God; and it has bent its energies to discrediting, in every way, the veracity and the authority of our Scriptures. But much of this criticism has been thoroughly candid and reverent, even conservative in its temper and purpose. It has not been unwilling to look at the facts; but it has held toward the Bible a devout and sympathetic attitude; it believes it to contain, as no other book in the world contains, the message of God to men; and it has only sought to learn from the Bible itself how that message has been conveyed.

It is this conservative criticism whose leadership will be followed in these studies. No conclusions respecting the history of these writings will be stated which are not accepted by conservative scholars. Nevertheless it must be remembered that the results of conservative scholarship have been very imperfectly reported to the laity of the churches. Many facts about the Bible are now known by intelligent ministers of which their congregations do not hear. An anxious and not unnatural feeling has prevailed that the faith of the people in the Bible would be shaken if the facts were known. The belief that the truth is the safest thing in the world, and that the things which cannot be shaken will remain after it is all told, has led to the preparation of this volume.

I have no doubt, however, that some of the statements which follow will fall upon some minds with a shock of surprise. The facts which will be brought to light will conflict very sharply with some of the traditional theories about the Bible. Some of my readers may be inclined to fear that the foundations of faith are giving way. Let me, at the outset, request all such to suspend their judgment and read the book through before they come to such a conclusion. Doubtless it will be necessary to make some readjustment of theories; to look at the Bible less as a miraculous and more as a spiritual product; to put less emphasis upon the letter and more upon the spirit; but after all this is done it may appear that the Bible is worth more to us than it ever was before, because we have learned how rightly to value it.

The word "Bible" is not a biblical word. The Old Testament writings were in the hands of the men who wrote the books of the New Testament, but they do not call these writings the Bible; they name them the Scriptures, the Holy Scriptures, the Sacred Writings, or else they refer to them under the names that were given to specific parts of them, as the Law, the Prophets, or the Psalms. Our word Bible comes from a word which began to be applied to the sacred writings as a whole about four hundred years after Christ. It is a Greek plural noun, meaning the books, or the little books. These writings were called by this plural name for about eight hundred years; it was not till the thirteenth century that they began to be familiarly spoken of as a single book. This fact, of itself, is instructive. For though a certain spiritual unity does pervade these sacred writings, yet they are a collection of books, rather than one book. The early Christians, who honored and prized them sufficiently, always spoke of them as "The Books," rather than as "The Book,"—and their name was more accurate than ours.

The names Old and New Testament are Bible words; that is to say we find the names in our English Bibles, though they are not used to describe these books. Paul calls the old dispensation the old covenant; and that phrase came into general use among the early Christians as contrasted with the Christian dispensation which they called the new covenant; therefore Greek-speaking Christians used to talk about "the books of the old covenant," and "the books of the new covenant;" and by and by they shortened the phrase and sometimes called the two collections simply "Old Covenant" and "New Covenant." When the Latin-speaking Christians began to use the same terms, they translated the Greek word "covenant" by the word "testament" which means a will, and which does not fairly convey the sense of the Greek word. And so it was that these two collections of sacred writings began to be called The Old Testament and The New Testament. It is the former of these that we are first to study.

When Jesus Christ was on the earth he often quoted in his discourses from the Jewish Scriptures, and referred to them in his conversations. His apostles and the other New Testament writers also quote freely from the same Scriptures, and books of the early Christian Fathers are full of references to them. What were these Jewish Scriptures?

At the time when our Lord was on the earth, the sacred writings of the Jews were collected in two different forms. The Palestinian collection, so called, was written in the Hebrew language, and the Alexandrian collection, called the Septuagint, in the Greek. For many years a large colony of devout and learned Jews had lived in Alexandria; and as the Greek language was spoken there, and had become their common speech, they translated their sacred writings into Greek. This translation soon came into general use, because there were everywhere many Jews who knew Greek well enough but knew no Hebrew at all. When our Lord was on earth, the Hebrew was a dead language; it may have been the language of the temple, as Latin is now the language of the Roman Catholic mass; but the common people did not understand it; the vernacular of the Palestinian Jews was the Aramaic, a language similar to the Hebrew, sometimes called the later Hebrew, and having some such relation to it as the English has to the German tongue. There is some dispute as to the time when the Jews lost the use of their own language and adopted the Aramaic; many of the Jewish historians hold the view that the people who came back from the captivity to Jerusalem had learned to use the Aramaic as their common speech, and that the Hebrew Scriptures had to be interpreted when they were read to them. Others think that this change in language took place a little later, and that it resulted in great measure from the close intercourse of the Jews with the peoples round about them in Palestine, most of whom used the Aramaic. At any rate the change had taken place before the coming of Christ, so that no Hebrew was then spoken familiarly in Palestine. When "the Hebrew tongue" is mentioned in the New Testament it is the Aramaic that is meant, and not the ancient Hebrew. The Greek, on the other hand, was a living language; it was spoken on the streets and in the markets everywhere, and many Jews understood it almost as well as they did their Aramaic vernacular, just as many of the people of Constantinople and the Levant now speak French more fluently than their native tongues. The Greek version of the Scriptures was, for this reason, more freely used by the Jews even in Palestine than the Hebrew original; it was from the Septuagint that Christ and his apostles made most of their quotations. Out of three hundred and fifty citations in the New Testament from the Old Testament writings about three hundred appear to be directly from the Greek version made at Alexandria. Between these two collections of sacred writings, the one written in Hebrew, then a dead language, and the other in Greek,—the one used by scholars only, and the other by the common people,—there were some important differences, not only in the phraseology and in the arrangement of the books, but in the contents themselves. Of these I shall speak more fully in the following chapters. It is to the Hebrew collection, which is the original of these writings, and from which our English Old Testament was translated, that we shall now give our attention. What were these Hebrew Scriptures of which all the writers of the New Testament knew, and from which they sometimes directly quote?

The contents of this collection were substantially if not exactly the same as those of our Old Testament, but they were arranged in very different order. Indeed they were regarded as three distinct groups of writings, rather than as one book, and the three groups were of different degrees of sacredness and authority. Two of these divisions are frequently referred to in the New Testament, as The Law and The Prophets; and the threefold division is doubtfully hinted at in Luke xxiv. 44, where our Lord speaks of the predictions concerning himself which are found in the Law and the Prophets and in the Psalms.

The first of these holy books of the Jews was, then, *the Law* contained in the first five books of our Bible, known among us as the Pentateuch, and called by the Jews sometimes simply "The Law," and sometimes "The Law of Moses." This was supposed to be the oldest portion of their Scriptures, and was by them regarded as much more sacred and authoritative than any other portion. To Moses, they, said, God spake face to face; to the other holy men much less distinctly. Consequently their appeal is most often to the law of Moses.

The group of writings known as "The Prophets" is subdivided into the Earlier and the Later Prophets. *The Earlier Prophets* comprise Joshua, the Judges, the two books of Samuel, counted as one, and the two books of the Kings, counted also as one. *The Later Prophets* comprise Isaiah, Jeremiah, Ezekiel, and the twelve Minor Prophets, the last books in our Old Testament,—Hosea, Joel, Amos, Obadiah, Jonah, Micah, Nahum, Habakkuk, Zephaniah, Haggai, Zechariah, and Malachi. These twelve *were counted as one book;* so that there were four volumes of the earlier and four of the later prophets. Why the Jews should have called Joshua, Judges, Samuel, and the Kings books of the Prophets is not clear; perhaps because they were supposed to have been written by prophets; perhaps because prophets have a conspicuous place in their histories. This portion of the Hebrew Scriptures, containing the four historical books named and the fifteen prophetical books (reckoned, however, as four), was regarded by the Jews as standing next in sacredness and value to the book of the Law.

The third group of their Scriptures was known among them as Kethubim, or Writings, simply. Sometimes, possibly, they called it The Psalms, because the book of the Psalms was the initial book of the collection. It consisted of the Psalms, the Proverbs, Job, the Song of Solomon, Ruth, Lamentations, Ecclesiastes, Esther, Daniel, Ezra, Nehemiah, and the Chronicles. This group of writings was esteemed by the Jews as less sacred and authoritative than either of the other two groups; the authors were supposed to have had a smaller measure of inspiration. Respecting two or three of these books there was also some dispute among the rabbis, as to their right to be regarded as sacred Scripture.

Such, then, were the Hebrew Scriptures in the days of our Lord, and such was the manner of their arrangement.

They had, indeed, other books of a religious character, to which reference is sometimes made in the books of the

Bible. In Numbers xxi. 14, 15, we have a brief war song quoted from "The Book of the Wars of Jehovah," a collection of which we have no other knowledge. In Joshua x. 13, the story of the sun standing still over Gibeon is said to have been quoted from "The Book of Jasher," and in 2 Samuel i. 18, the beautiful "Song of the Bow," written by David on the death of Saul and Jonathan, is said to be contained in the "Book of Jasher." It is evident that this must have been a collection of lyrics celebrating some of the great events of Hebrew history. The title seems to mean "The Book of the Just." The exploits of the worthies of Israel probably furnished its principal theme.

In 1 Chronicles xxix. 29, we read: "Now the acts of David the king, first and last, behold they are written in the History of Samuel the Seer, and in the History of Nathan the Prophet, and in the History of Gad the Seer." There is no reason to doubt that the first named of these is the history contained in the books of Samuel in our Bible; but the other two books are lost. We have another reference to the "History of Nathan," in 2 Chronicles ix. 29,— the concluding words of the sketch of King Solomon's life. "Now the rest of the acts of Solomon, first and last, are they not written in the History of Nathan the Prophet, and in the Prophecy of Abijah the Shilonite, and in the Visions of Iddo the Seer concerning Jeroboam the son of Nebat?" Here are two more books of which we have no other knowledge; their titles quoted upon the page of this chronicle are all that is left of them. A similar reference, in the last words of the sketch of Solomon's son Rehoboam, gives us our only knowledge of the "Histories of Shemaiah the Prophet."

In the Kings and in the Chronicles, reference is repeatedly made to the "Books of the Chronicles of the Kings of Israel," and the "Books of the Chronicles of the Kings of Judah," under which titles volumes that are now lost are brought to our notice. Undoubtedly much of the history in the biblical books of Kings and Chronicles was derived from these ancient annals. They are the sources from which the writers of these books drew their materials.

We are also told in 2 Chronicles xxvi. 22, that Isaiah wrote a history of the "Acts of Uzziah," which is wholly lost.

Other casual references are made to historical writings of various sorts, composed by prophets and seers, and thus apparently accredited by the biblical writers as authoritative utterances of divine truth. Why were they suffered to perish? Has not Emerson certified us that

"One accent of the Holy Ghost
The heedless world has never lost"?

But this is a fond exaggeration. Mr. Emerson was certainly not himself inspired when he uttered it. Many and many an accent of the Holy Ghost has been lost by this heedless world. And it is not at all improbable that some of these histories of Nathan and Gad and Shemaiah held vital and precious truth,—truth that the world has needed. The very fact that they are hopelessly lost raises some curious questions about the method of revelation. Is it to be supposed that the Providence which suffers whole books to be lost by men would infallibly guarantee those that remain against errors in the copies, and other imperfections? As a matter of fact, we know that He has not so protected any of them.

Still I doubt not that Providence has kept for us the best of this Hebrew literature. To say that it is the best literature that the world has produced is to say very little. It is separated widely from all other sacred writings. Its constructive ideas are as far above those of the other books of religion as the heavens are above the earth. I pity the man who has had the Bible in his hand from his infancy, and who has learned in his maturer years something of the literature of the other religions, but who now needs to have this statement verified. True it is that we find pure maxims, elevated thoughts, genuine faith, lofty morality, in many of the Bibles of the other races. True it is that in some of them visions are vouchsafed us of the highest truths of religion, of the very substance of the gospel of the Son of God. But when we take the sacred books of the other religions in their entirety, and compare them with the sacred writings of the Hebrews, the superiority of these in their fundamental ideas, in the conceptions that dominate them, in the grand uplifting visions and purposes that vitalize them, can be felt by any man who has any discernment of spiritual realities. It is in these great ideas that the value of these writings consists, and not in any petty infallibility of phrase, or inerrancy of statement. They are the record, as no other book in the world is a record, of that increasing purpose of God which runs through the ages. I hope that it will appear as the result of our studies, that one may continue to reverence the Scriptures as containing a unique and special revelation from God to men, and yet clearly see and frankly acknowledge the facts concerning their origin, and the human and fallible elements in them, which are not concealed, but lie upon their very face.

Chapter 2

What Did Moses Write?

We are now to study the first five books of the Bible, known as the Pentateuch. This word "Pentateuch" is not in the Bible; it is a Greek word signifying literally the Five-fold Work; from *penta*, five, and *teuchos*, which in the later Greek means roll or volume.

The Jews in the time of our Lord always considered these five books as one connected work; they called the whole sometimes "Torah," or "The Law," sometimes "The Law of Moses," sometimes "The Five-fifths of the Law." It was originally one book, and it is not easy to determine at what time its division into five parts took place.

Later criticism is also inclined to add to the Pentateuch the Book of Joshua, and to say that the first six books of the Bible were put into their present form by the same hand. "The Hexateuch," or Six-fold Work, has taken the place in these later discussions of the Pentateuch, or Five-fold Work. Doubtless there is good reason for the new classification, but it will be more convenient to begin with the traditional division and speak first of the five books reckoned by the later Jews as the "Torah," or the Five-fifths of the Law.

Who wrote these books? Our modern Hebrew Bibles give them the general title, *"Quinque Libri Mosis."* This means "The Five Books of Moses." But Moses could never have given them this title, for these are Latin words, and it is not possible that Moses should have used the Latin language because there was no Latin language in the world until many hundreds of years after the day of Moses. The Latin title was given to them, of course, by the editors who compiled them. The preface and the explanatory notes in these Hebrew Bibles are also written in Latin.

But over this Latin title in the Hebrew Bible is the Hebrew word "Torah." This was the name by which these books were chiefly known among the Jews; it signifies simply "The Law." This title gives us no information, then, concerning the authorship of these books.

When we look at our English Bibles we find no separation, as in the Hebrew Bible, of these five books from the rest of the Old Testament writings, but we find over each one of them a title by which it is ascribed to Moses as its author,—"The First Book of Moses, commonly called Genesis;" "The Second Book of Moses, commonly called Exodus;" and so on. But when I look into my Hebrew Bible again no such title is there. Nothing is said about Moses in the Hebrew title to Genesis.

It is certain that if Moses wrote these books he did not call them "Genesis," "Exodus," "Leviticus," "Numbers," "Deuteronomy;" for these words, again, come from languages that he never heard. Four of them are Greek words, and one of them, Numbers, is a Latin word. These names were given to the several books at a very late day. What are their names in the Hebrew Bible? Each of them is called by the first word, or some of the first words in the book. The Jews were apt to name their books, as we name our hymns, by the initial word or words; thus they called the first of these five books, "Bereshith," "In the Beginning;" the second one "Veelleh Shemoth," "Now these are the names;" the third one "Vayikra," "And he called," and so on. The titles in our English Bible are much more significant and appropriate than these original Hebrew titles; thus Genesis signifies origin, and Genesis is the Book of Origins; Exodus means departure, and the book describes the departure of Israel from Egypt; Leviticus points out the fact that the book is mainly occupied with the Levitical legislation; Numbers gives a history of the numbering of the people, and Deuteronomy, which means the second law, contains what seems to be a recapitulation and reenactment of the legislation of the preceding books. But these English titles, which are partly translated and partly transferred to English from older Latin and Greek titles, tell us nothing trustworthy about the authorship of the books.

How, then, you desire to know, did these books come to be known as the books of Moses?

"They were quoted," answer some, "and thus accredited by our Lord and his apostles. They are frequently mentioned in the New Testament as inspired and authoritative books; they are referred to as the writings of Moses; we have the testimony of Jesus Christ and of his apostles to their genuineness and authenticity." Let us see how much truth this answer contains. It confronts us with a very important matter which may as well be settled before we go on.

It is true, to begin with, that Jesus and the Evangelists do quote from these books, and that they ascribe to Moses some of the passages which they quote. The soundest criticism cannot impugn the honesty or the intelligence of such quotations. There is good reason, as we shall see, for believing that a large part of this literature was written in the time of Moses, and under the eye of Moses, if not by his hand. In a certain important sense, which will be clearer to us as we go on, this literature is all Mosaic. The reference to it by the Lord and his apostles is therefore legitimate.

But this reference does by no means warrant the sweeping conclusion that the five books of the law were all and entire from the pen of the Lawgiver. Our Lord nowhere says that the first five books of the Old Testament were all written by Moses. Much less does he teach that the contents of these books are all equally inspired and authoritative. Indeed he quotes from them several times for the express purpose of repudiating their doctrines and repealing their legislation. In the very forefront of his teaching stands a stern array of judgments in which undoubted commandments of the Mosaic law are expressly condemned and set aside, some of them because they are inadequate and superficial, some of them because they are morally defective. "Ye have heard that it was said to them of old time" thus and thus; "but I say unto you"—and then follow words that directly contradict the old legislation. After quoting two of the commandments of the Decalogue and giving them an interpretation that wholly transforms them, he proceeds to cite several old laws from these Mosaic books, in order to set his own word firmly against them. One of these also is a law of the Decalogue itself. There can be little doubt that the third commandment is quoted and criticised by our Lord, in this discourse. That commandment forbids, not chiefly profanity, but perjury; by implication it permits judicial oaths. And Jesus expressly forbids judicial oaths. "Swear not at all." I am aware that this is not the usual interpretation of these words, but I believe that it is the only meaning that the words will bear. Not to insist upon this, however, several other examples are given in the discourse concerning which there can be no question.

Jesus quotes the law of divorce from Deuteronomy xxiv. 1, 2. "When a man taketh a wife and marrieth her, then it shall be, if she find no favour in his eyes, because he hath found some unseemly thing in her, that he shall write her a bill of divorcement, and give it in her hand, and send her out of his house. And when she is departed out of his house she may go and be another man's wife." These are the words of a law which Moses is represented as uttering by the authority of Jehovah. This law, as thus expressed, Jesus Christ unqualifiedly repeals. "I say unto you that every one that putteth away his wife, saving for the cause of fornication, maketh her an adulteress, and whosoever shall marry her when she is put away committeth adultery."

The law of revenge is treated in the same way. "Ye have heard that it was said, An eye for an eye and a tooth for a tooth." Who said this? Was it some rabbin of the olden time? It was Moses; nay, the old record says that this is the word of the Lord by Moses: "The Lord spake unto Moses, saying [among other things], If a man cause a blemish in his neighbor, as he hath done so shall it be done to him; breach for breach, eye for eye, tooth for tooth; as he hath caused a blemish in a man, so shall it be rendered unto him." (Lev. xxiv. 19, 20.) So in Exodus xxi. 24, "Thou shalt give life for life, eye for eye, tooth for tooth, hand for hand, burning for burning, wound for wound, stripe for stripe." It is sometimes said that these retaliations were simply permitted under the Mosaic law, but this is a great error; they were enjoined: "Thine eye shall not pity," it is said in another place (Deut. xix. 21); "life shall go for life, eye for eye, tooth for tooth, hand for hand, foot for foot." This law of retaliation is an integral part of the moral legislation of the Pentateuch. It is no part of the ceremonial law; it is an ethical rule. It is clearly ascribed to Moses; it is distinctly said to have been enacted by command of God. But Christ in the most unhesitating manner condemns and countermands it.

"Ye have heard," he continues, "that it was said, Thou shalt love thy neighbor and hate thine enemy; but I say unto you, Love your enemies, and pray for them that persecute you." "But this," it is objected, "is not a quotation from the Old Testament. These words do not occur in that old legislation." At any rate Jesus introduces them with the very same formula which he has all along been applying to the words which he has quoted from the Mosaic law. It is evident that he means to give the impression that they are part of that law. He is not careful in any of these cases to quote the exact words of the law, but he does give the meaning of it. He gives the exact meaning of it here. The Mosaic law commanded Jews to love their neighbors, members of their own tribe, but to hate the people of surrounding tribes: "An Ammonite or a Moabite shall not enter into the assembly of the Lord; even to the tenth generation shall none belonging to them enter into the assembly of the Lord for ever. . . . Thou shalt not seek their peace nor their prosperity all thy days for ever." (Deut. xxiii. 3–6.)

"When the Lord thy God shall bring thee into the land whither thou goest to possess it, and shalt cast out many nations before thee, . . . then thou shalt utterly destroy them; thou shalt make no covenant with them, nor show mercy unto them." (Deut. vii. 1, 2.) This is the spirit of much of this ancient legislation; and these laws were, if the record is true, literally executed, in after times, by Joshua and Samuel, upon the people of Canaan. And these bloody commands, albeit they have a "Thus said the Lord" behind every one of them, Jesus, in the great discourse which is the charter of his kingdom, distinctly repeals.

Such is the method by which our Lord sometimes deals with the Old Testament. It is by no means true that he assumes this attitude toward all parts of it. Sometimes he quotes Lawgiver and Prophets in confirmation of his own words; often he refers to these ancient Scriptures as preparing the way for his kingdom and foreshadowing his person and his work. Nay, he even says of that law which we are now studying that not one jot or tittle shall in any wise pass from it till all things be accomplished. What he means by that we shall be able by and by to discover. But these passages which I have cited make it clear that Jesus Christ cannot be appealed to in support of the traditional view of the nature of these old writings.

The common argument by which Christ is made a witness to the authenticity and infallible authority of the Old Testament runs as follows:

Christ quotes Moses as the author of this legislation; therefore Moses must have written the whole Pentateuch.

Moses was an inspired prophet; therefore all the teaching of the Pentateuch must be infallible.

The facts are, that Jesus nowhere testifies that Moses wrote the whole of the Pentateuch; and that he nowhere guarantees the infallibility either of Moses or of the book. On the contrary, he sets aside as inadequate or morally defective certain laws which in this book are ascribed to Moses.

It is needful, thus, on the threshold of our argument, to have a clear understanding respecting the nature of the testimony borne by our Lord and his apostles to this ancient literature. It is upon this that the advocates of the traditional view of the Old Testament wholly rely. "Christ was authority," they say; "the New Testament writers were inspired; you all admit this; now Christ and the New Testament writers constantly quote the Scriptures of the Old Testament as inspired and as authoritative. Therefore they must be the infallible word of God." To this it is sufficient to reply, Christ and the apostles do quote the Old Testament Scriptures; they find a great treasure of inspired and inspiring truth in them, and so can we; they recognize the fact that they are organically related to that kingdom which Christ came to found, and that they record the earlier stages of that great course of revelation which culminates in Christ; but they nowhere pronounce any of these writings free from error; there is not a hint or suggestion anywhere in the New Testament that any of the writings of the Old Testament are infallible; and Christ himself, as we have seen, clearly warns his disciples that they do not even furnish a safe rule of moral conduct. After this, the attempt to prove the inerrancy of the Old Testament by summoning as witnesses the writers of the New Testament may as well be abandoned.

But did not Jesus say, "Search the Scriptures, for in them ye think ye have eternal life, and they are they that testify of me?" Well, if he had said that, it would not prove that the Scriptures they searched were errorless. The injunction would have all the force to-day that it ever had. One may very profitably study documents which are far from infallible. This was not, however, what our Lord said. If you will look into your Revised Version you will see that his words, addressed to the Jews, are not a command but an assertion: "Ye search the Scriptures, for in them ye think ye have eternal life" (John v. 39); if you searched them carefully you would find some testimony there concerning me. It is not an injunction to search the Scriptures; it is simply the statement of the fact that the Jews to whom he was speaking did search the Scriptures, and searched them as many people in our own time do, to very little purpose.

But does not Paul say, in his letter to Timothy, that "All Scripture is given by inspiration of God?" No, Paul does not say that. Look again at your Revised Version (2 Tim. iii. 16): "Every Scripture inspired of God is also profitable for teaching, for reproof, for correction, for instruction, which is in righteousness." Every writing inspired of God is profitable reading. That is the whole statement.

But Paul says in the verses preceding, that Timothy had known from a child the Sacred Writings which were able to make him wise unto salvation through faith in Jesus Christ. Was there not, then, in his hands, a volume or collection of books, known as the Sacred Writings, with a definite table of contents; and did not Paul refer to this collection, and imply that all these writings were inspired of God and profitable for the uses specified?

No, this is not the precise state of the case. These Sacred Writings had not at this time been gathered into a volume by themselves, with a fixed table of contents. What is called the Canon of the Old Testament had not yet been finally determined.[1] There were, indeed, as we saw in the last chapter, two collections of sacred writings, one in Hebrew and the other in Greek. The Hebrew collection was not at this time definitely closed; there was still a dispute among the Palestinian Jews as to whether two or three of the books which it now contains should go into it; that dispute was not concluded until half a century after the death of our Lord. The other collection, as I have said, was in the Greek language, and it included, not only our Old Testament books, but the books now known as the Old Testament Apocrypha. This was the collection, remember, most used by our Lord and his apostles. Which of these collections was in the hands of Timothy we do not certainly know. But the father of Timothy was a Greek, though his mother was a Jewess; and it is altogether probable that he had studied from his childhood the Greek version of the Old Testament writings. Shall we understand Paul, then, as certifying the authenticity and infallibility of this whole collection? Does he mean to say that the "Story of Susanna" and "Bel and the Dragon,"

---

1. See chapter xi.

and all the rest of these fables and tales, are profitable for teaching and instruction in righteousness? This text, so interpreted, evidently proves too much. Doubtless Paul did mean to commend to Timothy the Old Testament Scriptures as containing precious and saving truth. But we must not force his language into any wholesale endorsement of every letter and word, or even of every chapter and book of these old writings.

So far, therefore, as our Lord himself and his apostles are concerned, we have no decisive judgment either as to the authorship of these old writings or as to their absolute freedom from error. They handled these Scriptures, quoted from them, found inspired teaching in them; but the Scriptures which they chiefly handled, from which they generally quoted, in which they found their inspired teaching, contained, as we know, worthless matter. It is not to be assumed that they did not know this matter to be worthless; and if they knew this, it is not to be asserted that they intended to place upon the whole of it the stamp of their approval.

We have wandered somewhat from the path of our discussion, but it was necessary in order to determine the significance of those references to the Old Testament with which the New Testament abounds. The question before us is, Why do we believe that Moses wrote the five books which bear his name in our Bibles? We have seen that the New Testament writers give us no decisive testimony on this point. On what testimony is the belief founded?

Doubtless it rests wholly on the traditions of the Jews. Such was the tradition preserved among them in the time of our Lord. They believed that Moses wrote every word of these books; that God dictated the syllables to him and that he recorded them. But the traditions of the Jews are not, in other matters, highly regarded by Christians. Our Lord himself speaks more than once in stern censure of these traditions by which, as he charges, their moral sense was blunted and the law of God was made of none effect. Many of these old tales of theirs were extremely childish. One tradition ascribes, as we have seen, to Moses the authorship of the whole Pentateuch; another declares that when, during an invasion of the Chaldeans, all the books of the Scripture were destroyed by fire, Ezra wrote them all out from memory, in an incredibly short space of time; another tradition relates how the same Ezra one day heard a divine voice bidding him retire into the field with five swift amanuenses,—"how he then received a full cup, full as it were of water, but the color of it was like fire, . . . and when he had drank of it, his heart uttered understanding and wisdom grew in his breast, for his spirit strengthened his memory, . . . and his mouth was opened and shut no more and for forty days and nights he dictated without stopping till two hundred and four books were written down."[2] These fables had wide currency among the Jews; they were believed by Irenaeus, Tertullian, Augustine, and others of the great fathers of the Christian Church; but they are not credited in these days. It is evident that Jewish tradition is not always to be trusted. We shall need some better reason than this for believing that Moses was the author of the Pentateuch.

I do not know where else we can go for information except to the books themselves. A careful examination of

---

2. 2 Esdras xiv. See, also, Stanley's *Jewish Church*, iii, 151.

them may throw some light upon the question of their origin. A great multitude of scholars have been before us in their examination; what is their verdict?

First we have the verdict of the traditionalists,—those, I mean, who accept the Jewish tradition, and believe with the rabbins that Moses wrote the whole of the first five books of the Bible. Some who hold this theory are ready to admit that there may be a few verses here and there interpolated into the record by later scribes; but they maintain that the books in their substance and entirety came in their present form from the hands of Moses. This is the theory which has been generally received by the Christian church. It is held to-day by very few eminent Christian scholars.

Over against this traditional theory is the theory of the radical and destructive critics that Moses wrote nothing at all; that perhaps the ten commandments were given by him, but hardly anything more; that these books were not even written in the time of Moses, but hundreds of years after his death. Moses is supposed to have lived about 1400 B.C.; these writings, say the destructive critics, were first produced in part about 730 B.C., but were mainly written after the Exile (about 444 B.C.), almost a thousand years after the death of Moses. "Strict and impartial investigation has shown," says Dr. Knappert, "that . . . nothing in the whole Law really comes from Moses himself except the ten commandments. And even these were not delivered by him in the same form as we find them now."[3] This is, to my mind, an astounding statement. It illustrates the lengths to which destructive criticism can go. And I dare

---

3. *The Religion of Israel*, p. 9.

say that we shall find in our study of these books reason for believing that such views as these are as far astray on the one side as those of the traditionalists are on the other.

Let us test these two theories by interrogating the books themselves.

First, then, we find upon the face of the record several reasons for believing that the books cannot have come, in their present form, from the hand of Moses.

Moses died in the wilderness, before the Israelites reached the Promised Land, before the Canaanites were driven out, and the land was divided among the tribes.

It is not likely that he wrote the account of his own death and burial which we find in the last chapter of Deuteronomy. There are those, it is true, who assert that Moses was inspired to write this account of his own funeral; but this is going a little farther than the rabbins; they declare that this chapter was added by Joshua. It is conceivable that Moses might have left on record a prediction that he would die and be buried in this way; but the Spirit of the Lord could never inspire a man to put in the past tense a plain narrative of an event which is yet in the future. The statement when written would be false, and God is not the author of falsehood.

It is not likely either that Moses wrote the words in Exodus xi. 3: "Moreover the man Moses was very great in the land of Egypt, in the sight of all the people;" nor those in Numbers xii. 3: "Now the man Moses was very meek above all the men which were on the face of the earth." It has been said, indeed, that Moses was directed by inspiration to say such things about himself; but I do not believe that egotism is a supernatural product; men take that in the natural way.

Other passages show upon the face of them that they must have been added to these books after the time of Moses. It is stated in Exodus xvi. 35, that the Israelites continued to eat manna until they came to the borders of the land of Canaan. But Moses was not living when they entered that land.

In Genesis xii. 6, in connection with the story of Abraham's entrance into Palestine, the historical explanation is thrown in: "And the Canaanite was then in the land." It would seem that this must have been written at a day when the Canaanite was no longer in the land,—after the occupation of the land and the expulsion of the Canaanites. In Numbers xv. 32, an incident is related which is prefaced by the words, "While the children of Israel were in the wilderness." Does not this look back to a past time? Can we imagine that this was written by Moses? Again, in Deuteronomy iii. 11, we have a description of the bedstead of Og, one of the giants captured and killed by the Israelites, just before the death of Moses; and this bedstead is referred to as if it were an antique curiosity; the village is mentioned in which it is kept. In Genesis xxxvi. we find a genealogy of the kings of Moab, running through several generations, prefaced with the words: "These are the kings that reigned in the land of Edom before there reigned any king over the children of Israel." This is looking backward from a day when kings were reigning over the children of Israel. How could it have been written five hundred years before there ever was a king in Israel? In Genesis xiv. 14, we read of the city of Dan; but in Judges xviii. 29, we are told that this city did not receive its name until hundreds of years later, long after the time of Moses. Similarly the account of the naming of the villages of Jair, which we find in Deuteronomy iii. 14, is quite inconsistent with another account in Judges x. 3, 4. One of them must be erroneous, and it is probable that the passage in Deuteronomy is an anachronism.

Most of these passages could be explained by the admission that the scribes in later years added sentences here and there by way of interpretation. But that admission would of course discredit the infallibility of the books. Other difficulties, however, of a much more serious kind, present themselves.

In the first verse of the twentieth chapter of Numbers we read that the people came to Kadesh in the first month. The first month of what year? We look back, and the first note of time previous to this is the second month of the second year of the wandering in the wilderness. Their arrival at Kadesh described in the twentieth chapter would seem, then, to have been in the first month of the third year. In the twenty-second verse of this chapter the camp moves on to Mount Hor, and Aaron dies there. There is no note of any interval of time whatever; yet we are told in the thirty-third chapter of this book that Aaron died in the fortieth year of the wandering. Here is a skip of thirty-eight years in the history, without an indication of anything having happened meantime. On the supposition that this is a continuous history written by the man who was a chief actor in it, such a gap is inexplicable. There is a reasonable way of accounting for it, as we shall see, but it cannot be accounted for on the theory that the book in its present form came from the hand of Moses.

Some of the laws also bear internal evidence of having originated at a later day than that of Moses. The law forbidding the removal of landmarks presupposes a long occupation of the land; and the law regulating military enlistments is more naturally explained on the theory that it was framed in the settled period of the Hebrew history, and not during the wanderings. This may, indeed, have been anticipatory legislation, but the explanation is not probable.

Various repetitions of laws occur which are inexplicable on the supposition that these laws were all written by the hand of one person. Thus in Exodus xxxiv. 17–26, there is a collection of legal enactments, all of which can be found, in the same order and almost the same words, in the twenty-third chapter of the same book. Thus, to quote the summary of Bleek, we find in both places, (*a*) that all the males shall appear before Jehovah three times in every year; (*b*) that no leavened bread shall be used at the killing of the Paschal Lamb, and that the fat shall be preserved until the next morning; (*c*) that the first of the fruits of the field shall be brought into the house of the Lord; (*d*) that the young kid shall not be seethed in its mother's milk.[4]

We cannot imagine that one man, with a fairly good memory, much less an infallibly inspired man, should have written these laws twice over, in the same words, within so small a space, in the same legal document. In Leviticus we have a similar instance. If any one will take that book and carefully compare the eighteenth with the twentieth chapter, he will see some reason for doubting that both chapters could have been inserted by one hand in this collection of statutes. "It is not probable," as Bleek has said, "that Moses would have written the two chapters one after the other, and would so shortly after have

---

4. *Introduction to the Old Testament*, i. 240.

repeated the same precepts which he had before given, only not so well arranged the second time."[5]

There are also quite a number of inconsistencies and contradictions in the legislation, all of which may be easily explained, but not on the theory that the laws all came from the pen of one infallibly inspired lawgiver. We find also several historical repetitions and historical discrepancies, all of which make against the theory that Moses is the author of all this Pentateuchal literature. A single author, if he were a man of fair intelligence, good common sense, and reasonably firm memory, could not have written it. And unless tautology, anachronisms, and contradictions are a proof of inspiration, much less could it have been written by a single inspired writer. The traditional theory cannot therefore he true. We have appealed to the books themselves, and they bear swift witness against it.

Now let us look at the other theory of the destructive critics which not only denies that Moses wrote any portion of the Pentateuch, but alleges that it was written in Palestine, none of it less than six or seven hundred years after he was dead and buried.

In the first place the book expressly declares that Moses wrote certain portions of it. He is mentioned several times as having written certain historical records and certain words of the law. In Exodus xxiv., we are told that Moses not only rehearsed to the people the Covenant which the Lord had made with them, but that he wrote all the words of the Covenant in a book, and that he took the book of the Covenant and read it in the audience of all the people. After the idolatry of the people Moses was again

---

5. *Introduction to the Old Testament*, i. 240.

commanded to write these words, "and" it is added, "he wrote upon the tables the words of the Covenant, the ten commandments." In Exodus xvii. 14, we are told that Moses wrote the narrative of the defeat of Amalek in a book; and again in Numbers xxxiii. 21, we read that Moses recorded the various marches and halts of the Israelites in the wilderness. We have also in the Book of Deuteronomy (xxxi. 24–26) a statement that Moses wrote "the words of the law" in a book, and put it in the ark of the covenant for preservation. Precisely how much of the law this statement is meant to cover is not clear. Some have interpreted it to cover the whole Pentateuch, but that interpretation, as we have seen, is inadmissible. We may concede that it does refer to a body or code of laws,— probably that body or code on which the legislation of Deuteronomy is based.

These are all the statements made in the writings themselves concerning their origin. They prove, if they are credible, that portions of these books were written by Moses; they do not prove that the whole of them came from his hand.

I see no reason whatever to doubt that this is the essential fact. The theory of the destructive critics that this literature and this legislation was all produced in Palestine, about the eighth century before Christ, and palmed off upon the Jews as a pious fraud, does not bear investigation. In large portions of these laws we are constantly meeting with legal provisions and historical allusions that take us directly back to the time of the wandering in the wilderness, and cannot be explained on any other theory. "When," says Bleek, "we meet with laws which refer in their whole tenor to a state of things utterly

unknown in the period subsequent to Moses, and to circumstances existing in the Mosaic age, and in that only,
it is in the highest degree likely that these laws not only
in their essential purport proceeded from Moses, but also
that they were written down by Moses or at least in the
Mosaic age. Of these laws which appear to carry with
them such clear and exact traces of the Mosaic age, there
are many occurring, especially in Leviticus, and also in
Numbers and Exodus, which laws relate to situations
and surrounding circumstances only existing whilst the
people, as was the case in Moses' time, wandered in the
wilderness and were dwellers in the close confinement of
camps and tents."[6] It is not necessary to draw out this evidence at length; I will only refer to a few out of scores of
instances. The first seven chapters of Leviticus, containing laws regulating the burnt offerings and meat offerings, constantly assume that the people are in the camp
and in the wilderness. The refuse of the beasts offered in
sacrifice was to be carried out of the camp to the public
ash heap, and burned. The law of the Great Day of Atonement (Lev. xvi.) is also full of allusions to the fact that
the people were in camp; the scapegoat was to be driven
into the wilderness, and the man who drove it out was
to wash his clothes and bathe, and afterward come into
the camp; the bullock and the goat, slain for the sacrifice,
were to be carried forth without the camp; he who bears
them forth must also wash himself before he returns to
the camp. Large parts of the legislation concerning lep-
rosy are full of the same incidental references to the fact
that the people were dwelling in camp.

---

6. Vol. i. p. 212.

There are also laws requiring that all the animals killed for food should be slaughtered before the door of the Tabernacle. There was a reason for this law; it was intended to guard against a debasing superstition; but how would it have been possible to obey it when the people were scattered all over the land of Palestine? It was adapted only to the time when they were dwelling in a camp in the wilderness.

Besides, it must not be overlooked that in all this legislation "the priests are not at all referred to in general, but by name, as Aaron and his sons, or the sons of Aaron the priests."

All the legislation respecting the construction of the tabernacle, the disposition of it in the camp, the transportation of it from place to place in the wilderness, the order of the march, the summoning of the people when camp was to be broken, with all its minute and circumstantial directions, would be destitute of meaning if it had been written while the people were living in Palestine, scattered all over the land, dwelling in their own houses, and engaged in agricultural pursuits.

The simple, unforced, natural interpretation of these laws takes us back, I say, to the time of Moses, to the years of the wandering in the wilderness. The incidental references to the conditions of the wilderness life are far more convincing than any explicit statement would have been. Can any one conceive that a writer of laws, living in Palestine hundreds of years afterwards, could have fabricated these allusions to the camp life and the tent life of the people? Such a novelist did not exist among them; and I question whether Professor Kuenen and Professor Wellhausen, with all their wealth of imagination, could have done any such thing. Many of these laws were certainly written in the time of Moses; and I do not believe that any man was living in the time of Moses who was more competent to write such laws than was Moses himself. The conclusion of Bleek seems therefore to me altogether reasonable: "Although the Pentateuch in its present state and extent may not have been composed by Moses, and also many of the single laws therein may be the product of a later age, still the legislation contained in it is genuinely Mosaic in its entire spirit and character."[7] We are brought, therefore, in our study, to these inevitable conclusions:

1. The Pentateuch could never have been written by any one man, inspired or otherwise.

2. It is a composite work, in which many hands have been engaged. The production of it extends over many centuries.

3. It contains writings which are as old as the time of Moses, and some that are much older. It is impossible to tell how much of it came from the hand of Moses, but there are considerable portions of it which, although they may have been somewhat modified by later editors, are substantially as he left them.

I have said that the Pentateuch is a composite work. In the next chapter we shall find some curious facts concerning its component parts, and the way in which they have been put together. And although it did not come into being in the way in which we have been taught by the traditions of the rabbins, yet we shall see that it contains some wonderful evidence of the superintending care of

---

7. Vol. i. p. 221.

God,—of that continuous and growing manifestation of his truth and his love to the people of Israel, which is what we mean by revelation.

Revelation, we shall be able to understand, is not the dictation by God of words to men that they may be written down in books; it is rather the disclosure of the truth and love of God to men in the processes of history, in the development of the moral order of the world. It is the Light that lighteth every man, shining in the paths that lead to righteousness and life. There is a moral leadership of God in history; revelation is the record of that leadership. It is by no means confined to words; its most impressive disclosures are in the field of action. "Thus *did* the Lord," as Dr. Bruce has said, is a more perfect formula of revelation than "Thus said the Lord." It is in that great historical movement of which the Bible is the record that we find the revelation of God to men.

Chapter 3

Sources of the Pentateuch

In the last chapter we found evidence that the Pentateuch as it stands could not have been the work of Moses, though it contains much material which must have originated in the time of Moses, and is more likely to have been dictated by him than by any one else; that large portions of the Mosaic law were of Mosaic authorship; that the entire system of Levitical legislation grew up from this Mosaic germ, though much of it appeared in later generations; and that, therefore, the habit of the Jews of calling it all the law of Moses is easily understood. We thus discovered in this study that the Pentateuch is a composite book.

The Christian Church in all the ages has been inclined to pin its faith to what the rabbins said about the origin of this book, and this is not altogether surprising; but in these days when testimony is sifted by criticism we find that the traditions of the rabbins are not at all trustworthy; and when we go to the Book itself, and ask it to tell us what it can of the secret of its origin, we find that it has a very different story to tell from that with which the rabbins have beguiled us. A careful study of the Book makes it perfectly certain that it is not the production of any one man, but a growth that has been going on for many centuries; that it embodies the work of many hands, put together in an artless way by various editors and compilers. The framework is Mosaic, but the details of the work were added by reverent disciples of Moses, the last of whom must have lived and written many hundred years after Moses' day.

Some of the evidences of composite structure which lie upon the very face of the narrative will now come under our notice. It is plain that the whole of this literature could not have been written by any one man without some kind of assistance. All the books, except the first, are indeed a record of events which occurred mainly during the lifetime of Moses, and of most of which he might have had personal knowledge. But the story of Genesis goes back to a remote antiquity. The last event related in that book occurred four hundred years before Moses was born; it was as distant from him as the discovery of America by Columbus is from us; and other portions of the narrative, such as the story of the Flood and the Creation, stretch back into the shadows of the age which precedes history. Neither Moses nor any one living in his day could have given us these reports from his own knowledge. Whoever wrote this must have obtained his materials in one of three ways.

1. They might have been given to him by direct revelation from God.

2. He might have gathered them up from oral tradition, from stories, folk-lore, transmitted from mouth to mouth, and so preserved from generation to generation.

3. He might have found them in written documents existing at the time of his writing.

The first of these conjectures embodies the rabbinical theory. The later form of that theory declared, however, that God did not even dictate while Moses wrote, but simply handed the law, all written and punctuated, out of heaven to Moses; the only question with these rabbins was whether he handed it down all at once, or one volume at a time. It is certain that this is not the correct theory. The repetitions, the discrepancies, the anachronisms, and the errors which the writing certainly contains prove that it could not have been dictated, word for word, by the Omniscient One. Those who maintain such a theory as this should beware how they ascribe to God the imperfections of men. It seems to me that the advocacy of the verbal theory of inspiration comes perilously near to the sin against the Holy Ghost.

The second conjecture, that the writer of these books might have gathered up oral traditions of the earlier generations and incorporated them into his writings, is more plausible; yet a careful examination of the writings themselves does not confirm this theory. The form of this literature shows that it must have had another origin.

The only remaining conjecture, that the books are compilations of written documents, has been established beyond controversy by the most patient study of the writings themselves. In the Book of Genesis the evidence of the combination of two documents is so obvious that he who runs may read. These two documents are distinguished from each other, partly by the style of writing, and partly by the different names which they apply to the Supreme Being. One of these old writers called the

Deity Elohim, the other called him Yahveh, or Jehovah. These documents are known, therefore, as the Elohistic and the Jehovistic narratives. Sometimes it is a little difficult to tell where the line runs which separates these narratives, but usually it is distinct. Readers of Genesis find many passages in which the name given to the Deity is "God," and others in which it is "LORD," in small capitals. The first of these names represents the Hebrew Elohim, the second the Hebrew Yahveh or Jehovah. In one important section, beginning with the fourth verse of the second chapter, and continuing through the chapter, the two names are combined, and we have the Supreme Being spoken of as "The LORD God," Jehovah-Elohim. It is evident to every observing reader that we have in the beginning of Genesis two distinct accounts of the Creation, the one occupying the first chapter and three verses of the second, the other occupying the remainder of the second chapter with the whole of the third. The difference between these accounts is quite marked. The style of the writing, particularly in the Hebrew, is strongly contrasted; and the details of the story are not entirely harmonious. In the first narrative the order of creation is, first the earth and its vegetation, then the lower animals, then man, male and female, made in God's image. In the second narrative the order is, first the earth and its vegetation, then man, then the lower orders of animals, then woman. In the first story plant life springs into existence at the direct command of God; in the second it results from a mist which rose from the earth and watered the whole face of the ground. These striking differences would be hard to explain if we had not before our faces the clear evidence of two old documents joined together.

I spoke in the last chapter of certain historical discrepancies which are not explicable on the supposition that this is the work of a single writer. Such are the two accounts of the origin of the name of Beersheba, the one in the twenty-first and the other in the twenty-sixth chapter of Genesis. The first account says that it was named by Abraham, and gives the reason why he called the place by this name. The second account says that it received its name from Isaac, about ninety years later, and gives a wholly different explanation of the reason why he called it by this name. When we find that in the first of these stories God is called Elohim,[1] and in the second Jehovah, we can readily explain this discrepancy. The compiler took one of these narratives from one of these old documents, and the other from the other, and was not careful to reconcile the two.

A similar duplication of the narrative is found in chapters xx. and xxvi., with respect to the incident of Abimelech; in the first of these narratives a serious complication is described as arising between Abimelech King of Gerar on the one hand and Abraham and Sarah on the other; in the second Abimelech is represented as interfering, in precisely the same way and with the same results, in the domestic felicity of Isaac and Rebekah. The harmonizers have done their work, of course, upon these two passages; they have said that there were two Abimelechs, and that Isaac repeated the blunder of his father; but it is a little singular, if this were so, that no reference is made in the latter narrative to the former. It is altogether probable

---

1. In the last verse of this narrative the word Jehovah is used, but this is probably an interpolation.

that we have the same story ascribed to different actors; and when we find that the one narrative is Elohistic and the other Jehovistic, the problem is solved.

More curious than any other of these combinations is the account of the Flood, in which the compiler has taken the narratives of these two old writers and pieced them together like patchwork. Refer to your Bibles and note this piece of literary joiner-work. At the fifth verse of the sixth chapter of Genesis this story begins; from this verse to the end of the eighth verse the Jehovistic document is used. The name of the Deity is Jehovah, translated LORD. From the ninth verse to the end of the chapter the Elohistic document is used. The word applied to God is Elohim, translated God. With the seventh chapter begins again the quotation from the other document, "And the LORD [Jehovah] said unto Noah." This extends only to the sixth verse; then the Elohistic narrative begins again, and continues to the nineteenth verse of the eighth chapter, including it; then the Jehovistic narrative begins again, and continues through the chapter; then the Elohist takes up the tale for the first seventeen verses of the ninth chapter; then the Jehovist goes on to the twenty-seventh verse, and the Elohist closes the chapter. It is true that we have in the midst of some of these Elohistic passages a verse or two of the other document inserted by the compiler; but the outlines of the different documents are marked as I have told you. If you take this story and dissect out of it the portions which I have ascribed to the Elohist and put them together, you will have a clear, complete, consecutive story of the Flood; the portions of the Jehovistic narrative inserted rather tend to confusion. "The consideration of the context here," says Bleek, "quite apart from the changes in the naming of God, shows that the Jehovistic passages of the narrative did not originally belong to it. It cannot fail to be observed that the connection is often interrupted by the Jehovistic passages, and that by cutting them out a more valuable and clearer continuity of the narrative is almost always obtained. For instance, in the existing narrative certain repetitions keep on occurring; one of these, especially, is connected with a difference in the matters of fact related, introducing no slight difficulty and obscurity."[2]

Hear the Jehovist: "And Jehovah saw that the wickedness of man was great in the earth" (ch. vi. 5). Now hear the Elohist (vi. 11): "And the earth was corrupt before Elohim, and the earth was filled with violence." The Jehovist says (vi. 7): "And Jehovah said, I will destroy man whom I have created from the face of the ground." The Elohist says (vi. 13): "The earth is filled with violence through them, and behold I will destroy them with the earth." In the ninth verse of the sixth chapter we read: "Noah was a righteous man and perfect in his generations; Noah walked with Elohim." In the first verse of the seventh chapter, we read, "And Jehovah said unto Noah, Come thou and all thy house into the ark; for thee have I seen righteous before me in this generation." These repetitions show how the same story is twice told. But the contradictions are more significant. Here the one narrative represents Elohim as saying (vi. 19): "And of every living thing of all flesh, two of every kind shalt thou bring into the ark to keep them alive with thee; they shall be male and female. Of the fowl after their kind and of the

---

2. Vol. i. p. 273.

cattle after their kind, of every creeping thing of the earth after its kind, two of every sort shall come unto thee to keep them alive." But the other narrative represents Jehovah as saying, "Of every clean beast thou shalt take to thee seven and seven, the male and the female; and of the beasts that are not clean, two, the male and the female; of the fowl also of the air seven and seven, male and female, to keep seed alive upon the face of all the earth." The one story says that of every kind of living creature one pair should be taken into the ark; the other says that of *clean* beasts, seven pairs of each species should be received, and of unclean beasts only one pair. The harmonists have wrestled with this passage also; some of them say that perhaps the first passage only meant that they should *walk in* two and two; others say that a good many years had elapsed between the giving of the two commands (of which there is not a particle of evidence), and we are left to infer that in the mean time the Almighty either forgot his first orders, or else changed his mind. It is a pitiful instance of an attempt to evade a difficulty that cannot be evaded. One of the very conservative commentators, Dr. Perowne, in Smith's "Bible Dictionary," concludes to face it: "May we not suppose," he timidly asks, "that we have here traces of a separate document, interwoven by a later writer, with the former history? The passage has not, indeed, been incorporated intact, but there is a coloring about it which seems to indicate that Moses, or whoever put the book of Genesis into its present shape, had here consulted a different narrative. The distinct use of the divine names in the same phrase (vi. 22; vii. 5), in the former

Elohim, in the latter Jehovah, suggests that this may have been the case."[3]

"May we not suppose," the good doctor asks, that we have traces of two documents here? Certainly, your reverence. It is just as safe to suppose it, as it is to suppose, when you see a nose on a man's face, that it is a nose. There is no more doubt about it than there is about any other palpable fact. The truth is, that the composite character of Genesis is no longer, in scholarly circles, an open question. The most cautious, the most conservative of scholars concede the point. Even President Bartlett, of Dartmouth College, a Hebraist of some eminence, and as sturdy a defender of old-fashioned orthodoxy as this country holds, made this admission more than twenty years ago: "We may accept the traces of earlier narratives as having been employed and authenticated by him [Moses]; and we may admit the marks of later date as indications of a surface revision of authorized persons not later than Ezra and Nehemiah." And Dr. Perowne, the conservative scholar already quoted, in the article on the "Pentateuch" in "Smith's Bible Dictionary," sums up as follows:—

"1. The Book of Genesis rests chiefly on documents much earlier than the time of Moses, though it was probably brought to very nearly its present shape either by Moses himself, or by one of the elders who acted under him.

"2. The books of Exodus, Leviticus, and Numbers are to a great extent Mosaic. Besides those portions which are expressly declared to have been written by him, other

---

3. Art. "Noah," iii. 2179, American Edition.

portions, and especially the legal sections, were, if not actually written, in all probability dictated by him.

"3. Deuteronomy, excepting the concluding part, is entirely the work of Moses, as it professes to be.

"4. It is not probable that this was written before the three preceding books, because the legislation in Exodus and Leviticus, as being the more formal, is manifestly the earlier whilst Deuteronomy is the spiritual interpretation and application of the law. But the letter is always before the spirit; the thing before its interpretation.

"5. The first *composition* of the Pentateuch as a whole could not have taken place till after the Israelites entered Canaan.

"6. The whole work did not finally assume its present shape till its revision was undertaken by Ezra after the return from the Babylonish captivity."

The volume from which I have quoted these words bears the date of 1870. Twenty years of very busy work have been expended upon the Pentateuch since Dr. Perowne wrote these words; if he were to write to-day he would be much less confident that Moses wrote the whole of Deuteronomy, and he would probably modify his statements in other respects; but he would retract none of these admissions respecting the composite character of these five books.

The same fact of a combination of different documents can easily be shown in all the three middle books of the Pentateuch, as well as in Genesis. This is the fact which explains those repetitions of laws, and those singular breaks in the history, to which I called your attention in the last chapter. There is, as I believe, a large element of purely Mosaic legislation in these books; many of these laws were written either by the hand of Moses or under his eye; and the rest are so conformed to the spirit which he impressed upon the Hebrew jurisprudence that they may be fairly called Mosaic; but many of them, on the other hand, were written long after his day, and the whole Pentateuch did not reach its present form until after the exile, in the days of Ezra and Nehemiah.

The upholders of the traditional theory—that Moses wrote the Pentateuch, just as Blackstone wrote his Commentaries—are wont to make much account of the disagreements of those critics who have undertaken to analyze it into its component parts. "These critics," they say, "are all at loggerheads; they do not agree with one another; none of them even agrees with himself very long; most of them have several times revised their theories, and there seems to be neither certainty nor coherency in their speculations." But this is not quite true. With respect to some subordinate questions they are not agreed, and probably never will be; but with respect to the fact that these books are composite in their origin they are perfectly agreed, and they are also remarkably unanimous in their judgments as to where the lines of cleavage run between these component parts. The consensus of critical opinion now is that there are at least four great documents which have been combined in the Pentateuch; and the critics agree in the main features of the analysis, though they do not all call these separated parts by the same names, nor do they all think alike concerning the relative antiquity of these portions. Some think that one of these documents is the oldest, and some give that distinction to another; nor do they agree as to how old the oldest is, some bringing the earliest composition down to a recent period; but on the main question that the literature is composite they are at one. The closeness of their agreement is shown by Professor Ladd in a series of tables[4] in which he displays to the eye the results of the analysis of four independent investigators, Knobel, Schrader, Dillmann, and Wellhausen. He goes through the whole of the Pentateuch and the Book of Joshua,—the Hexateuch, as it is now called,—and picks out of every chapter those verses assigned by these several authorities to that ancient writing which we have been calling the Elohistic narrative, and arranges them in parallel columns. You can see at a glance when they agree in this analysis, and when they disagree. I think that you would be astonished to find that the agreements are so many and the disagreements so few. So much unity of judgment would be impossible if the lines of cleavage between these old documents were not marked with considerable distinctness. "The only satisfactory explanation," says Professor Ladd, "of the possibility of accomplishing such a work of analysis is the fact that the analysis is substantially correct."[5]

Professor C. A. Briggs, of the Union (Presbyterian) Theological Seminary in New York, bore this testimony three years ago in the "Presbyterian Review:" "The critical analysis of the Hexateuch is the result of more than a century of profound study of the documents by the greatest critics of the age. There has been a steady advance until the present position of agreement has been

---

4. *The Doctrine of Sacred Scripture,* Part II. chap. vii.
5. *What is the Bible?* p. 311.

reached, in which Jew and Christian, Roman Catholic and Protestant, Rationalistic and Evangelical scholars, Reformed and Lutheran, Presbyterian and Episcopal, Unitarian, Methodist, and Baptist all concur. The analysis or the Hexateuch into several distinct original documents is a purely literary question in which no article of faith is involved. Whoever in these times, in the discussion of the literary phenomena of the Hexateuch, appeals to the ignorance and prejudices of the multitude as if there were any peril to faith in these processes of the Higher Criticism, risks his reputation for scholarship by so doing. There are no Hebrew professors on the continent of Europe, so far as I know, who would deny the literary analysis of the Pentateuch into the four great documents. The professors of Hebrew in the Universities of Oxford, Cambridge, and Edinburgh, and tutors in a large number of theological colleges, hold to the same opinion. A very considerable number of the Hebrew professors of America are in accord with them. There are, indeed, a few professional scholars who hold to the traditional opinion, but these are in a hopeless minority. I doubt whether there is any question of scholarship whatever in which there is greater agreement among scholars than in this question of the literary analysis of the Hexateuch."

I have but one more witness to introduce, and it shall be the distinguished German professor Delitzsch, who has long been regarded as the bulwark of evangelical orthodoxy in Germany. "His name," says Professor Ladd, "has for many years been connected with the conception of a devout Christian scholarship used in the defense of the faith against attacks upon the supernatural character of the Old Testament religion and of the writings which record its development." In a preface to his commentary on Isaiah published since his recent death, he speaks with great humility of the work that he has done, adding, "Of one thing only do I think I may be confident,—that the spirit by which it is animated comes from the good Spirit that guides along the everlasting way." The opinion of such a scholar ought to have weight with all serious-minded Christians. When I give you his latest word on this question, you will recognize that you have all that the ripest and most devout scholarship can claim. Let me quote, then, Professor Ladd's abstract of his verdict:—

"In the opinion of Professor Delitzsch only the basis of the several codes . . . incorporated in the Pentateuch is Mosaic; the form in which these codes . . . are presented in the Pentateuch is of an origin much later than the time of Moses. The Decalogue and the laws forming the Book of the Covenant are the most ancient portions; they preserve the Mosaic type in its relatively oldest and purest form. Of this type Deuteronomy *is a development.* The statement that Moses 'wrote' the Deuteronomic law (Deut. xxxi. 9, 24) *does not refer to the present Book of Deuteronomy, but to the code of laws which underlies it.*

"The Priest's Code, which embodies the more distinctively ritualistic and ceremonial legislation, is the result of a long and progressive development. Certain of its principles originated with Moses, but its form, which is utterly unlike that of the other parts of the Pentateuch, was received at the hands of the priests of the nation. Probably some particular priest, at a much later date, indeed, than the time of Moses, but prior to the composition of Deuteronomy, was especially influential in shaping it. But the last stages of its development may belong to the period after the Exile.

"The historical traditions which are incorporated into the Hexateuch were committed to writing at different times and by different hands. The narratives of them are superimposed, as it were, stratum upon stratum, in the Pentateuch and the Book of Joshua. For the Book of Joshua is connected intimately with the Pentateuch, and when analyzed shows the same composite structure. The differences which the several codes exhibit are due to modifications which they received in the course of history as they were variously collected, revised, and passed from generation to generation. . . . The Pentateuch, like all the other historical books of the Bible, is composed of documentary sources, differing alike in character and age, which critical analysis may still be able, with greater or less certainty, to distinguish and separate from one another."[6]

That such is the fact with respect to the structure of these ancient writings is now beyond question. And our theory of inspiration must be adjusted to this fact. Evidently neither the theory of verbal inspiration, nor the theory of plenary inspiration can be made to fit the facts which a careful study of the writings themselves bring before us. These writings are not inspired in the sense which we have commonly given to that word. The verbal theory of inspiration was only tenable while they were supposed to be the work of a single author. To such a composite literature no such theory will apply. "To make this claim," says Professor Ladd, "and yet accept

---

6. *What is the Bible?* pp. 489–491.

the best ascertained results of criticism, would compel us to take such positions as the following: The original authors of each one of the writings which enter into the composite structure were infallibly inspired; every one who made any changes in any one of these fundamental writings was infallibly inspired; every compiler who put together two or more of these writings was infallibly inspired, both as to his selections and transmissions [omissions?], and as to any connecting or explanatory words which he might himself write; every redactor was infallibly inspired to correct and supplement and omit that which was the product of previous infallible inspirations. Or perhaps it might seem more convenient to attach the claim of a plenary inspiration to the last redactor of all; but then we should probably have selected of all others the one least able to bear the weight of such a claim. Think of making the claim for a plenary inspiration of the Pentateuch in its present form on the ground of the infallibility of that one of the Scribes who gave it its last touches some time subsequent to the date of Ezra!"[7]

And yet this does not signify that these books are valueless. When it was discovered that the Homeric writings were not all the work of Homer, the value of the Homeric writings was not affected. As pictures of the life of that remote antiquity they had not lost their significance. The value of these Mosaic books is of a very different sort from that of the Homeric writings, but the discoveries of the Higher Criticism affect them no more seriously. Even their historical character is by no means overthrown. You can find in Herodotus and in Livy discrepancies and con-

---

7. *The Doctrine of Sacred Scripture*, i. 499.

tradictions, but this does not lead you to regard their writings as worthless. There are no infallible histories, but that is no reason why you should not study history, or why you should read all history with the inclination to reject every statement which is not forced on your acceptance by evidence which you cannot gainsay.

These books of Moses are the treasury, indeed, of no little valuable history. They are not infallible, but they contain a great deal of truth which we find nowhere else, and which is yet wonderfully corroborated by all that we do know. Ewald declares that in the fourteenth chapter of Genesis Abraham is brought before us "in the clear light of history." From monuments and other sources the substantial accuracy of this narrative is confirmed; and the account of the visit of Abraham to Egypt conforms, in all its minute incidents, to the life of Egypt at that time. The name Pharaoh is the right name for the kings reigning then; the behavior of the servants of Pharaoh is perfectly in keeping with the popular ideas and practices as the monuments reveal them. The story of Joseph has been confirmed, as to its essential accuracy, as to the verisimilitude of its pictures of Egyptian life, by every recent discovery. Georg Ebers declares that "this narrative contains nothing which does not accurately correspond to a court of Pharaoh in the best times of the Kingdom." Many features of this narrative which a rash skepticism has assailed have been verified by later discoveries.

We are told in the Exodus that the Israelites were impressed by Pharaoh into building for him two store-cities ("treasure cities," the old version calls them), named Pithom and Rameses, and that in this work they were made to "serve with rigor;" that their lives were embittered "with hard service in mortar and brick and all manner of hard service in the field;" that they were sometimes forced to make brick without straw. The whereabouts of these store-cities, and the precise meaning of the term applied to them, has been a matter of much conjecture, and the story has sometimes been set aside as a myth. To Pithom there is no clear historical reference in any other book except Exodus. Only four or five years ago a Genovese explorer unearthed, near the route of the Suez Canal, this very city; found several ruined monuments with the name of the city plainly inscribed on them, "Pi Tum," and excavating still further uncovered a ruin of which the following is Mr. Rawlinson's description: "The town is altogether a square, enclosed by a brick wall twenty-two feet thick, and measuring six hundred and fifty feet along each side. Nearly the whole of the space is occupied by solidly built, square chambers, divided one from another by brick walls, from eight to ten feet thick, which are unpierced by window or door or opening of any kind. About ten feet from the bottom the walls show a row of recesses for beams, in some of which decayed wood still remains, indicating that the buildings were two-storied, having a lower room which could only be entered by a trap-door, used probably as a store-house, or magazine, and an upper one in which the keeper of the store may have had his abode. Therefore this discovery is simply that of a 'store-city,' built partly by Rameses II.; but it further appears from several short inscriptions, that the name of the city was Pa Tum, or Pithom; and thus there is no reasonable doubt that one of the two cities built by the Israelites has been laid bare, and answers completely to the description given of it."[8]

The walls of Egypt were not all laid with mortar, but the record speaks of mortar in this case, and here it is: the several courses of these buildings were usually "laid with mortar in regular tiers." More striking still is the fact that in some of these buildings, while the lower tiers are composed of bricks having straw in them, the upper tiers consist of a poorer quality of bricks without straw. Photographs may be seen in this country of some of these brick granaries of this old store-city of Pithom, with the line of division plainly showing between the two kinds of bricks; and thus we have before our eyes a most striking confirmation of the truth of this story of the bondage of the Israelites in Egypt. Quite a number of such testimonies to the substantial historical verity of these Old Testament records have been discovered in recent years as old mounds have been opened in Egypt and in Chaldea, and the monuments of buried centuries have told their story to the wondering world. The books are not infallible, but he who sets them all aside as a collection of myths or fables exposes his ignorance in a lamentable way.

But what is far more to the purpose, the ideas running all through the old literature, the constructive truths of science, of ethics, of religion, are pure and lofty and full of saving power. Even science, I say, owes much to Genesis. The story of the Creation in the first chapter of Genesis must not indeed be taken for veritable history; but it is a solemn hymn in which some great truths of the

---

8. Quoted by Robinson in *The Pharaohs of the Bondage*, p. 97.

world's origin are sublimely set forth. It gives us the distinct idea of the unity of Creation,—sweeping away, at one mighty stroke, the whole system of naturalistic polytheism, which makes science impossible, when it declares that "In the beginning God created the heavens and the earth." In the same words it sets forth the truth by whose light science alone walks safely, that the source of all things is a spiritual cause. The God from whose power all things proceed is not a fortuitous concourse of atoms, but a spiritual intelligence. From this living God came forth matter with its forces, life with its organisms, mind with its freedom. And although it may not be possible to force the words of this ancient hymn into scientific statements of the order of creation, it is most clear that it implies a continuous process, a law of development, in the generations of the heaven and the earth. This is not a scientific treatise of creation, but the alphabet of science is here, as Dr. Newman Smyth has said; and it is correct. The guiding lights of scientific study are in these great principles.

Similarly the ethical elements and tendencies of these old writings are sound and strong. I have shown you how defective many of the Mosaic laws are when judged by Christian standards; but all this legislation contains formative ideas and principles by which it tends to purify itself. Human sacrifices were common among the surrounding nations; the story of Abraham and Isaac banishes that horror forever from Hebrew history. Slavery was universal, but the law of the Jubilee Year made an end of domestic slavery in Israel. The family was foundationless; the wife's rights rested wholly on the caprice of her husband; but that law of divorce which I quoted to you, and which our Lord repealed, set some bounds to this caprice, for the husband was compelled to go through certain formalities before he could turn his wife out of doors. The law of blood vengeance, though in terms it authorized murder, yet in effect powerfully restrained the violence of that rude age, and gave a chance for the development of that idea of the sacredness of life which to us is a moral commonplace, but which had scarcely dawned upon the minds of those old Hebrews. Thus the history shows a people moving steadily forward under moral leadership, out of barbarism into higher civilization, and we can trace the very process by which the moral maxims which to us are almost axioms have been cleared of the crudities of passion and animalism, and stamped upon the consciousness of men. Is not God in all this history?

Those first principles which I have called the guiding lights of science are also the elements of pure religion. Science and religion spell out different messages to men, but they start with the same alphabet. And the religious purity of that hymn of the Creation is not less wonderful than its scientific verity. Compare it with the other traditional stories of the origin of things; compare it with the mythologies of Egypt, of Chaldea, of Greece and Rome, and see how far above them it stands in spiritual dignity, in moral beauty. "We could more easily, indeed," says Dr. Newman Smyth, "compute how much a pure spring welling up at the source of a brook that widens into a river, has done for meadow and grass and flowers and overhanging trees, for thousands of years, than estimate the influence of this purest of all ancient traditions of the Creation, as it has entered into the lives and revived the consciences of men; as it has purified countries of idolatries and swept away superstition; and has flowed on and on with the increasing truth of history, and kept fresh and fruitful, from generation to generation, faith in the One God and the common parentage of men."[9]

Above all, we find in all this literature the planting and the first germination of that great hope which turned the thought of this people from the earliest generations toward the future, and made them trust and pray and wait, in darkest times, for better days to come. "Speak unto the children of Israel that they go forward!" This is the voice that is always sounding from the heights above them, whether they halt by the shore of the sea, or bivouac in the wilderness. They do not always obey the voice, but it never fails to rouse and summon them. No people of all history has lived in the future as Israel did. "By faith" they worshiped and trusted and wrought and fought, the worthies of this old religion; towards lands that they had not seen they set their faces; concerning things to come they were always prophesying; and it is this great hope that forms the germ of the Messianic expectation by which they reach forth to the glories of the latter day. This attitude of Israel, in all the generations, is the one striking feature of this history. No soulless sphinx facing a trackless desert with blind eyes—no impassive Buddha ensphered in placid silence—is the genius of this people, but some strong angel poised on mighty pinion above the highest peak of Pisgah, and scanning with swift glances the beauty of the promised land. Now any people of which this is true must be, in a large sense of the word, an inspired people; and their literature, with all the signs

9. *Old Faiths in New Light*, p. 73.

of imperfection which must appear in it, on account of the medium through which it comes, will give proof of the divine ideas and forces that are working themselves out in their history.

It is in this large way of looking at the Hebrew literature that we discover its real preciousness. And when we get this large conception, then petty questions about the absolute accuracy of texts and dates no longer trouble us. "He who has once gained this broader view of the Bible," says Dr. Newman Smyth, "as the development of a course of history itself guided and inspired by Jehovah, will not be disconcerted by the confused noises of the critic. His faith in the Word of God lies deeper than any difficulties or flaws upon the surface of the Bible. He will not be disturbed by seeing any theory of its mechanical formation, or school-book infallibility broken to fragments under the repeated blows of modern investigation; the water of life will flow from the rock which the scholar strikes with his rod. He can wait, without fear, for a candid and thorough study of these sacred writings to determine, if possible, what parts are genuine, and what narratives, if any, are unhistorical. His belief in the Word of God, from generation to generation, does not depend upon the minor incidents of the Biblical stories; it would not be destroyed or weakened, even though human traditions could be shown to have overgrown some parts of this sacred history, as the ivy, creeping up the wall of the church, does not loosen its ancient stones."[10]

---

10. *Old Faiths in New Light*, p. 59.

Chapter 4

The Earlier Hebrew Histories

We found reasons, in previous chapters, for believing that considerable portions of the Levitical legislation came from the hands of Moses, although the narratives of the Pentateuch and many of its laws were put into their present form long after the time of Moses. The composite character of all this old literature has been demonstrated. The fact that its materials were collected from several sources, by a process extending through many centuries, and that the work of redaction was not completed until the people returned from the exile about five centuries before Christ, and almost a thousand years after the death of Moses, are facts now as well established as any other results of scholarly research.

Nevertheless, we have maintained that the Israelites possessed, when they entered Canaan, a considerable body of legislation framed under the eye of Moses and bearing his name. Throughout the Book of Joshua this legislation is frequently referred to. If the Book of Joshua was, as we have assumed, originally connected with the first five books, constituting what is now called the Hexateuch, if these six books were put into their present form by the same writers, we should expect that the Mosaic legislation would be clearly traced through all these books.

But when we go forward in this history we come at once upon a remarkable fact. The Book of Judges, the Book of Ruth, and the two books of Samuel cover a period of Jewish history estimated in our common chronology at more than four hundred years, and in these four books there is no mention whatever of that Mosaic legislation which constituted, as we have supposed, the germ of the Pentateuch. The name of Moses is mentioned only six times in these four books; twice in the early chapters of the Judges in connection with the settlement of the kindred of his wife in Canaan; once in a reference to an order given by Moses that Hebron should be given to Caleb; twice in a single passage in I Samuel xii., where Moses and Aaron are referred to as leaders of the people out of Egyptian bondage, and once in Judges iii. 4, where it is said that certain of the native races were left in Canaan, "to prove Israel by them, whether they would hearken to the commandments of the Lord which he commanded their fathers by the hand of Moses." This last is the only place in all these books where there is the faintest allusion to any legislation left to the Israelites by Moses; and this reference does not make it clear whether the "commandments" referred to were written or oral. The word "law" is not found in these four books. There is nothing in any of these books to indicate that the children of Israel possessed any written laws. There are, indeed, in Ruth and in the Judges frequent accounts of observances that are enjoined in the Pentateuch; and in Samuel we read of the tabernacle and the ark and the offering of sacrifices; the history tells us that some of the things commanded in the Mosaic law were observed during this period; but when we look in these books for any reference or appeal to the sacred writings of Moses, or to any other sacred writings, or to any laws or statutes or written ordinances for the government of the people, we look in vain. Samuel the Prophet anointed Saul and afterward David as Kings of Israel; but if, on these solemn occasions, he said anything about the writings of Moses or the law of Moses, the fact is not mentioned. The records afford us no ground for affirming that either Samuel or Saul was aware of the existence of such sacred writings.

This is a notable fact. That the written law of Moses should, for four centuries of Hebrew history, have disappeared so completely from notice that the historian did not find it necessary to make any allusion to it, is a circumstance that needs explanation.

It is true, as I have said, that during this period certain observances required by the law were kept more or less regularly. But it is also true that many of the most specific and solemn requirements of the law were neglected or violated during all these years by the holiest men. The Mosaic law utterly forbids the offering of sacrifices at any other place than the central sanctuary, the tabernacle or the temple; but the narrative of these early historical books shows all the saints and heroes of the earlier history building altars, and offering sacrifices freely in many places, with no apparent consciousness of transgression,—nay, with the strongest assurance of the divine approval. "Samuel," says Professor Robertson Smith, "sacrifices on many high places, Saul builds altars, David and his son Solomon permit the worship at the high places to continue, and the historian recognizes this as legitimate because the temple was not yet built (I Kings iii. 2–4). In Northern Israel this state of things was never changed. The high places were an established feature in the Kingdom of Ephraim, and Elijah himself declares that the destruction of the altars of Jehovah—all illegitimate according to the Pentateuch—is a breach of Jehovah's covenant."[1]

According to the Levitical law it was positively unlawful for any person but the high priest ever to go into the innermost sanctuary, the holy of holies, where the ark of God was kept; and the high priest could go into that awful place but once a year. But we find the boy Samuel actually sleeping "in the temple of the Lord where the ark of the Lord was." The old version conceals this fact by a mistranslation. These are only a few of many violations of the Pentateuchal legislation which we find recorded in these books.

From the silence of these earlier histories concerning the law of Moses, and from these many transgressions, by the holiest men, of the positive requirements of the Pentateuchal legislation, the conclusion has been drawn by recent critics that the Pentateuchal legislation could not have been in existence during this period of history; that it must have been produced at a later day. It must be admitted that they make out a strong case. For reasons presented in the second chapter, I am unable to accept their theory. It is probable, however, that the code of laws in existence at this time was a limited and simple code—no such elaborate ritual as that which we now find

---

1. *The Old Testament in the Jewish Church*, pp. 220, 221.

in the Pentateuch; and that those particular requirements with respect to which the earlier Judges and Samuel and David appear to behave themselves so disorderly, had not then been enacted.

Moreover, it seems to be necessary to admit that there was a surprising amount of popular ignorance respecting even those portions of the law which were then in existence. This is the astonishing phenomenon. Attempts are made to illustrate it by the ignorance of the Bible which prevailed among our own ancestors before the invention of printing; but no parallel can be found, as I believe, in the mediaeval history of Europe. It is true that many of the common people were altogether unfamiliar with the Bible in mediaeval times; but we cannot conceive of such a thing as that the priests, the learned men, and the leaders of the church at that time, should have been unaware of the existence of such a book.

On his death-bed David is said to have admonished Solomon (I Kings ii. 3), that he should keep the statutes and commandments of the Lord, "according to that which is written in the law of Moses." This is the first reference to the Mosaic law which we find in connection with the history of David; the first mention of a written law since the death of Joshua, four centuries before. After this there are three other casual allusions to the law of Moses in the first book of Kings, and four in the second book. The books of Chronicles, which follow the Kings, contain frequent allusions to the law; but these books, as we shall see by and by, were written long afterward; and the tradition which they embody cannot be so safe a guide as that of the earlier histories. It is in Chronicles that we learn of the attempt which was made by one of the good kings of Judah, Jehoshaphat, to have certain princes, priests, and Levites appointed to teach the law; they went about the land, it is said, teaching the people, "and had the book of the law of Jehovah with them." I think that this is the first intimation, after the death of Moses, that the law delivered by him had been publicly taught or even read in connection with the ordinances of worship. The earlier narrative of Jehoshaphat's reign, which we find in the Book of the Kings, makes no allusion to this circumstance.

Nearly three hundred years after Jehoshaphat, and nearly five hundred years after David, the young King Josiah was reigning in Jerusalem. The temple had fallen into ruin, and the good king determined to have it repaired. Hilkiah, the high priest, who was rummaging among the rubbish of the dilapidated sanctuary, found there the Book of the Law of the Lord. The surprise which he manifests at this discovery, the trepidation of Shaphan the scribe, who hastens to tell the king about it, and the consternation of the king when he listens for the first time in his life to the reading of the book, and discovers how grievously its commandments have been disobeyed, form one of the most striking scenes of the old history. "How are we to explain," asks Dr. Perowne, "this surprise and alarm in the mind of Josiah, betraying, as it does, such utter ignorance of the Book of the Law and the severity of its threatenings,—except on the supposition that as a written document it had well-nigh perished?"[2] Undoubtedly "the Book of the Law" thus discovered was that body of legislation which lies at the

---

2. Smith's *Bible Dictionary*, art. "Pentateuch."

heart of the Deuteronomic code; and this was never again lost sight of by the Jewish people. It was less than fifty years after this that Nebuchadnezzar destroyed the city and the temple and carried the people away into captivity. And it was not until their return from the Captivity, seventy years later, that these sacred writings began to assume that place of eminence in the religious system of the Jews which they have held in later times. The man by whom the Jews were taught to cherish and study these writings was Ezra, one of the returning exiles. This Ezra, the record says, "was a ready scribe in the law of Moses which the Lord God of Israel had given," and "he had prepared his heart to seek the law of the Lord, and to do it and to teach in Israel statutes and judgments." He it was, no doubt, who gave to these laws their last revision, and who put the Pentateuch substantially into the shape in which we have it now. Doubtless much was added at this time; ritual rules which had been handed down orally were written out and made part of the code; the Pentateuch, after the Exile, was a more elaborate law book than that which Hilkiah found in the old temple. Under the presidency of Ezra in Jerusalem, and in the days which followed, the Book of the Law was exalted; it was the standard of authority; it was read in the temple and explained in the synagogues; its writings were woven into all the thought and life of the people of Israel; there never has been a time since that day when the history of the reign of any king could have been written without mentioning the law of Moses; there never has been a decade when any adequate account of the life of the Jewish people could have been given which would not bring this book constantly into view.

This Book of the Law, as finally completed by Ezra and his co-laborers, was the foundation of the Hebrew Scriptures; it possessed a sacredness in the eyes of the Jews far higher than that pertaining to any other part of their writings. Next to this in age and importance was the great division of their Scriptures known by them as *"The Prophets."*

After the Book of the Law was given to the people with great solemnity, in the days of Ezra, and the public reading and explanation of it became a principal part of the worship of the Jews, it began to be noised abroad that there were certain other sacred writings worthy to be known and treasured. The only information we have concerning the beginning of this second collection is found in one of the apocryphal books, the second of Maccabees (ii. 14), in which we are told that Neemias (Nehemiah), in "founding a library, gathered together the acts of the kings, and [the writings of] the prophets, and of David, and the epistles of the kings concerning the holy gifts." These last named documents are not now in existence. They appear to have been the letters and commissions of Babylonian and Persian kings respecting the return of the people to Jerusalem and the rebuilding of the temple. The other writings mentioned are, however, all known to us, and are included in our collection. It is not certain that Nehemiah began this collection; it may have been initiated before his day, and the "founding" of the library may have been only the work of providing for the preservation and arrangement of books already in his possession. This second collection of sacred writings, called The Prophets, was divided, as I have before stated, into the Earlier and the Later Prophets; the former subdivision containing the books of Joshua,[3] Judges, Samuel, and Kings; the latter, the books which we now regard and class as the prophecies. Ruth was at first considered as a part of the Judges, and was included among the "Earlier Prophets," and Lamentations was appended to Jeremiah, and included among the "Later Prophets." These two books were afterward removed from this collection, for liturgical reasons, and placed in the third group of writings, of which we shall speak farther on.

It is probable that the prophetic writings proper were first collected; but it will be more convenient to speak first of the books known to the Jews as the "Earlier Prophets," and to us as the Old Testament Histories,—Judges, Ruth, Samuel, and the Kings.

These books take up the history of Israel at the death of Joshua, and continue it to the time of the Captivity, a period of more than eight centuries. Some of the critics are inclined to connect them all together as successive volumes of one great history; but there is not much foundation for this judgment, and it is better to treat them separately.

The Book of Judges contains the annals of the Israelites after the death of Joshua, and covers a period of three or four centuries. It was a period of disorder and turbulence,—the "Dark Ages" of Jewish history; when every man, as the record often says, "did that which was right in his own eyes." There is frequent mention of the keeping of various observances enjoined in the laws of Moses; but there is no express mention of these laws in

---

3. Joshua, although originally a portion of the pentateuchal literature, was, about the time of the Exile, separated from the first five books, and put into this later collection.

the book. The story is chiefly occupied with the northern tribes; no mention is made of Judah after the third chapter; and it is largely a recital of the various wars of deliverance and defense waged by these northern Hebrews against the surrounding peoples, under certain leaders who arose, in a providential way, to take command of them.

The questions, Who wrote it? and When was it written? are not easily answered. It would appear that portions of it must have been written after the time of Saul, for the phrase, frequently repeated, "there was then no king in the land," looks back from a period when there *was* a king in the land. And it would appear that the first chapter must have been written before the middle of the reign of King David; for it tells us that the Jebusites had not yet been driven out of Jerusalem; that they still held that stronghold; while in 2 Samuel v. 6, 7, we are told of the expulsion of the Jebusites by David, who made the place his capital from that time. The tradition that Samuel wrote the book rests on no adequate foundation.

The evidence that this book also was compiled, by some later writer, from various written documents, is abundant and convincing. There are two distinct introductions, one of which comprises the first chapter and five verses of the second, and the other of which occupies the remainder of the second chapter. The first of these begins thus: "And it came to pass after the death of Joshua that the children of Israel asked of the Lord, saying, Who shall go up for us against the Canaanites, to fight against them?" The second of these introductions begins by telling how Joshua sent the people away, after his farewell address, and goes on (ii. 8) to say, "And

Joshua the son of Nun the servant of the Lord died, being an hundred and ten years old." After recounting a number of events which happened, as it tells us, after the death of Joshua, the narrative goes on to give us as naively as possible an account of Joshua's death. If this were a consecutive narrative from the hand of one writer, inspired or otherwise, such an arrangement would be inexplicable; but if we have here a combination of two or more independent documents, the explanation is not difficult. It is a little puzzling, too, to find the circumstances of the death of Joshua repeated here, in almost the same words as those which we find in the Book of Joshua (xxiv. 29–31). It would seem either that the writer of Joshua must have copied from Judges, or the writer of Judges from Joshua, or else that both copied from some older document this account of Joshua's death.

Another still more striking illustration of the manner in which these old books are constructed is found in the account given in the first chapter of the capture of Debir, by Caleb (i. 11–15). Here it is expressly said that this capture took place after the death of Joshua, as a consequence of the leadership assigned by Jehovah to the tribe of Judah in this war against the Canaanites. But the same narrative, in the same words, is found in the Book of Joshua (xv. 15–19), and here we are told no less explicitly that the incident happened during the lifetime of Joshua. There is no doubt that the incident happened; it is a simple and natural story, and carries the marks of credibility upon its face; but if it happened after the death of Joshua it did not happen before his death; one of these narrators borrowed the story from the other, or else both borrowed it from a common source; and one of them, certainly, put it in the wrong place,—one of them must have been mistaken as to the time when it occurred. Such a mistake is of no consequence at all to one who holds a rational theory of inspiration; he expects to find in these old documents just such errors and misplacements; they do not in the least affect the true value of the book; but it must be obvious to any one that instances of this nature cannot be reconciled with the theory of an infallible book, which has been generally regarded as the only true theory.

The book is of the utmost value as showing us the state of morals and manners in that far-off time, and letting us see with what crude material the great ideas committed to Israel—the unity and spirituality and righteousness of God—were compelled to work themselves out.

The Book of Ruth, which was formerly, in the Jewish collections, regarded as a part of the Book of Judges, is a beautiful pastoral idyll of the same period. Its scene is laid in Judea, and it serves to show us that in the midst of all those turbulent ages there were quiet homes and gentle lives. No sweeter story can be found in any literature; maternal tenderness, filial affection, genuine chivalry, find in the book their typical representatives. The first sentence of the book gives us the approximate date of the incidents recorded: it was "in the days when the judges judged." The concluding verses give us the genealogy of King David, showing that Ruth was his great-grandmother; it must, therefore, have been written as late as the reign of David,—probably much later; for it describes, as if they belonged to a remote antiquity, certain usages of the Jews which must needs have shaped themselves after the occupation of Canaan. Yet it could scarcely have been written so late as the Captivity, for the marriage of Ruth, who is a Moabitess, to Boaz, is mentioned as if it were a matter of course, with no hint of censure. In the latter days of Israel such an alliance of a Jew with a foreigner would have been regarded as highly reprehensible. Indeed the Deuteronomic law most stringently forbids all social relations with that particular tribe to which Ruth belonged. "An Ammonite or a Moabite shall not enter into the assembly of the Lord; even to the tenth generation shall none belonging to them enter into the assembly of the Lord for ever. . . . Thou shalt not seek their peace nor their prosperity all thy days for ever." (Deut. xxiii. 3, 6.) But Ruth, the Moabitess, becomes the wife of one of the chief men of Bethlehem, with the applause of all the Bethlehemites, and the highest approval of the author of this narrative; nay, she becomes, in the fourth generation, the ancestress of the greatest of all the kings of Israel. This certainly shows that the people of Bethlehem did not know of the Deuteronomic law, for they were a God-fearing and a law-abiding people; and it also makes it probable that the incident occurred, and that the book which describes the incident was written, before this part of the Deuteronomic code was in existence. It is therefore valuable, not only as throwing light on the life of the people at that early period, but also as illustrating the growth of the pentateuchal literature.

The two Books of Samuel and the two Books of Kings appear in the Septuagint and in the Latin Vulgate as one work in four volumes,—they are called the Four Books of Kings. In the recent Hebrew Bibles they are divided, however, as in our Bible, and bear the same names. They constitute, it is true, a continuous history; but the supposition that they were all written at one time and by one author is scarcely credible. The standpoint of the writer of the Kings is considerably shifted from that occupied by the writer of Samuel; we find ourselves in a new circle of ideas when we pass from the one book to the other.

The Books of Samuel are generally ascribed to Samuel as their author. This is a fair sample of that lazy traditionalism which Christian opinion has been constrained to follow. There is not the slightest reason for believing that the Books of Samuel were written by Samuel any more than that the Odyssey was written by Ulysses, or the Aeneid by Aeneas, or Bruce's Address by Bruce, or Paracelsus by Paracelsus, or St. Simeon Stylites by Simeon himself. Even in Bible books we do not hold that the Book of Esther was written by Esther, or the Book of Ruth by Ruth, or the Book of Job by Job, or the Books of Timothy by Timothy. The fact that Samuel's name is given to the book proves nothing as to its authorship. It may have been called Samuel because it begins with the story of Samuel. The Hebrews were apt to name their books by some word or fact at the beginning of them, as we have seen in their naming of the books of the Pentateuch.

It is true that certain facts are mentioned in this book of which Samuel would have better knowledge than any one else; and he is said to have made a record of certain events, (I Sam. x. 25.) But his death is related in the first verse of the twenty-fifth chapter of First Samuel; and it is certain, therefore, that considerably more than half of the document ascribed to him must have been written by some one else.

As to the name of the writer we are wholly ignorant, and it is not easy to determine the date at which he wrote. If we regarded this as a continuous history from the hand of one writer, we should be compelled to ascribe it to a date somewhat later than the separation of the two kingdoms; for in I Sam. xxvii. 6, we read of the present made by the king of Gath to David of the city of Ziklag, at the time when David was hiding from Saul; "where-fore," it is added, "Ziklag pertaineth unto the kings of Judah even unto this day." Now there were no "kings of Judah" until after the ten tribes seceded; Rehoboam was the first of the kings of Judah, therefore this must have been written after the time of Rehoboam. Doubtless this sentence was written after that time; and in all probabil-ity the books of Samuel did not receive their present form until some time after the secession of the ten tribes. The materials from which the writer composed the book are hinted at here and there; it is almost certain that here, as in the other books, old documents are combined by the author, and not always with the best editorial care. Sev-eral old songs are quoted: the "Song of Hannah," David's exquisite lament over Saul and Jonathan, which is known as "The Bow;" David's "Song of Deliverance," after he had escaped from Saul, which we find in the Psalter as the Eighteenth Psalm, and "The Last Words of David." The books contain a vivid narrative of the times of Eli and Samuel and Saul, and of the splendid reign of King David. No portion of the Old Testament has been more diligently studied, and the moral teaching of the books is clear and luminous. The ethical thoroughness of these writings when compared with almost any literature of equal antiq-uity is always remarkable. Take, as an example, the treatment which David receives at the hands of the writer. He is a great hero, the one grand figure of Hebrew history; but there is nothing of the demigod in this picture of him; his faults and crimes are exposed and denounced, and he gains our respect only by his hearty contrition and amendment. Verily the God of Israel whom this book reveals is a God who loveth righteousness and hateth iniquity.

The Books of the Kings were originally one book, and ought to have remained one. The manuscript was torn in two by some scribe or copyist long ago, in the middle of the story of the reign of King Ahaziah; the first word of Second Kings goes on without so much as taking breath, from the last word of First Kings. There is no excuse for this bisection of the narrative; it must be due to some accident, or to the arbitrary and unintelligent act of some person who paid no attention to the meaning of the document. As the Books of Samuel carry the history from the birth of Samuel down to the end of David's reign, so the Books of the Kings take up the story in the last days of David and carry it on to the time of the Exile, a period of four hundred and fifty years. The name of the author is concealed from us; there is a tradition, not altogether improbable, that it was written by the Prophet Jeremiah. If you will compare the last chapter of Second Kings with the last chapter of Jeremiah, you will discover that they are almost verbally the same. Here, again, if Jeremiah was not the author, either writer may have copied the passage from the other, or both may have taken it from some older book. But this passage gives us a note of time. It tells us that Evil-Merodach, king of Babylon, in the first year of his reign, released the captive king of Judah, Jehoiachin, from his long confinement, and gave him a seat at his own table. The book must have been written, then, after the beginning of the reign of Evil-Merodach; and there is plenty of history to show that his reign began 561 B.C. And inasmuch as the book gives no hint of the return of the Jews from their captivity, which began in 538 B.C., we may fairly conclude that the book was written some time between those dates. Let us suppose that Jeremiah wrote it; even he, as prophet of the Lord, certainly used the materials of history which had accumulated in the archives of the two nations.

It is evident that, after the establishment of the kingdom, considerable attention was paid to the preservation of the records of important national events. The kings kept chroniclers who not only preserved and edited old documents, but who wrote the annals of their own times. In I Kings xi. 41, at the conclusion of the narrative of Solomon's reign, we read, "Now the rest of the acts of Solomon, and all that he did, and his wisdom, are they not written in the Book of the Acts of Solomon?" For his history of Jeroboam the writer refers in the same way to "The Book of the Chronicles of the Kings of Israel," and for his history of Rehoboam to "The Book of the Chronicles of the Kings of Judah." The same is true of the reigns of other kings. These were not, of course, our Books of Chronicles, for these were not written for two hundred years after the Book of Kings was finished. It is thus evident, as one modern writer has said, "that the author laboriously employed the materials within his reach, very much as a modern historian might do, and further that he was as much puzzled by chronological difficulties as a modern historian frequently is."[4] Prophet or not, he took the materials at his hands, and put them together in this history.

The splendid but corrupt reign of the son of David; the secession of the ten tribes under Jeroboam; the hostile relations of the two kingdoms of Israel and Judah for two hundred and fifty years, by which both were weakened, and through unholy alliances corrupted, and the result of which was the final destruction of both, are described in this book in a spirited and evidently veracious manner. The two great prophets, Elijah and Elisha, are grand figures in this narrative; much of the story revolves around them. As witnesses for the righteous Jehovah they stand forth, warning, rebuking, counseling kings and people; the moral leadership by which Israel is chastened and corrected and led in the way of righteousness expresses itself largely through their ministry. The words of Lord Arthur Hervey, in Smith's "Bible Dictionary," none too strongly convey the historian's sense of the value of this part of the Old Testament:—

"Considering the conciseness of the narrative and the simplicity of the style, the amount of the knowledge which these books convey of the characters, conduct, and manners of kings and people during so long a period is truly wonderful. The insight which they give us into the aspect of Judah and Jerusalem, both natural and artificial, with the religious, military, and civil institutions of the people, their arts and manufactures, the state of education and learning among them, their resources, commerce, exploits, alliances, the causes of their decadence,

---

4. Horton's *Inspiration and the Bible*, p. 182.

and finally of their ruin, is most clear, interesting, and instructive. In a few brief sentences we acquire more accurate knowledge of the affairs of Egypt, Tyre, Syria, Assyria, Babylon, and other neighboring nations than had been preserved to us in all the other remains of antiquity up to the recent discoveries in hieroglyphical and cuneiform monuments."[5]

The substantial historical veracity of these books has been confirmed in many ways by these very monuments to which Lord Hervey refers. And yet this substantial historical accuracy is found, as in other histories of the olden time, in the midst of many minor errors and discrepancies. It would seem as if Providence had taken the utmost pains to show us that the essential truth and the moral and religious value of this history could not be identified with any theory of verbal or even plenary inspiration.

Take, for example, some of the chronological items of this record. Mr. Horton's clear statement will bring a few of them before us:—

"The author seems to have been content, in dealing with an Israelite king, to give the date reckoned by the year of the reigning king in Judah just as he found it stated in the Israelite chronicles, and then to do the same in dealing with the dates of the reigning kings of Israel; but he did not consider whether the two chronicles harmonized. We may take some illustrations from the latter part of the work. Hoshea began to reign in Israel (2 Kings xv. 30) in the twentieth year of Jotham the king of Judah. So far writes our author, following the records of the Northern Kingdom. For his next paragraph he turns

5. Vol. iii. p. 1561, American Edition.

to his records of the Southern Kingdom, and naively tells us that Jotham never reached a twentieth year, but only reigned sixteen years (xv. 33); but even this is not the end of the difficulty; in chapter xvii. he goes back to the Northern Kingdom and tells us that Hoshea began to reign, not in Jotham's reign at all, but in the reign of Ahaz, Jotham's successor; and if now he had said, 'in the fourth year of Ahaz,' we might see our way through the perplexity, for the fourth year of Ahaz would, at any rate, be twenty years from the beginning of Jotham's reign, though Jotham himself had died after reigning sixteen years; but he says, not in the fourth, but 'in the twelfth year of Ahaz king of Judah.' We may give it up, and exclaim with the Speaker's commentator, 'The chronological confusion of the history, as it stands, is striking,' and then perhaps we may exclaim at the Speaker's commentator, that he and the like of him have given us so little account of these unmistakable phenomena, and the cause of them, in the history.

"One other illustration may suffice. King Ahaz, according to one authority, lived twenty years and then came to the throne and reigned for sixteen years. (2 Kings xvi. 2.) At his death, therefore, Ahaz was thirty-six years of age. In that year he was succeeded by his son Hezekiah, who was twenty-five years of age. This would mean that King Ahaz was married at the age of ten, which, making all allowance for the earlier puberty of Eastern boys, does not seem probable; and the explanation is much more likely to be found in the chronological inaccuracies of our author, to which, if we have been observantly reading his book through, we shall by this time have become quite accustomed."[6]

Observe that we are not going to any hostile or foreign sources for these evidences of inaccuracy; we are simply letting the book tell its own story. Such phenomena as these appear throughout this history. They lie upon the very face of the narrative. Probably few of the readers of these pages have noted them. For myself, I must confess that I read the Bible through, from cover to cover, several times before I was thirty years old, but I had never observed these inaccuracies. The commentators, for the most part,—the orthodox commentators,—carefully keep these facts out of sight. Sometimes they attempt, indeed, to explain or reconcile them, but such explanations generally increase the incredibility of the narrative. The latest verdict of ultra-conservatism is that these dates and chronological notes are interpolated by some later hand; but this, too, is quite out of the question. The only true account of the matter is, that the author took these records from the Chronicles of the Kings of Judah and the Chronicles of the Kings of Israel, and pieced them together without noticing or caring whether they agreed. His mind was not fixed upon scientific accuracy of dates. He was thinking only of the great ethical and spiritual problems working themselves out in this history,—of the question whether or not these kings "did that which was right in the sight of the Lord," and of the effects of their right doing and their evil doing upon the lives of the people. What difference, indeed, does it make to you and me whether Jotham reigned sixteen years or twenty years?

6. Inspiration and the Bible, pp. 189–191.

It seems to me that these inaccuracies are suffered to lie upon the face of the narrative that our thoughts may be turned away from these details of the record to the great principles of morality and religion whose development it reveals to us.

These errors which appear upon the surface are obvious enough to any careful reader. But other facts, most important and suggestive, are brought to light when we compare these narratives of Samuel and Kings as we find them in the Hebrew text with the same narrative in the Greek text, the Septuagint. The Old Testament, as we have seen, was translated into the Greek language, for the benefit of those Jews who spoke only Greek, early in the third century before Christ. Undoubtedly it was a pretty faithful translation at the time when it was made. But a careful comparison of the two texts as they exist at the present time shows that considerable additions have been made to both of them; and that some changes and misplacements have occurred in both of them. Sometimes it is evident that the Hebrew is the more correct, because the story is more orderly and consistent; and sometimes it is equally evident that the Greek version, which, as you remember, was commonly used by our Lord and his apostles, is the better. This comparison gives us a vivid and convincing illustration of the freedom with which the text was handled by scribes and copyists; how bits of narrative—most commonly legends and popular tales concerning the heroes of the nation—were thrust into the text, sometimes quite breaking its continuity; they make it plain that that preternatural supervision of it, for the prevention of error, which we have frequently heard about, is itself a myth. It is in these books of Samuel and the Kings that these variations of the Septuagint from the Hebrew text are most frequent and most instructive.

In the story of David's introduction to Saul, for example, our version, following the Hebrew, tells us (I Sam. xvi. 14–23), that when David was first made known to Saul he was "a mighty man of valor, and a man of war, and prudent in speech, and a comely person." He comes into Saul's household; Saul loves him greatly, and makes him his armor-bearer. In the next chapter David is represented as a mere lad, and it appears that Saul had never seen or heard of him. Indeed, he asks his general, Abner, who this stripling is. The contradiction in these narratives is palpable and irreconcilable. When we turn now to the Septuagint, we find that it omits from the seventeenth chapter verses 12–31 inclusive; also from the 55th verse to the end of the chapter and the first five verses of the next chapter. Taking out these passages, the main difficulties of the narrative are at once removed. It appears probable that these passages were not in the narrative when it was translated into Greek, but that they embodied a current and a very beautiful tradition about David which some later Hebrew transcriber ventured to incorporate into the text.

In the Books of the Kings the variations between these two versions are also extremely suggestive. You can see distinctly, as if it were done before your eyes, how supplementary matter has been inserted into the one text or the other, since the Greek translation was made. In the sixth chapter of First Kings, the Septuagint omits verses 11–14, which is an exhortation to Solomon, injected into the specifications respecting the temple building. Omit these verses, and the description goes on smoothly. Similarly in the ninth chapter of the same book the Septuagint omits verses 15–25. This passage breaks the connection; the narrative of Solomon's dealings with Hiram is consecutively told in the Greek version; in the Hebrew it is interrupted by this extraneous matter. You can readily see which is the original form of the writing.

Now what does all this signify? Of course it signifies most distinctly that this history must not be judged by the canons of modern historical criticism. Mr. Horton quotes some strenuous advocate of the traditional theory of the Bible as maintaining that "when God writes history he will be at least as accurate as Bishop Stubbs or Mr. Gardiner; and if we are to admit errors in his historical work, then why not in his plan of salvation and doctrine of atonement?" It is this kind of reasoning that drives intelligent men into infidelity. For the errors are here; they speak for themselves; nothing but a mole-eyed dogmatism can evade them; and if we link the great doctrines of the Bible with this dogma of the historical inerrancy of the Scriptures, they will all go down together.

But what, after all, do these errors amount to? What is the meaning and purport of this history? What are these writers trying to do? "It seems," says Mr. Horton, "as if their purpose was not so much to tell us what happened as to emphasize for us the lesson of what happened. It is *applied* history, rather than history pure and simple; and on this ground we can understand the tendency to irritation which critical historians sometimes betray in approaching it. . . . The prophetic historian would never dream, like a modern historian, of writing interminable monographs about a disputed name or a doubtful date; he might even take a story which rested on very doubtful authority, finding in it more that would suit his purpose than the bare and accurate statement of the fact which could be authenticated. The standpoint of the prophetic historian and of the scientific historian are wholly different; they cannot be judged by the same canons of criticism. . . . To the prophetic eye the significance of all events seems to be in their relation to the will of God. The prophet may not always discern what the will of God is; he may interpret events in a quite inadequate manner. But his predominant thought makes itself felt; and consequently the study of these histories leaves us in a widely different frame of mind from that which Thucydides or Mr. Freeman would produce. We do not feel to know, perhaps, so accurately about the wars between Israel and Judah as we know about the wars between Athens and Sparta; we do not feel to know, perhaps, so much about the monarchy of Israel as we know about the Anglo-Norman monarchy; but, on the other hand, we seem to be more aware of God, we seem to recognize his hand controlling the wavering affairs of states, we seem to comprehend that obedience to his will is of more importance than any political consideration, and that in the long course of history disobedience to his will means national distress and national ruin. The study of scientific histories has its advantages; but it is not quite certain that these advantages are greater than those which the study of prophetic history yields. Perhaps, after all, the one fact of history is God's work in it; in which case the scientific histories, with all their learning, with all their toil, will look rather small by the side of these imperfect compositions which at least saw vividly and recognized faithfully *the one fact.*"

Chapter 5

The Hebrew Prophecies

In the last chapter the opinion was expressed that the first books collected by Nehemiah, when he made up his "library," a century after the Exile, were the writings of the prophets. We studied the historical books first, because they stand first in the Hebrew Bible, and are there named the "Earlier Prophets;" but the probabilities are that the prophetical writings proper, called by the Jews the "Later Prophets," were first gathered.

When was this collection made? If it was made by Nehemiah (and there is nothing to discredit the statement of the author of 2 Maccabees that he was the collector), then it was not compiled until one hundred years after the Exile, or only about four hundred and twenty years before Christ. Most of the prophets had written before or during the Exile. Joel, Hosea, and Amos had flourished three or four hundred years before this collection was made; Isaiah, the greatest of them all, had been in his grave almost three centuries; Micah, nearly as long; Nahum, Habakkuk, and Zephaniah had been silent from one to two hundred years; Jeremiah, who was alive when the seventy years' captivity began, and Ezekiel, who prophesied and perished among the captives on the banks of the Euphrates, were more remote from Nehemiah than Samuel Johnson and Jonathan Edwards are from us; even Haggai and Zechariah, who came back with the returning exiles and helped to build the second temple, had passed away from fifty to one hundred years before the time of Nehemiah. Malachi alone,—"The Messenger,"—and the last of the prophets, may have been alive when the compilation of the prophetic writings was made.

It may be safely conjectured that the Jews, although they had never possessed any collection of the books of the prophets, had known something of their contents. Several of the prophets had foretold the desolation and the captivity, and there had been abundant time during the Exile to recall the words they had spoken and to wish that their fathers had heeded them. These remembered words of the prophets, passing from lip to lip, would thus have acquired peculiar sacredness. It seems clear, also, that copies of these books must have been kept,—perhaps in the schools of the prophets; for the later prophets quote, verbally, from the earlier ones. It may, therefore, have been in response to a popular wish that this collection of their writings was undertaken. Words so momentous as these ought to be sacredly treasured. Furthermore, there were reasons to apprehend that the holy flame of prophecy was dying out. Malachi may have been speaking still, but there was not much promise that he would have a successor, and the expectation of prophetic voices was growing dim among the people.

The Levitical ritual, now so elaborate and cumbersome, had supplanted the prophetic oracle. The ritualist is never a prophet; and out of such a formal cult no words of inspiration are apt to flow. With all the greater carefulness, therefore, would the people treasure the messages that had come to them from the past. Accordingly these prophetic writings, which had existed in a fragmentary and scattered form, were gathered into a collection by themselves.

It must be admitted that when we try to tell how these writings had been preserved and transmitted through all these centuries, we have but little solid ground of fact to go upon. The Scriptures themselves are entirely silent with respect to the manner of their preservation; the traditions of the Jews are wholly worthless. We must not imagine that these books of Isaiah and Jeremiah and Hosea were written and published as our books are written and published; there was no book trade then through which literature could be marketed, and no subscription agencies hawking books from door to door. You must not imagine that every family in Judea had a copy of Isaiah's Works,—nor even that a copy could be found in every village; it is possible that there were not, when the people were carried into captivity, more than a few dozen copies of these prophecies in existence, and these were in the hands of some of the prophets or literary dignitaries of the nation, or in the archives of some of the prophetical schools. The notion that these works were distributed among the people for study and devotional reading is not to be entertained. No such general use of the prophetical writings was ever conceived of by the Jews before the Captivity.

Indeed, many of these prophecies, as we call them, were not, primarily, literature at all. They were sermons or addresses, delivered orally to the individuals concerned, or to assemblies of the people. You can see the evidence, in many cases, that they must have been thus delivered.

We speak of the "prophecy" of Isaiah, or the "prophecy" of Jeremiah; but the books bearing their names are made up of a number of "prophecies," uttered on various occasions. The division between these separate prophecies is generally indicated by the language; in all Paragraph Bibles it is marked by blank lines. In each of these earlier prophetical books we thus have, in all probability, a succession of deliverances, extending through long periods of time and prepared for various occasions.

After the oracle was spoken to those for whom it was designed, it was written down by the prophet or by his friends and disciples, and thus preserved. This supposition seems, at any rate, more plausible than any other that I have found. Manifestly many of these prophecies were originally sermons or public addresses; it is natural to suppose that they were first delivered, and then, for substance, reduced to writing, that a record might be made of the utterance.

It is sometimes alleged that these prophecies, as soon as they were produced, were at once added to a collection of sacred Scriptures which was preserved in the sanctuary. There was a "Book" or "Scripture," it is said, "which from the time of Moses was kept open, and in which the writings of the prophets may have been recorded as they were produced."[1]

---

1. Alexander on Isaiah, i. 7.

The learned divine who ventures this conjecture admits that it would be as hard to prove it as to disprove it. My own opinion is that it would be much harder. If there had been any such official receptacle of sacred writings, the prophets were not generally in a position to secure the admission of their documents into it. They were often in open controversy with the people who kept the sanctuary; the political and the religious authorities of the nation were the objects of their severest denunciations; it is not likely that the priests would make haste to transcribe and preserve in the sanctuary the sermons and lectures of the men who were scourging them with censure. This national *bibliotheca sacra* in which the writings of the prophets were deposited as soon as they were composed is the product of pure fiction. It was not thus that the prophetical utterances were preserved; rather is it to be supposed that the pupils and friends of the prophet faithfully kept his manuscripts after he was gone; that occasional copies were made of them by those who wished to study them, and that thus they were handed down from generation to generation.

When Nehemiah made his collection he found these manuscripts, in whose hands we know not, and brought them together in one place. We may presume that the writings of each prophet were copied upon a separate roll, and that the rolls were kept together in some receptacle in the temple. Most of these prophets had now been dead some hundreds of years; the truth of their messages was no longer disputed even by the priests and the scribes; their heresy was now the soundest orthodoxy; the custodians of orthodoxy would of course now make a place for their writings in the national archives.

The priests have always been ready to build sepulchres for the prophets after they were dead, and to pay them plenty of *post mortem* reverence.

The books of the prophets stand in the later Hebrew Bibles in the same order as that in which they are placed in our own; they occupy a different place in the whole collection: they are in the middle of the Hebrew Bible, and they are at the end of ours; but their relation to one another is the same in both Bibles. This order is not chronological; in part, at least, it seems to represent what was supposed to be the relative importance of the books. Isaiah, Jeremiah, and Ezekiel are placed first, perhaps because they are longest, although several of the minor prophets are of earlier date than they. "Daniel" is not among the prophets in the Hebrew Bible; the book which bears this name is one of the books of the third collection,—the Hagiographa,—of which we shall speak at another time.

"When we follow further the same collection," says Professor Murray, "we find Hosea immediately following Ezekiel [although Hosea lived more than two centuries before Ezekiel] and in turn followed by Joel and Amos, mainly on the principle of comparative bulk. Haggai, Zechariah, and Malachi were placed at the end for reasons purely chronological, after the rest of the collection had been made up. We cannot see any clear or consistent reason for the position of Obadiah, Jonah, Micah, Nahum, Habakkuk, and Zephaniah, which stand together in the middle of the collection."

An examination of the chronological notes on the margin of our English Bibles (which are not always correct though they are approximately so) will show that these prophetical books are not arranged in the order of time. It would be a great improvement to have them so arranged. Pupils in the Sunday-schools who attempted a few years ago to follow the "International" lessons through these prophecies, *seriatim*, found themselves skipping back and forward over the centuries in a history-defying dance which was quite bewildering to all but the clearest heads. We could understand these prophecies much better if they were arranged in the order of their dates. And as no one supposes that the present arrangement, made by Jewish scribes, is in any wise inspired, there seems to be no good reason why the late revisers might not have altered it, and set these books in a historical and intelligible order.

Who were these prophets and what was their function? To give any adequate answer to this inquiry would require a treatise; it is only in the most cursory manner that we can deal with it in this place.

The prophet is the man who speaks for God. He is the interpreter of the divine will. By some means he has come to understand God's purpose, and his function is to declare it. Thus in Exodus iv. 16, Jehovah says to Moses, "Aaron thy brother . . . shall be thy spokesman unto the people, and it shall come to pass that he shall be to thee a mouth and thou shalt be to him as God." And again (vii. i), "See, I have made thee a god to Pharaoh, and Aaron thy brother shall be thy prophet." These passages indicate the Biblical meaning of the word. The prophet is the spokesman or interpreter of some superior authority. In Classic Greek, also, Apollo is called the prophet of Jupiter, and the Pythia is the prophetess of Apollo. Almost universally, in the Old Testament, the word is used to signify an expounder or interpreter of the divine will.

"The English words 'prophet, prophecy, prophesying,'" says Dean Stanley, "originally kept tolerably close to the Biblical use of the word. The celebrated dispute about 'prophesyings' in the sense of 'preachings' in the reign of Elizabeth, and the treatise of Jeremy Taylor on 'The Liberty of Prophesying,' *i.e.*, the liberty of preaching, show that even down to the seventeenth century the word was still used as in the Bible, for preaching or speaking according to the will of God. In the seventeenth century, however, the limitation of the word to the sense of prediction had gradually begun to appear. This secondary meaning of the word had by the time of Dr. Johnson so entirely superseded the original Scriptural signification that he gives no other special definition of it than 'to predict, to foretell, to prognosticate,' 'a predicter, a foreteller,' 'foreseeing or foretelling future events;' and in this sense it has been used almost down to our own day, when the revival of Biblical criticism has resuscitated, in some measure, the Biblical use of the word."[2] The predictive function of the prophet is not, then, the only, nor the prominent feature of his work. By far the larger portion of the prophetic utterances were concerned with the present, and made no reference to the future.

The prophet exercised his office in many ways. Moses was a prophet, the first and greatest of the prophets; but we have from him few predictions; he interpreted the will of God in the enactment of laws. Samuel was a great prophet; but Samuel was not employed in foretelling future events; he sought to know the will of God,

2. *History of the Jewish Church*, i. 459, 460.

that he might administer the affairs of the Jewish commonwealth in accordance with it. Elijah and Elisha were great prophets, but they were not prognosticators; they were preachers of righteousness to kings and people, and they delivered their message in a way to make the ears of those who heard them to tingle. And this, for all the prophets who succeeded them, was the one great business. The ethical function of these men of God came more and more distinctly into view.

When Paul admonished Timothy (2 Tim. iv. 2) to "preach the word; be instant in season, out of season; reprove, rebuke, exhort with all long-suffering and teaching," he was calling on him to be a follower of the prophets. When kings became profligate and faithless, when priests grew formal and greedy, when the rich waxed extortionate and tyrannical, these men of God arose to denounce the transgressors and threaten them with the divine vengeance. They might arise in any quarter, from any class. They were confined to no tribe, to no locality, to no calling. Neither sex monopolized this gift. Miriam, Deborah, Huldah were shining names upon their roll of honor. To no ecclesiasticism or officialism did they owe their authority; no man's hands had been laid upon them in ordination; they were Jehovah's messengers; from him alone they received their messages, to him alone they held themselves responsible.

No such preachers of politics ever existed as these Hebrew prophets; with all the affairs of state they constantly intermeddled; bad laws and unholy policies found in them sharp and unsparing critics; the entangling alliances of Israel with the surrounding nations were denounced by them in season and out of season. The people of their own time often stigmatized them as unpatriotic; because they would not approve popular iniquities, or refrain their lips from rebuking even "favorite sons," or the idols of the populace, they often found themselves under the ban of public opinion; they lived lonely lives; not a few of them died violent deaths. "Which of the prophets did not your fathers persecute?" demanded Stephen, "and they killed them which showed before of the coming of the Righteous One; of whom ye have now become betrayers and murderers."[3]

The relation of the prophets to the political life of the Jewish people is brought out in a striking way by John Stuart Mill in his book on "Representative Government." In that chapter in which he discusses the criterion of a good government, he shows how the Egyptian hierarchy and the Chinese paternal despotism destroyed those countries by stereotyping their institutions. Then he goes on:—

"In contrast with these nations let us consider the example of an opposite character, afforded by another and a comparatively insignificant Oriental people, the Jews. They, too, had an absolute monarchy and a hierarchy, and their organized institutions were as obviously of sacerdotal origin as those of the Hindoos. These did for them what was done for other Oriental races by their institutions, subdued them to industry and order, and gave them a national life. But neither their kings nor their priests ever obtained, as in those other countries, the exclusive moulding of their character. Their religion, which

---

3. Acts vii. 52.

enabled persons of genius and a high religious tone to be regarded and to regard themselves as inspired from heaven, gave existence to an inestimably precious unorganized institution,—the Order (if it may be so termed) of Prophets. Under the protection, generally though not always effectual, of their sacred character, the Prophets were a power in the nation, often more than a match for kings and priests, and kept up in that little corner of the earth the antagonism of influences which is the only real security for continued progress. Religion, consequently, was not then what it has been in so many other places, a consecration of all that was once established, and a barrier against further improvement. The remark of a distinguished Hebrew, M. Salvador, that the Prophets were in church and state the equivalent of the modern liberty of the press, gives a just but not an adequate conception of the part fulfilled in national and universal history by this great element of Jewish life; by means of which, the canon of inspiration never being complete, the persons most eminent in genius and moral feeling could not only denounce and reprobate, with the direct authority of the Almighty, whatever appeared to them deserving of such treatment, but could give forth better and higher interpretations of the national religion, which thenceforth became part of the religion. Accordingly, whoever can divest himself of the habit of reading the Bible as if it was one book, which until lately was equally inveterate in Christians and unbelievers, sees with admiration the vast interval between the morality and religion of the Pentateuch, or even of the historical books (the unmistakable work of Hebrew Conservatives of the Sacerdotal order), and the morality and religion of the Prophecies. Conditions more favorable to progress could not easily exist; accordingly, the Jews, instead of being stationary like other Asiatics, were, next to the Greeks, the most progressive people of antiquity, and, joint with them, have been the starting-point and main propelling agency of modern civilization."[4]

Not only in the sphere of politics, but in that of religion also, were they constantly appearing as critics and censors. The tendency of religion to become merely ritual, to divorce itself from righteousness, is inveterate. Against this tendency the prophets were the constant witnesses. The religious "machine" is always in the same danger of becoming corrupt and mischievous as is the political "machine;" the man with the sledge-hammer who will smash it and fling it into the junk-pile has a work to do in every generation. This was the work of the Hebrew prophets. "I desired mercy, and not sacrifice," cries Hosea, speaking for Jehovah. "I hate, I despise your feast days," says Amos, "and I will not smell in your solemn assemblies, . . . but let judgment run down as waters, and righteousness as a mighty stream." "Your new moons and your appointed feasts my soul hateth," proclaims Isaiah; "they are a trouble unto me; I am weary to bear them. Wash ye, make you clean; cease to do evil; learn to do well. Is not this the fast that I have chosen, to loose the bands of wickedness, to undo the heavy burden, and to let the oppressed go free?"

This is, then, the chief function of the Hebrew prophet; he is the expounder of the righteous will of God, not

---

4. *Considerations on Representative Government*, pp. 51–53, American Edition.

mainly with respect to future events, but with respect to present transgressions and present obligations of kings and priests and people. And yet it would be an error to overlook or disparage his dealings with the future. As a teacher of righteousness he saw that present disobedience would bring future retribution, and he pointed it out with the utmost fidelity. Any man who carefully studies the laws of God can make some predictions with great confidence. He knows that certain courses of conduct will be followed by certain consequences. Some of the predictions of the Hebrew prophets were of this nature. Yet predictions of this nature were always conditional. The condition was not always expressed, but it was always understood. The threatening of destruction to the disobedient was withdrawn when the disobedient turned from their evil ways. The predictions of the prophets were not always fulfilled for this good reason. The rule is explicitly laid down by the Prophet Jeremiah: "At what instant I shall speak concerning a nation . . . to destroy it; if that nation . . . turn from their evil, I will repent of the evil that I thought to do unto them. And at what instant I shall speak concerning a nation . . . to build and to plant it; if it do evil in my sight, that it obey not my voice, then I will repent of the good wherewith I said I would benefit them."[5]

And there is something more than this. Instances are here recorded of specific predictions of future events, which came to pass as they were predicted,—predictions which cannot be explained on naturalistic principles. "Of this sort," says Bleek, "are the prophecies of Isaiah as to

---

5. Jeremiah xviii. 7–9.

the closely impending destruction of the kingdoms of Israel and Syria, which he predicted with great confidence at a time when the two kingdoms appeared particularly strong by their treaty with each other, . . . besides the repeated predictions as to the destruction of the mighty hosts of Sennacherib, king of Assyria, which besieged Jerusalem, and the deliverance of the state from the greatest distress. Among these predictions, those in Isaiah xxix. 1–8, appear to me particularly noteworthy, where he foretells that a long time hence Jerusalem should be besieged by a foreign host and pressed very hard, but that the latter, just as they believed they were getting possession of the city, should be scattered and annihilated; for this prediction, from its whole character, appears to have been uttered before any danger showed itself from this quarter."[6]

Beyond and above all this is the gradual rise in Israel of that great Messianic hope, of which the prophets were the inspired and inspiring witnesses. We find, at a very early day, an expectation of a future revelation of the glory of God, dawning upon the consciousness of the nation, and expressing itself by the words of its most devout spirits. Even in prosperous days there was a dim outreaching after something better; in times of disaster and overthrow this hope was kindled to a passionate longing. Of this Messianic hope, its nature and its fulfillment, no words of mine can tell so eloquently as these words of Dean Stanley:—

"It was the distinguishing mark of the Jewish people that their golden age was not in the past, but in the future; that their greatest hero (as they deemed him to be)

---

6. *Introduction to the Old Testament*, ii. 27.

was not their Founder, but their Founder's latest Descendant. Their traditions, their fancies, their glories, gathered round the head, not of a chief or warrior or sage that had been, but of a King, a Deliverer, a Prophet who was to come. Of this singular expectation the Prophets were, if not the chief authors, at least the chief exponents. Sometimes he is named, sometimes he is unnamed; sometimes he is almost identified with some actual Prince of the present or the coming generation, sometimes he recedes into the distant ages. But again and again, at least in the late prophetic writings, the vista is closed by this person, his character, his reign. And almost everywhere the Prophetic spirit in the delineation of his coming remains true to itself. He is to be a King, a Conqueror, yet not by the common weapons of earthly warfare, but by those only weapons which the Prophetic order recognized; by justice, mercy, truth, and goodness; by suffering, by endurance, by identification of himself with the joys, the sufferings of his nation; by opening a wider sympathy to the whole human race than had ever been offered before. That this expectation, however explained, existed in a greater or less degree amongst the Prophets is not doubted by any theologians of any school whatever. It is no matter of controversy. It is a simply and universally recognized fact that, filled with these Prophetic images, the whole Jewish nation—nay, at last, the whole Eastern world—did look forward with longing expectation to the coming of this future Conqueror. Was this unparalleled expectation realized? And here again I speak only of facts which are acknowledged by Germans and Frenchmen no less than by Englishmen, by critics and by skeptics even more than by theologians and ecclesiastics. There did arise out of this nation a Character as unparalleled as the expectation which had preceded him. Jesus of Nazareth was, on the most superficial no less than on the deepest view of his coming, the greatest name, the most extraordinary power that has ever crossed the stage of History. And this greatness consisted not in outward power, but precisely in those qualities in which from first to last the Prophetic order had laid the utmost stress,—justice and love, goodness and truth."[7]

This is the great fact from which the student of the Old Testament must never remove his attention. That this wonderful hope and expectation did suffuse all the utterances of the prophets is not to be gainsaid by any candid man. That the expectation assumed, as the ages passed, a more and more definite and personal form is equally certain. Isaiah was perhaps the first to give distinct shape to this prophetic hope. Ewald thus summarizes the Messianic idea in the writings of Isaiah:—

"There must come some one who should perfectly satisfy all the demands of the true religion, so as to become the centre from which all its truth and force should operate. His soul must possess a marvelous and surpassing nobleness and divine power, because it is his function perfectly to realize in life the ancient religion, the requirements of which no one has yet satisfied, and that, too, with that spiritual glorification which the great prophets had announced. Unless there first comes some one who shall transfigure this religion into its purest form, it will never be perfected, and its kingdom will never come. But he will and must come, for otherwise the religion which

---

7. *History of the Jewish Church*, i. 519, 520.

demands him would be false; he is the first true King of the community of the true God, and as nothing can be conceived of as supplanting him, he will reign forever in irresistible power; he is the divine-human King, whose coming had been due ever since the true community had set up a human monarchy in its midst, but who had never come. He is to be looked for, to be longed for, to be prayed for; and how blessed it is simply to expect him devoutly, and to trace out every feature of his likeness. To sketch the nobleness of his soul is to pursue in detail the possibility of perfecting all religion; and to believe in the necessity of his coming is to believe in the perfecting of all divine agency on earth."[8]

It is precisely here that we get at the heart of the Old Testament; this wonderful fore-looking toward the Messianic manifestations of God upon the earth, which kindled the hearts of the people and found clearest utterance by the lips of its most inspired men, which binds this literature all together, histories, songs, precepts, allegories. This it is which reveals the true inspiration of these old writings, and which makes them, to every Christian heart, precious beyond all price.

Such being the character of these prophetic books, let us glance for a moment at a few of them, merely for the purpose of locating the prophecy in the history, and of discerning, when it is possible, the providential causes which called it forth.

It is difficult to tell which of these fifteen prophets, whose utterances are treasured in this collection, first appeared upon the scene. The probability seems to be that

---

8. *The History of Israel,* iv. 203, 204.

the earliest of them was Joel. Opinions differ widely; I cannot discuss them nor even cite them; but the old theory that Joel lived and preached about eight hundred and seventy-five years before Christ does not seem to me to be invalidated by modern criticism. He was a native of the Southern Kingdom; and at the time we have named, the King of Judea was Joash, whose dramatic elevation to the throne in his seventh year, by Jehoiada the priest, is narrated in the Book of Kings. It was a time of disturbance and disaster in Judah and Jerusalem; the boy-king was but a nominal ruler; the regent was Jehoiada; and incursions of the surrounding tribes, who carried away the people and sold them as slaves, kept the land in a constant state of alarm. Worse than this was the visitation of locusts, continuing, as it would seem, for several years, by which the country was stripped and devastated. This visitation furnishes the theme of the short discourse which is here reported. The description of the march of the locusts over the land is full of poetic beauty; and the people are admonished to accept this as a divine chastisement for their sins, and to do the works meet for repentance. Then comes the promise of the divine forgiveness, and of that great gift of the Spirit, whose fulfillment Peter claimed on the day of Pentecost: "In the midst of the deepest woes which then afflicted the kingdom," says Ewald, "his great soul grasped all the more powerfully the eternal hope of the true community, and impressed it all the more indelibly upon his people, alike by the fiery glow of his clear insight and the entrancing beauty of his passionate utterance."[9]

---

9. *The History of Israel,* iv. 139.

The next prophet in the order of time is undoubtedly Amos. He tells us that he lived in the days of Uzziah, King of Judah, about seventy years after Joel. He was a herdsman of Tekoa, a small city of Judah, twelve miles south of Jerusalem. In these days the Northern Kingdom was far more prosperous and powerful than the Southern; under Jeroboam II. Israel had become rich and luxurious; and the prophet was summoned, as he declares, by the call of Jehovah himself to leave his herds upon the Judean hills, and betake himself to the Northern Kingdom, there to bear witness against the pride and oppression of its people. This messenger and interpreter of Jehovah to his people is a poor man, a laboring man; but he knows whose commission he bears, and he is not afraid. Stern and terrible are the woes that fall from his lips: the words vibrate yet with the energy of his righteous wrath.

"Ye that put far away the evil day, and cause the seat of violence to come near; that lie upon beds of ivory, and stretch themselves upon their couches, and eat the lambs out of the flock, and the calves out of the midst of the stall; that sing idle songs to the sound of the viol; that devise for themselves instruments of music, like David; that drink wine in bowls, and anoint themselves with the chief ointments; but they are not grieved for the affliction of Joseph."

Such luxury always goes hand in hand with contempt of the lowly and oppression of the poor; it is so to-day; it was so in that far-off time; and this prophet pours upon it the vials of the wrath of God:—

"Forasmuch therefore as ye trample upon the poor, and take exactions from him of wheat: ye have built houses of hewn stone, but ye shall not dwell in them; ye have planted pleasant vineyards, but ye shall not drink the wine thereof. For I know how manifold are your transgressions and how mighty are your sins; ye that afflict the just, that take a bribe, and that turn aside the needy in the gate from their right."

It is no wonder that Amaziah, the priest of Bethel, writhed under the scourge of the herdsman prophet, and wanted to be rid of him: "O thou seer," he cried, "go, flee thee away into the land of Judah, and there eat bread, and prophesy there: but prophesy not again any more in Bethel." But the prophet stood his ground and delivered his message, and it still resounds as the very voice of God through every land where the greed of gold makes men unjust, and the love of pleasure banishes compassion from human hearts.

The nearest successor of Amos, in this collection, seems to have been Hosea, who tells us in the opening of his prophecy that the word of the Lord came unto him in the days of Uzziah, Jotham, Ahaz, and Hezekiah, kings of Judah, and in the days of Jeroboam, son of Joash, king of Israel. There is some doubt about the genuineness of this superscription; but it was about this time, undoubtedly, that Hosea flourished. To which kingdom he belonged it is not known; probably, however, to Israel, with whose affairs his teaching is chiefly concerned. He must have followed close upon the herdsman of Tekoa; possibly they were contemporaries. His prophecy, too, is a blast from the trumpet of the Lord our Righteousness. Such an indictment of a people has not often been heard.

"Hear the word of the Lord, ye children of Israel: for the Lord hath a controversy with the inhabitants of the land, because there is no truth, nor mercy, nor knowledge of God in the land. There is nought but swearing and breaking faith, and killing, and stealing, and committing adultery; they break out, and blood toucheth blood."

Especially severe is the prophet in his denunciation of the priesthood.

"They feed on the sin of my people, and set their heart on their iniquity. And it shall be, like people, like priest: and I will punish them for their ways, and will reward them their doings."

These prophecies of Hosea are instinct with a severe morality; the ethical thoroughness with which he chastises the national sins is unflinching; but it is not all threatening; now and again we hear the word of tenderness, the promise of the divine forgiveness:—

"I will heal their backsliding. I will love them freely; for mine anger is turned away from him. I will be as the dew unto Israel; he shall blossom as the lily, and cast forth his roots as Lebanon."

Micah follows Hosea, at an interval of perhaps fifty years. He lived in a little village of Judah, west of Jerusalem, and exercised his ministry in both kingdoms, testifying impartially against the wickedness of Jerusalem and Samaria, though the weight of his censure seems to rest upon the Judean capital. His strain is an echo of the outcry of Amos and Hosea; it is the same intense indignation against the violence and rapacity of the rich, against corrupt judges, false prophets, rascally traders, treacherous friends. For all these sins condign punishment is threatened; and yet, after these retributive woes are past, there is promise of a better day. The great Messianic hope here begins to find clear utterance; the former prophets have seen in their visions only the restoration of the people of

Israel; to Micah there comes the anticipation of an individual Leader and Deliverer.

"But thou, Bethlehem Ephratah, which art little to be among the thousands of Judah, out of thee shall one come forth that is to be ruler in Israel, whose goings forth are from old, from everlasting. . . . And he shall stand and shall feed his flock in the strength of the Lord, in the majesty of the name of the Lord his God; and they shall abide; for now shall he be great unto the ends of the earth."

Thus slowly broadens the dawn of the Messianic hope.

The first part of the fourth chapter of Micah, which is a prediction of the glory that shall come to Zion in the latter day, is verbally identical with the first part of the second chapter of Isaiah. One of the prophets must have quoted from the other or else, as Dr. Geikie suggests, both copied from some older prophet.

After Micah comes the greatest of the prophets, Isaiah. He appeared upon the scene in his native city of Jerusalem about the middle of the eighth century before Christ. His work was mainly done during the reigns of Ahaz, "the Grasper," one of the vilest and most ungodly of the Judean monarchs, and of Hezekiah, the good king, about a century and a half before the destruction of Jerusalem.

About this time Judea was constantly exposed to the rapacity of the great Assyrian power before whose armies she finally fell; sometimes her rulers entered into coalitions with the surrounding nations to resist the Assyrian; sometimes they submitted and paid heavy tribute. Egypt, on the south, was also a mighty empire at this time, constantly at war with Assyria; and the kings of Judah sometimes sought alliances with one of these great powers, as a means of protection against the other. They proved to be the upper and nether millstones between which the Jewish nationality was ground to powder. It was in the midst of these alarming signs of national destruction that Isaiah arose. Of the prophetic discourses which he delivered in Jerusalem we have about thirty; his words are the words of a patriot, a statesman, a servant and messenger of Jehovah. He warned the kings against these entangling alliances with foreign powers; he admonished them to stand fast in their allegiance to Jehovah, and obey his laws; yet he saw that they would not heed his word, and that swift and sure destruction was coming upon the nation. And his expectation was not like that of the other prophets, that the nation as a whole would be saved out of these judgments; to him it was made plain that only a remnant would survive; but that from that remnant should spring a noble race, with a purer faith, in whom all the nations of the earth should be blessed. Of the Messianic hope as it finds expression in these words of Isaiah I have already spoken.

This Book of Isaiah contains thirty-one prophetic discourses, some of them mere fragments. There is reason for doubt as to whether they were all spoken by Isaiah; when they were gathered up, two hundred years later, some utterances of other prophets may have been mingled with them. Indeed it is now regarded as well-nigh certain that the last twenty-seven chapters are the work of a later prophet,—of one who wrote during the Captivity. Professor Delitzsch, in the last edition of his commentary on Isaiah, finally concedes that this is probable. The Book of Isaiah, he is reported as saying, "may have been an anthology of prophetic discourses by different authors; that is, it may have been composed partly and directly by Isaiah, and partly by other later prophets whose utterances constitute a really homogeneous and simultaneous continuation of Isaian prophecy. These later prophets so closely resemble Isaiah in prophetic vision that posterity might, on that account, well identify them with him,—his name being the correct common denominator for this collection of prophecies."

These words of the most distinguished and devout of the Old Testament critics throw a flood of light on the structure not only of Isaiah, but of other Old Testament writings; they show how unlike our own were the primitive ideas of authorship; and how the Pentateuch, for example, drawn from many sources and revised by many editors, could be called the law of Moses; how *his* name may have been the "common denominator" of all that collection of laws.

I have shown, perhaps, in these hasty notices, something of the nature and purpose of five of these prophetic books. Of the rest I must speak but a single word, for the time fails me to tell of Zephaniah, who in the time of good King Josiah, denounced the idolatry of the people, the injustice of its princes and judges, and the corruption of its prophets and priests, threatened the rebellious with extermination, and promised to the remnant an enduring peace; of Jeremiah, who about the same time first lifted up his voice, and continued speaking until after the destruction of Jerusalem,—from whose writings we may derive a more complete and intelligible account of the period preceding the Exile than from any other source; of Nahum, who, just before the fall of Jerusalem, uttered his oracle against Nineveh; of Obadiah, who, after the fall of the holy city, launched his thunderbolts against the perfidious Edomites because of their rejoicing over the fate of Jerusalem; of Ezekiel, the prophet of the Exile, who wrote among the captives by the rivers of Babylon; of Haggai and Zechariah, who came back with the returning exiles, and whose courageous voices cheered the laborers who wrought to restore the city and the temple; of Malachi, whose pungent reproofs of the people for their lack of consecration followed the erection of the second temple, and closed the collection of the Hebrew prophets.

The limits of this small volume forbid us to enter upon several interesting critical inquiries respecting the component parts of Isaiah and Zechariah, and especially the matter of the variations of the Septuagint from the Hebrew text in the Book of Jeremiah. In this last named book we find the same phenomena that we encountered in our study of Samuel and The Kings: the Greek version differs considerably from the Hebrew; a comparison of the two illustrates, as nothing else can do, the processes through which the text of these old documents has passed, and the freedom with which they have been handled by scribes and copyists. The Hebrew text, from which our English version was made, is generally better than the Greek; but there are several cases in which the Greek is manifestly more accurate.

There is one book, reckoned among these minor prophets, of which I have not spoken, and to which I ought to make some reference. That is the book of Jonah.

It is found among the minor prophets, but it is not in any sense prophetical; it is neither a sermon nor a prediction; it is a narrative. Probably it was placed by the

Jews among these prophetical books because Jonah was a prophet. But this book was not written by Jonah; there is not a word in the book which warrants the belief that he was its author. It is a story about Jonah, told by somebody else long after Jonah's day. Jonah, the son of Amittai, was a prophet of the Northern Kingdom in the days of Jeroboam II., far back in the ninth century. The only reference to him contained in the Old Testament is found in 2 Kings xiv. 25. But this book was almost certainly written long after the destruction of Nineveh, which took place two hundred years later. One reason for this belief is in the fact that the writer of the book feels it necessary to explain what kind of a city Nineveh was. He stops in the midst of his story to say: "Now Nineveh was an exceeding great city of three days' journey." That explanation would have been superfluous anywhere in Israel in the days of Jeroboam II., and the past tense indicates that it was written by one who was looking back to a city no longer in existence. "Nineveh was." The character of the Hebrew also favors the theory of a later date for the book. We have, therefore, a tale that was told about Jonah probably three or four hundred years after his day.

Is it a true tale, or is it a work of didactic fiction? I believe that it is the latter. It is a very suggestive apologue, full of moral beauty and spiritual power, designed to convey several important lessons to the minds of the Jewish people. I cannot regard it as the actual experience of a veritable prophet of God, because I can hardly imagine that such a prophet could have supposed, as the Jonah of this tale is said to have supposed, that by getting out of the bounds of the Kingdom of Israel, he would get out of the sight of Jehovah. This is precisely what this Jonah of the story undertook to do. When he was bidden to go to Nineveh and cry against it, "he rose up to flee unto Tarshish *from the presence of the Lord; and he went down to Joppa, and found a ship going to Tarshish: so he paid the fare thereof, and went down into it, to go with them unto Tarshish from the presence of the Lord" (ch. i. 3). Is this actual history? Is this the belief of a genuine prophet of the Lord? What sort of a prophet is he who holds ideas as crude as this concerning the Being with whom he is in constant communication and from whom he receives his messages? If Jonah did entertain this belief, then it is not likely that he can teach us anything about God which it is important that we should know.*

Thus, without touching the miraculous features of the story, we have sound reasons for believing that this cannot be the actual experience of any veritable prophet of God; that it is not history, but fiction. Why not? Can any one who has read the parable of the Prodigal Son or the Good Samaritan doubt that fiction may be used in Sacred Scripture for the highest purpose?

But it is argued that the references to this story which are found in the words of Christ authenticate the story. Our Lord, in Matt. xii, 39–42, refers to this book. He speaks of the repentance of the Ninevites under the preaching of Jonah as a rebuke to the Jews who had heard the word of life from him and had not repented; and he uses these words: "An evil and adulterous generation seeketh a sign; and there shall no sign be given to it but the sign of Jonah the prophet: for as Jonah was three days and three nights in the belly of the whale; so shall the Son of man be three days and three nights in the heart of the earth."

This confirms, say the orthodox commentators, the historical accuracy of the story of Jonah. "If," says Canon Liddon, "he would put his finger on a fact in past Jewish history which, by its admitted reality, would warrant belief in his own resurrection, he points to Jonah's being three days and three nights in the belly of the whale." This use of the incident by our Lord clearly authenticates the incident as an actual historical fact. So say the conservative theologians. And so say also the men who labor to destroy the authority of Christ. Mr. Huxley perfectly agrees with Canon Liddon. He praises the Canon's penetration and consistency; he agrees that there can be no other possible interpretation of Christ's words. The ultra-conservative and the anti-Christian critics are at one in insisting that Christ stands committed to the literal truth of the narrative in Jonah. The inference of the ultra-conservative is that the narrative is historically true; the inference of the anti-Christian critic is that Jesus is unworthy our confidence as a religious teacher; that one who fully indorsed such a preposterous tale cannot be divine. It is instructive to observe the ultra-conservative critics thus playing steadily into the hands of the anti-Christian critics, furnishing them with ammunition with which to assail the very citadel of the Christian faith. It is a kind of business in which, I am sorry to say, they have been diligently engaged for a good while.

Now I, for my part, utterly deny the proposition which these allied forces of skepticism and traditionalism are enlisted in supporting. I deny that Jesus Christ can be fairly quoted as authenticating this narrative. I maintain that he used it allegorically for purposes of illustration, without intending to express any opinion as to the historical verity of the narrative. It was used in a literary way, and not in a dogmatic way. Our Lord speaks always after the manner of men,—speaks the common speech of the people, takes up the phrases and even the fables that he finds upon their lips, and uses them for his own purposes. He does not stop to criticise all their stories, or to set them right in all their scientific errors; that would have been utterly aside from his main purpose, and would certainly have confused them and led them astray. He speaks always of the rising and the setting of the sun, using the phrases that were current at that time, and never hinting at the error underneath them. He knew what these people meant by these phrases. If he knew that these phrases conveyed an erroneous meaning, why did he not correct them? So, too, he quotes from the story of the Creation in Genesis, and never intimates that the six days there mentioned are not literal days of twenty-four hours each. He knew that those to whom he was speaking entertained this belief, and put this interpretation upon these words. Why does he not set it aside?

These questions may admit of more than one answer; but, taking the very highest view of Christ's person, it is certainly enough to say that any such discussion of scientific questions would have been, as even we can see, palpably unwise. There was no preparation in the human mind at that day for the reception and verification of such a scientific revelation. It could not have been received. It would not have been preserved. It would only have confused and puzzled the minds of his hearers, and would have shut their minds at once against that moral and spiritual truth which he came to impart. And what we have said about scientific questions applies with equal force to questions of Old Testament criticism. To have entered upon the discussion of these questions with the Jews would have thwarted his highest purpose. In the largest sense of the word these Scriptures were true. Their substantial historical accuracy he wished to confirm. Their great converging lines of light united in him. He constantly claimed their fulfillment in his person and his kingdom. Why, then, should he enter upon a kind of discussion which would have tended to confuse and obscure the main truths which he came to teach? If, then, he refers to these Scriptures, he uses them for his own ethical and spiritual purposes,—not to indorse their scientific errors; not to confirm the methods of interpretation in use among the Jews.

But Mr. Huxley insists, and all the ultra-conservative commentators join him in insisting, that Christ could not, if he had been an honest man, have spoken thus of Jonah if the story of Jonah had not been historically accurate. This is the way he puts it: "If Jonah's three days' residence in the whale is not an 'admitted fact,' how could it 'warrant belief' in the 'coming resurrection'?"[10] Mr. Huxley is using Canon Liddon's phrases here; but he is using them to confute those for whom, as he knows very well, Canon Liddon does not speak. Those who say that the story of Jonah is an "admitted reality" may, perhaps, be able to see that it "warrants belief" in the "coming resurrection." To my own mind, even this is by no means clear. I do not see how the one event, even if it were an "admitted reality," could "warrant belief" in the other. No past event can warrant belief in any future event, unless the

10. *The Nineteenth Century,* July, 1890.

two events are substantially identical. The growth of an acorn into an oak in the last century "warrants the belief" that an acorn will grow into an oak in the present century; but it does not "warrant the belief" that a city planted on an eligible site will grow to be a great metropolis. The one event might illustrate the other, but no conclusions of logic can be carried from the one to the other. It is precisely so with these two events. There is a certain analogy between the experience of Jonah, as told in the book, and that of our Lord; but it is ridiculous to say that the one event, if an "admitted reality," "warrants belief" in the other,—whether it is said by Mr. Huxley or Canon Liddon. Our Lord's words convey no such meaning. In truth, if we are here dealing with scientific comparisons, the one event, if taken as an "admitted reality," *warrants disbelief* in the other. What are our Lord's precise words? "*As* Jonah was three days and three nights in the whale's belly, *so* shall the Son of man be three days and three nights in the heart of the earth." We are told by Mr. Huxley and his orthodox allies that we must take this as a literal historical parallel, or not at all; that if we treat it in any other way, we accuse our Lord of dishonesty. What, then, was the condition of Jonah during these three days and nights? Was he dead or alive? He was certainly alive, if the tale is history—very thoroughly alive in all his faculties. He was praying part of the time, and part of the time he was writing poetry. We have a long and beautiful poem which he is said to have composed during that enforced retirement from active life. It would appear that his release took place immediately after the poem was finished. If, now, these events are bound together with the links of logic, if the one event is the historic counterpart

of the other, the Son of man, during the three days of his
sojourn in the heart of the earth, was not dead at all! He
was only hidden for a little space from the sight of men.
He was alive all the while, *and there was no resurrection!* It
is to this that you come when you begin to apply to these
parables and allegories of the Bible the methods of scientific exposition. This may be satisfactory enough to Mr.
Huxley. I should like to know how it suits his orthodox
allies.

The fact is, that you are not dealing here with equiva-
lents, but with analogies; not with laws of evidence, but
with figures of rhetoric: and it is absurd to say that one
member of an analogy "warrants belief" in the existence
of the other. There is no such logical nexus. The leaven in
the meal does not "warrant belief" in the spread of Christianity, but it serves to illustrate it. The story of the Prodigal Son does not "warrant belief" in the fatherly love of
God, but it helps us to understand something of that love,
and it helps us precisely as much as if it had been a veritable history, instead of being, as it is, a pure work of
fiction.

"What sort of value," asks Mr. Huxley, "as an illustration of God's methods of dealing with sin, has an account of an event that never happened?" Such an admonition, he says, is "morally about on a level with telling a
naughty child that a bogy is coming to fetch it away." Let
us apply this maxim to some of Mr. Huxley's homilies:—

"Surely," he says in one of his "Lay Sermons," "our in-
nocent pleasures are not so abundant in this life that we
can afford to despise this or any other source of them. We
should fear being banished for our neglect *to that limbo
where the great Florentine tells us are those who during this*

life wept when they might be joyful."[11] This limbo of Dante's is not, I dare say, an "admitted reality" in Mr. Huxley's physical geography. "What sort of value," therefore, has his reference to it? Is he merely raising the cry of bogy? He certainly does intend what he says as a dissuasive from a certain course of erroneous conduct. I venture to insist that he has a real meaning, and that, although the limbo is a myth, the condition which he intends to illustrate by his allusion to it is a reality.

Once more: "I do not suppose that the dead soul of Peter Bell, of whom the great poet of nature says,—

'A primrose by the river's brim
A yellow primrose was to him,
And it was nothing more,'

would have been a whit roused from its apathy by the information that the primrose is a Dicotyledonous Exogen, with a monopetalous corolla and a central placentation."[12]

Does Mr. Huxley believe that Peter Bell was a historical person? If he was not, how, in the name of biological theology, could his dead soul have been roused by any information whatever? Yet these sentences of his have a real and valuable meaning. It is evident that Mr. Huxley does understand the uses of allegory and fable for purposes of illustration; that he can employ characters and situations which are not historical, but purely imaginary, to illustrate the realities which he is trying to present,—

---

11. *Lay Sermons and Addresses*, p. 92.
12. *Ibid.* p. 91.

speaking of them all the while just as if they were historical persons or places, and trusting his readers to interpret him aright. Such a use of language is common in all literature. To affirm that our Lord could not resort to it without dishonesty is to deny to him the ordinary instruments of speech.

"We may conclude, then," with Professor Ladd, "that the reference to Jonah does not cover the question whether the prophet's alleged sojourn in the sea monster is an historical verity; and that it is no less uncritical than invidious to make the holding of any particular theory of the Book of Jonah a test of allegiance to the teachings of the Master."[13]

It is evident enough, as Professor Cheyne has said, that the symbolic meaning of the book was the most important part of it in the New Testament times. But other and more obvious meanings are conveyed by the narrative. Indeed, there is scarcely another book in the Old Testament whose meaning is so clear, whose message is so divine. Apologue though it is, it is full of the very truth of God. There is not one of the minor prophecies that has more of the real gospel in it. To the people who first received it, how full of admonition and reproof it must have been! That great city Nineveh—a city which was, in its day, as Dr. Geikie says, "as intensely abhorred by the Jews as Carthage was by Rome, or France under the elder Napoleon was by Germany"—was a city dear to God! He had sent his own prophet to warn it of its danger; and his prophet, instead of being stoned or torn asunder, as the prophets of God had often been by their own people, had

---

13. *The Doctrine of Sacred Scripture*, i. 67.

been heard and his message heeded. The Ninevites had turned to God, and God had forgiven them! God was no less ready to forgive and save Nineveh than Jerusalem. What a wonderful disclosure of the love of the universal Father! What a telling blow, even in those old days, at the "middle wall of partition" by which the Jew fenced out the Gentile from his sympathy!

And then the gentle rebuke of Jonah's petulant narrowness! How true is the touch that describes Jonah as angry because God had forgiven the Ninevites! His credit as a prophet was gone. I suppose that he was afraid also, like many theologians of more modern times, that if threatened penalty were remitted solely on the ground of the repentance of the sinners, the foundations of the divine government would be undermined. How marvelously does the infinite pity and clemency of God shine out through all this story, as contrasted with the petty consistency and the grudging compassion of man; and how clearly do we hear in this beautiful narrative the very message of the gospel: "Let the wicked forsake his way, and the unrighteous man his thoughts: and let him return to the Lord, and he will have mercy upon him; and to our God, for he will abundantly pardon. For my thoughts are not your thoughts, neither are your ways my ways, saith the Lord."

May I say, in closing, that the treatment which the Book of Jonah has received, alike from skeptics and from defenders of the faith, illustrates, in a striking way, the kind of controversy which is raised by the attempt to maintain the infallibility of the Bible. The *crux* of all the critics, orthodox and heterodox, is the story about the fish. The orthodox have assumed that the narrative without the miracle was meaningless, and the heterodox have taken them at their word. In their dispute over the question whether Jonah did really compose that psalm in the belly of the fish, with his head festooned with seaweed, they have almost wholly overlooked the great lessons of fidelity to duty, of the universal divine fatherhood, and the universal human brotherhood, which the story so beautifully enforces. How easy it is for saints as well as scoffers, in their dealing with the messages of God to men, to tithe the mint, anise, and cummin of the literal sense, and neglect the weightier matters of judgment, mercy, and truth which they are intended to convey!

Chapter 6

The Later Hebrew Histories

After the Book of the Law had been revised by Ezra, and the Book of the Prophets had been compiled by Nehemiah, there still remained a body of sacred writings, not Mosaic in their origin and not from the hands of any recognized prophet, but still of value in the eyes of the Jews. We cannot tell the time at which the work of collecting these Scriptures was begun; possibly it was going on while the Books of the Prophets were being compiled. This third collection was called from the first by the Jews, "Ketubim," meaning simply writings; the Greeks afterward called it by a name which has been anglicized, and which has become the common designation of these writings among us, "The Hagiographa," or the Holy Writings. The adjective holy was not a part of the Jewish title; it would have overstated, somewhat, their first estimate of this part of their Bible. For while the degree of sacredness attached to these books gradually increased, they were always held as quite inferior to the other two groups of Scriptures. For convenience the list of books in this collection may be here repeated:—

The Psalms
The Proverbs
Job
The Song of Solomon
Ruth
Lamentations
Ecclesiastes
Esther
Daniel
Ezra
Nehemiah
1 Chronicles
2 Chronicles

The arrangement is topical; first, three poetical books, The Psalms, The Proverbs, and Job; then five so-called Megilloth, or Rolls, read in the later synagogues on certain great feast days,—The Song of Songs at the Passover, Ruth at Pentecost, Lamentations on the anniversary of the burning of the temple, Ecclesiastes at the Feast of Tabernacles, and Esther at the Feast of Purim; lastly, the historical and quasi-historical books, Daniel, Ezra, Nehemiah, and the Chronicles.

Of Ruth I have already spoken in its proper historical connection, taking it with the Book of Judges.

In treating of the remaining books I shall not follow the order of the Hebrew Bible, which I have given above, but shall rather reverse it, treating first of the historical books, Ezra, Nehemiah, and the Chronicles, also of Esther and Daniel; then, in a subsequent chapter, of the poetical books, the Lamentations, the books attributed to Solomon,—Proverbs, Ecclesiastes, and Solomon's Song,—and finally of Job and the Psalms.

The histories which, under the title of the "Earlier Prophets," are contained in the middle group of the Hebrew Scriptures, have been studied in a former chapter. In this later group of writings we find certain other historical works which cover the same ground. In the words of Mr. Horton:—

"Taking historical excerpts from the first six books of the Bible, and then going on in a continuous narrative from the beginning of Judges to the end of the Second Book of Kings, we have a story—true, a story with many gaps in it, still a connected story—from the earliest times to the captivity of Judah. Then, starting from the First Book of Chronicles and reading on to the end of Nehemiah, we have, in a very compressed form, though enlarged in some parts, a complete record from Adam to the return from the Captivity; at the end of this long sweep of narrative comes the Book of Esther, which is a brief appendix containing a historical episode of the Captivity. Taking these two distinct histories, we have two lines of narrative, an older and a later, which run together up to the Captivity; the older, though covering a shorter time, is much the larger and fuller; the later, very thin in most parts, becomes very full in its account of the Temple-worship and Temple-kingship at Jerusalem, and then continues the story alone up to the end of the Captivity, and the reestablishment of the Temple-worship after the return."[1]

The older history, contained in Samuel and Kings, breaks off abruptly in the time of the Captivity; we know that it must have been written during the Exile, and could

---

1. *Inspiration and the Bible,* pp. 159, 160.

not have been written earlier than about 550 B.C. The later history, in Chronicles and Ezra-Nehemiah, begins with Adam, and goes on, by one or two genealogical tables, for almost two centuries after the Captivity. In 1 Chronicles iii. 19, the genealogy of Zerubbabel, who came back with the captives, is carried on for at least six generations. Counting thirty years for a generation, the table extends the time of the writing of this record to at least one hundred and eighty years after the return of the exiles. This occurred in 538 B.C., and the book must therefore have been written as late as 350 B.C., or very nearly two centuries after the earlier history was finished.

There are conclusive reasons for believing that the four books now under consideration, the two books of Chronicles, Ezra, and Nehemiah, were originally but one book. In the Hebrew Canon the Chronicles is now but one book; and in the old Hebrew collections Ezra and Nehemiah were but one book. It was in the Septuagint that they were first separated. Thus we have the four certainly reduced to two. And it is not difficult, on an inspection of the documents, to reduce the two to one. If you will open your Bible at the last verses of Second Chronicles, beginning with the twenty-second verse of the last chapter, and, fixing your eyes on this passage, will ask some one to read to you the first three verses of the Book of Ezra, you will see how these two books were formerly one; and how the manuscript was torn in two in the wrong place; so that the Book of Chronicles actually ends in the middle of a sentence. The period at the end of this book ought to be expunged.

The explanation of this curious phenomenon is not difficult. The last group of sacred writings, what the Jews call the Ketubim, was kept open for additions to a very late day. After this history was written (Chronicles-Ezra-Nehemiah) the question arose whether it should be admitted into the canon. The first answer to this question evidently was: "We do not need the first part of the history,—the Book of Chronicles,—for we have the substance of it already in the Books of Samuel and Kings and in the earlier writings; but we do need the last part of it, 'Ezra-Nehemiah,' for this carries the history on beyond the Captivity, and gives the account of the return of the exiles and the rebuilding of the city and the temple." So they tore the book in two, and put the last part of it into the growing collection of "Ketubim," or "Writings." The careless division of the manuscript, not at the beginning of a paragraph, but in the middle of a sentence, made it necessary, of course, for the scribe to copy at the beginning of the Ezra-roll the words belonging to it which had been torn off; but they were not erased from the first part, and have been left there, as the old historians say, "unto this day."

By and by there were requests that this first part—the Chronicles—be admitted to the Ketubim. The priests and the Levites of the temple would be sure to urge this request, for the Chronicles is the one book of the Old Testament in which their order is glorified; and at length the request was granted; the Chronicles were added to the collection, and as they went in last they follow Ezra-Nehemiah, although they belong, chronologically, before it. They stand to-day at the end of the Hebrew Bible, and thus testify, by their position, respecting the lateness of the date at which they were admitted to the canon. Thus the Hebrew Bible ends with an incomplete sentence.

What this later history may have been called before it was torn in two we have no means of knowing; but the Jews called the last part of it (which stands first in their collection) by the name of Ezra, and the first part of it (which is last in their canon) they named, "Events of the Times," or "Annals." In the Septuagint this book of the Chronicles was called "Paraleipomena," "Leavings," "Things Left Over," "Supplements." Jerome first gave it the name of "Chronicles," by which we know it.

The name of the author of this book is unknown. The strong probabilities are that he was a Levite, connected with the temple service in Jerusalem. The Levites had charge of the public religious services of the temple, especially of its music; and the fullness with which this writer expatiates upon all this part of the ritual shows that it was very dear to his heart.[2] Everything relating to the Levitical priesthood and its services is dwelt upon in this book with emphasis and elaboration; as the histories of Samuel and the Kings are written from the prophetical standpoint, this is most evidently written from the priestly point of view.

In these books of the Chronicles the author constantly points out the sources of his information. He tells us that he quotes from the "Book of the Kings of Judah and Israel," from the "Acts of the Kings of Israel," and from "The Story of the Book of the Kings." The identity of these books is a disputed question. It is supposed by some critics that he refers to the Books of Kings in our Bible; others maintain that he draws from another and much larger

---

2. See 1 Chron. vi. 31–48; xv. 16–24; xvi 4–42; xxv.2 Chron. v. 12, 13; vii. 6; viii. 14; xx. 19–21; xxiii. 13; xxix. 25–30; xxxi 2; zxxiv. 12; xxxv. 15.

book of a similar name which has been lost. The latter theory is generally maintained by the more conservative critics; and it is easier to vindicate the author's trustworthiness on this supposition; yet even so there are serious difficulties in the case; for it is hard to believe that he could have written these annals without having had before him the earlier record, and between the two are many discrepancies. The main facts of the history are substantially the same in the two narratives; but in minor matters the disagreements and contradictions are numerous. It is part of the purpose of this study to look difficulties of this kind fairly in the face; it is treason to the spirit of all truth to refuse to do so. Let us examine, then, a few of these discrepancies between the earlier and later history.

In 2 Samuel viii. 4, we are told that in David's victory over Hadadezer king of Zobah, he took from the latter "a thousand and seven hundred horsemen." In 1 Chronicles xviii. 4, he is said to have taken "a thousand chariots and seven thousand horsemen." In 2 Samuel xxiv. 9, David's census is said to have returned 800,000 warriors for Israel, and 500,000 for Judah. In 1 Chronicles xxi. 5, the number is stated as 1,100,000 for Israel, and 470,000 for Judah. In 2 Samuel xxiv. 24, David is said to have paid Araunah for his threshing-floor fifty shekels of silver, estimated at about thirty dollars of our money; in 1 Chronicles xxi. 25, he is said to have given him "six hundred shekels of gold by weight," amounting to a little more than thirty-four hundred dollars. In 2 Chronicles xiv. i, we read that Asa reigned in the stead of his father Abijah, and that in his days the land was quiet ten years. Again in the 10th and the 19th verses of the following chapter we learn that from the fifteenth to the thirty-fifth year of

Asa there was no war in the land. In 1 Kings xv. 32, we are explicitly told that "there was war between Asa and Baasha king of Israel all their days." In 1 Chronicles xx. the story of the taking of Rabbah seems to be abridged from 2 Samuel xi., xii.; but the abridgment is curiously done, so that the part taken by David in the siege and capture of the city is not brought out; and the whole narrative of David's relation to Uriah and Bathsheba, with the rebuke of Nathan and the death of David's child, is not alluded to. The relation of the two narratives at this point is significant; it deserves careful study. One more curious difference is found in the two accounts of the numbering of Israel. In 2 Samuel xxiv. 1, we read, "And the anger of the Lord was kindled against Israel, and he moved David against them, saying, Go, number Israel and Judah." In 1 Chronicles xxi., we read, "And Satan stood up against Israel and moved David to number Israel." The numbering in both narratives is assumed to be a grievous sin; and the penalty of this sin, which was David's, was visited upon the people in the form of a pestilence, which slew seventy thousand of them. I observe that the commentators try to reconcile these statements by saying that God *permitted* Satan to tempt David. I wonder if that explanation affords to any mind a shade of relief. But the older record utterly forbids such a gloss. "The anger of the Lord against Israel" prompted the Lord to "move David against them," and the Lord said, "Go, number Judah and Israel!" It was not a permission; it was a direct instigation. Then because David did what the Lord moved him to do, "the Lord sent a pestilence upon Israel," which destroyed seventy thousand men. We are not concerned to reconcile these two accounts, for neither of them can be true. Let us not suppose that we can be required, by any theory of inspiration, to blaspheme God by accusing him of any such monstrous iniquity. Let no man open his mouth in this day to declare that the Judge of all the earth instigated David to do a presumptuous deed, and then slew seventy thousand of David's subjects for the sin of their ruler. Such a view of God might have been held without censure three thousand years ago; it cannot be held without sin by men who have the New Testament in their hands. This narrative belongs to that class of crude and defective teachings which Jesus, in the Sermon on the Mount, points out and sets aside. We may, nay we must apply to the morality of this transaction the principle of judgment which Jesus gives us in that discourse, and say: "Ye have heard that it hath been said by them of old time that God sometimes instigates a ruler to do wrong, and then punishes his people for the wrong done by the ruler which he himself has instigated; but I say unto you that 'God cannot be tempted with evil, neither tempteth he any man;' moreover the ruler shall not bear the sin of the subject, nor the subject the sin of the ruler; for every man shall give account of himself unto God." It is by the higher standard that Christ has given us in the New Testament that we must judge all these narratives of the Old Testament, and when we find in these old writings statements which represent God as perfidious and unjust, we are not to try to "harmonize" them with other statements; we are simply to set them aside as the views of a dark age.

Such blurred and distorted ideas about God and his truth we do certainly find here and there in these old writings; the treasure which they have preserved for us is in earthen vessels; the human element, which is a necessary part of a written revelation, all the while displays itself. It is human to err; and the men who wrote the Bible were human. We may have a theory that God must have guarded them from every form of error, but the Bible itself has no such theory; and we must try to make our theories of inspiration fit the facts of the Bible as we find them lying upon its pages.

The second portion of this history, the Book of Ezra-Nehemiah, presents fewer of these difficulties than the Book of Chronicles. It is a fragmentary, but to all appearance a veracious record of the events which took place after the first return of the exiles to Jerusalem. The first caravan returned in the first year of King Cyrus; and the history extends to the last part of the reign of Artaxerxes Longimanus,—covering a period of more than a hundred years. The documents on which it is based were largely official; and there is no doubt that considerable portions of the first book came from the pen of Ezra himself, and that the second book was made up in part from writings left by Nehemiah. The language of the second book is Hebrew; that of the first is partly Hebrew and partly Chaldee or Aramaic. We read in the fourth chapter of Ezra that a certain letter was written to King Artaxerxes, and it is said that "the writing of the letter was written in the Syrian character." The margin of the revised version says "Aramaic." We find this letter in our Hebrew Bibles in the Aramaic language. And the writer, after copying the letter in Aramaic, goes right on with the history in Aramaic; from the twelfth verse of the fourth chapter to the eighteenth verse of the sixth chapter the language is all Aramaic; then the historian drops back into Hebrew again, and goes on to the twelfth verse of the seventh chapter, when he returns to Aramaic to record the letter of Artaxerxes, which extends to the twenty-seventh verse. The rest of the book is Hebrew. With the exception of some short sections of the Book of Daniel, this is the only portion of our Old Testament that was not written originally in the Hebrew tongue.

The contents of these two books may be briefly summarized. The first book tells us how the Persian king Cyrus, in the first year of his reign, issued a proclamation to the Jews dwelling in his kingdom, permitting and encouraging them to return to their own country and to rebuild the temple in Jerusalem. The conquest of the Babylonians by the Persians had placed the captive Jews in vastly improved circumstances. Between the faith of the Persians and that of the Jews there was close affinity. The Persians were monotheists; and "Cyrus," as Rawlinson says, "evidently identified Jehovah with Ormazd, and, accepting as a divine command the prophecy of Isaiah, undertook to rebuild their temple for a people who, like his own, allowed no image of God to defile the sanctuary. . . . The foundation was then laid for that friendly intimacy between the two peoples of which we have abundant evidence in the books of Ezra, Nehemiah, and Esther." The words of the decree of Cyrus, with which the Book of Ezra opens, show how he regarded the God of the Jews: "Whosoever there is among you of all his people, his God be with him, and let him go up to Jerusalem, which is in Judah, and build the house of the Lord, the God of Israel, (he is God,) which is in Jerusalem." The parenthetical clause is a clear confession of the faith of Cyrus that Jehovah was only another name for Ormazd; that there is but one God.

In consequence of this decree, a caravan of nearly fifty thousand persons, led by Zerubbabel, carrying with them liberal free-will offerings of those who remained in Babylon for the building of the temple, went back to Jerusalem, and in the second year began the erection of the second temple. With this pious design certain Samaritans interfered, finally procuring an injunction from the successor of Cyrus by which the building of the temple was interrupted for several years. On the accession of Darius, the prophets Haggai and Zechariah stirred up the people to resume the work, and at length succeeded in getting from the great king complete authority to proceed with it. In the sixth year of his reign the second temple was completed, and dedicated with great rejoicing. This closes the first section of the Book of Ezra. The rest of the book is occupied with the story of Ezra himself, who is said to have been "a ready scribe in the law of Moses," and who, "in the seventh year of Artaxerxes, king of Persia," led a second caravan of exiles home to Jerusalem, with great store of silver and gold and wheat and wine and oil for the resumption of the ritual worship of the Lord's house. The story of this return of the exiles is minutely told; and the remainder of this book is devoted to a recital of the matter of the mixed marriages between the Jewish men and the women of the surrounding tribes, which caused Ezra great distress, and which he succeeded in annulling, so that these "strange women," as they are called, were all put away. To our eyes this seems a piece of doubtful morality, but we must consider the changed standards of our time, and remember that these men might have done with the purest conscientiousness some things which we could not do at all.

The Book of Nehemiah is in part a recital by Nehemiah himself of the circumstances of his coming to Jerusalem, which seems to have taken place about thirteen years after the coming of Ezra. He was the cupbearer of Artaxerxes the king; he had heard of the distress and poverty of his people at Jerusalem, and in the fervid patriotism of his nature he begged the privilege of going up to Jerusalem to rebuild its walls. Permission was gained, and the first part of the book contains a stirring account of the experiences of Nehemiah in building the walls of Jerusalem. After this work was finished, Nehemiah undertook a census of the restored city, but he found, as he says, "the book of the genealogy of them that came up at the first,"—the list of families which appears in Ezra,—and this he copies. It may be instructive to take these two lists—the one in Ezra ii. and the one in Nehemiah vii.—and compare them. After this we have an account of a great congregation which assembled "in the broad place that was before the water gate," when Ezra the scribe stood upon "a pulpit of wood" from early morning until midday, and read to the assembled multitude from the book of the law. "And Ezra opened the book in the sight of all the people (for he was above all the people); and when he opened it all the people stood up, and Ezra blessed Jehovah the great God. And all the people answered, Amen, Amen, with the lifting up of their hands; and they bowed their heads, and worshiped Jehovah, with their faces to the ground." Other scribes stood by, apparently to take turns in the reading; and it is said that "they read in the book, in the law of the Lord distinctly [or, 'with an interpretation,' Marg.], and they gave the sense, so that they understood the reading." From this it has been inferred that the people had already become, in their sojourn in the East, more familiar with Aramaic than with their own tongue, and that they were unable to understand the Hebrew without some words of interpretation. It is doubtful, however, whether all this meaning can be read into this passage. At any rate, we have here, undoubtedly, the history of the inauguration of the reading of the law as one of the regular acts of public worship. And this must have been about 440 B.C.

The narrative of the first complete and formal observance of the Feast of Tabernacles since the days of Joshua; the narrative of the solemn league and covenant by which the people bound themselves to keep the law; the narrative of the dedication of the wall of the city, and the account of various reforms which Nehemiah prosecuted, with certain lists of priests and Levites, fill up the remainder of the book.

Taking it all in all it is a very valuable record; no historical book of the Old Testament gives greater evidence of veracity; none excels it in human interest. The pathetic tale of the return of this people from their long exile, of the rebuilding of their city and their temple, and of the heroic and self-denying labors of Zerubbabel and Nehemiah, the governors, and Haggai and Zechariah, the prophets, and Ezra the scribe, with all their coadjutors, is full of significance to all those who trace in the history of the people of Israel, more clearly than anywhere else, the increasing purpose of God which runs through all the ages.

That portions of the first book were written by Ezra, and of the second book by Nehemiah, is not doubted; but both books were revised somewhat by later hands; additions were undoubtedly made after the death of Nehemiah; for one, at least, of the genealogies shows us a certain Jaddua as high priest, and tells us that he was the great grandson of the man who was high priest when Nehemiah came to Jerusalem. It is not probable that Nehemiah lived to see this Jaddua in the high priest's office. It is probable that the last revision of the Bible was made some time after 400 B.C.

I have now to speak, in the conclusion of this chapter, of two other books of this last group, concerning which there has always been much misconception, the Book of Esther and the Book of Daniel. Esther stands in our Bibles immediately after Ezra-Nehemiah, while Daniel is included among the prophets. But in the Hebrew Bibles both books are found in the group which was last collected and least valued.

I have styled these historical books; are they truly historical? That they are founded upon fact I do not doubt; but it is, perhaps, safer to regard them both rather as historical fictions than as veritable histories. The reason for this judgment may appear as we go on with the study.

The Book of Esther may be briefly summarized. The scene is laid in Shushan the palace, better known as Susa, one of the royal residences of the kings of Persia. The story opens with a great feast, lasting one hundred and eighty days, given by the King Ahasuerus to all the nabobs of the realm. It is assumed that this king was Xerxes the Great, but the identification is by no means conclusive. At the close of this monumental debauch, the king, in his drunken pride, calls in his queen Vashti to show her beauty to the inebriated courtiers. She refuses, and the refusal ought to be remembered to her honor; but this book does not so regard it. The sympathy of the book is with the bibulous monarch, and not with his chaste and modest spouse. The king is very wroth, and after taking much learned advice from his counselors, puts away his queen for this act of insubordination, and proceeds to look for another. His choice falls upon a Jewish maiden, a daughter of the Exile, who has been brought up by her cousin Mordecai. Esther, at Mordecai's command, at first conceals her Jewish descent from the king. An opportunity soon comes for Mordecai to reveal to Esther a plot against the king's life; and the circumstance is recorded in the chronicles of the realm.

Soon after this a certain Haman is made Grand Vizier of the kingdom, and Mordecai the Jew refuses to do obeisance to him; in consequence of which Haman secures from the king an edict ordering the assassination of all the Jews in the kingdom. His wrath against Mordecai being still further inflamed, he erects a gallows fifty cubits high, with the purpose of hanging thereon the testy Israelite. The intervention of Esther puts an end to these malicious schemes. At the risk of her life she presents herself before the king, and gains his favor; then, while Haman's purpose halts, the king is reminded, when the annals of his kingdom are read to him on a wakeful night, of the frustration of the plot against his person by Mordecai, and learning that no recompense has been made to him, suddenly determines to elevate and honor him; and the consequence is, that Haman himself, his purposes being disclosed by the queen, is hanged on the gallows that he had prepared for Mordecai, and Mordecai is elevated to Hainan's place. The decree of an Eastern king cannot be annulled, and the massacre of the Jews still remains a legal requirement; yet Esther and Mordecai are permitted to send royal orders to all parts of the realm authorizing the Jews upon the day of the appointed massacre to stand for their lives, and to kill as many as they can of their enemies. Thus encouraged, and supported also by the king's officials in every province, who are now the creatures of Mordecai, the Jews turn upon their enemies, and slay in one day seventy-five thousand of them,—five hundred in the palace of Shushan,—among whom are the ten sons of Haman. On the evening of this bloody day, the king says to Esther the queen: "The Jews have slain five hundred men in Shushan the palace, and the ten sons of Haman; what then have they done in the rest of the king's provinces? [From this sample of their ferocity you can judge how much blood must have been shed throughout the kingdom.] Now what is thy petition? and it shall be granted thee; or what is thy request further? and it shall be done." It might be supposed that this fair Jewish princess would be satisfied with this banquet of blood, but she is not; she wants more. "Then said Esther, if it please the king, let it be granted to the Jews which are in Shushan to do to-morrow also, according unto this day's decree, and let Haman's ten sons be hanged upon the gallows." The request is granted; the next day three hundred more Persians are butchered in Shushan the palace; and the dead bodies of the ten sons of Haman, weltering in their gore, are lifted up and hanged upon the gallows, and all to please Queen Esther! If a single Jew loses his life in this outbreak, the writer forgets to mention it. It is idle to say that this is represented as a defensive act on the part of the Jews; the impression is given that the Persians, by the menacing action of their own officials under Mordecai's authority, were completely cowed, and were simply slaughtered in their tracks by the infuriated Jews.

As a memorial of this feast of blood, the Jewish festival of Purim was instituted, which is kept to this day; and the Book of Esther is read at this feast, in dramatic fashion, with passionate responses by the congregation.

Is this history? There is every reason to hope that it is not. That some deliverance of the Jews from their enemies in Persia may be commemorated by the feast of Purim is possible; that precisely such a fiendish outbreak of fanatical cruelty as this ever occurred, we may safely and charitably doubt. The fact that the story was told, and that it gained great popularity among the Jews, and by some of those in later ages came to be regarded as one of the most sacred books of their canon is, however, a revelation to us of the extent to which the most baleful and horrible passions may be cherished in the name of religion. It is precisely for this purpose, perhaps, that the book has been preserved in our canon. If any one wishes to see the perfect antithesis of the precepts and the spirit of the gospel of Christ, let him read the Book of Esther. Frederick Bleek is entirely justified in his statement that "a spirit of revenge and persecution prevails in the book, and that no other book of the Old Testament is so far removed as this is from the spirit of the gospel."[3] For it is not merely true that these atrocities are here recited; they are clearly indorsed. There is not a word said in deprecation of the beastliness of the king or the vindictiveness of

---

3. Introduction to the Old Testament, i. 450.

the hero and the heroine. It is clear, as Bleek says, "that the author finds a peculiar satisfaction in the characters and mode of acting of his Jewish compatriots, Esther and Mordecai; and that the disposition shown by them appears to him as the right one, and one worthy of their nation." "Esther the beautiful queen," whose praises have been sung by many of our poets, possesses, indeed, some admirable qualities; her courage is illustrious; her patriotism is beautiful; but her bloodthirstiness is terrible.

As to the time when this book was written, or who wrote it, I am not curious. Probably it was written long after the Exile, but by some one who was somewhat familiar with the manners of Oriental courts. The name of God is not once mentioned in the book; and it seems like blasphemy to intimate that the Spirit of God could have had anything to do with its composition. It is absolutely sickening to read the commentaries, which assume that it was dictated by the Holy Ghost, and which labor to justify and palliate its frightful narrative. One learns, with a sense of relief, that the Jews themselves long disputed its admission to their canon; that the school of Schammai would not accept it, and that several of the wisest and best of the early fathers of the Christian church, Athanasius and Melito of Sardis among the rest, denied it a place in sacred Scripture. Dr. Martin Luther is orthodox enough for me, and he, more than once, expressed the hearty wish that the book had perished. That, indeed, we need not desire; let it remain as a dark background on which the Christian morality may stand forth resplendent; as a striking example of the kind of ideas which Christians ought not to entertain, and of the kind of feelings which they ought not to cherish.

The Book of Daniel brings us into a very different atmosphere. Esther is absolutely barren of religious ideas or suggestions; Daniel is full of the spirit of faith and prayer. Whether the character of Daniel, as here presented, is a sketch from life or a work of the imagination, it is a noble personality. The self-control, the fidelity to conscience, the heroic purposes which are here attributed to him, make up a picture which has always attracted the admiration of generous hearts.

"As in the story of the Three Children," says Dean Stanley, "so in that of the Den of Lions, the element which has lived on with immortal vigor is that which tells how, 'when Daniel knew that the writing was signed, he kneeled upon his knees three times a day and prayed and gave thanks to God, as he did aforetime.' How often have these words confirmed the solitary protest, not only in the Flavian amphitheatre, but in the ordinary yet not more easy task of maintaining the right of conscience against arbitrary power or invidious insult! How many an independent patriot or unpopular reformer has been nerved by them to resist the unreasonable commands of king or priest! How many a little boy at school has been strengthened by them for the effort, when he has knelt down by his bedside for the first time to say his prayers in the presence of indifferent or scoffing companions. . . . Shadrach, Meshach, and Abednego in the court of Nebuchadnezzar, Daniel in the court of Darius, are the likenesses of 'the small transfigured band whom the world cannot tame,' who, by faith in the Unseen, have in every age 'stopped the mouths of lions, and quenched the violence of fire.' This was the example to those on whom, in all ages, in spirit if not in letter, 'the fire had no power, nor was an hair of their head singed, neither were their coats changed, nor the smell of fire passed upon them;' but it was 'as it were a moist, whistling wind, and the form of the fourth, who walked with them in the midst of the fire, was like a Son of God.'"[4]

Was Daniel a historical person? The question has been much disputed, but I think that we may safely answer it in the affirmative. It is true that in all these writings of the later period of Israel Daniel is mentioned but twice, both times in the Book of Ezekiel (xiv. 14; xxviii. 3). The first of these allusions is a declaration that a few righteous men cannot save a wicked city, when the decree of destruction against it has been issued; "though these three men, Noah, Daniel, and Job were in it, they should deliver but their own souls by their righteousness, saith the Lord God." The other is in a prophecy against the King of Tyre, in which he is represented as saying to himself that he is wiser than Daniel; that there is no secret that can be hidden from him. Whether these casual uses of the name of Daniel for purposes of illustration can be regarded as establishing his historical character may be questioned. And it is a singular fact that we have not in Ezra, or Nehemiah, or Haggai, or Zechariah, or Malachi, any reference to the existence of Daniel. Nevertheless, it is hardly to be supposed that such a character was wholly fictitious; we may well suppose that he existed, and that the narratives of his great fidelity and piety are at any rate founded upon fact.

The first six chapters of the book are not ascribed to Daniel as their author; he is spoken of in the third person,

---

4. *History of the Jewish Church,* pp. 41, 42.

and sometimes in a way that a good man would not be likely to speak about himself. The remainder of the book claims to be written by him. The question is whether this claim is to be taken as an assertion of historical fact, or as a device of literary workmanship. Ecclesiastes was undoubtedly written long after the Exile, yet it purports to have been composed by King Solomon. The author puts his words into the mouth of Solomon, to gain attention for them. It is not fair to call this a fraud; it was a perfectly legitimate literary device. It is entirely possible that this may be the case with the author of this book. Daniel was a person whose name was well-known among his contemporaries, and the author makes him his mouthpiece. There may have been a special reason why the author should have desired to send out these narratives and visions under the name of a hero of antiquity, a reason which we shall presently discover.

The Book of Daniel is not what is commonly called a prophecy; it is rather an apocalypse. It belongs to a class of literature which sprang up in the last days of the Jewish nationality, after the old prophets had disappeared; it is designed to comfort the people with hopes of future restoration of the national power; its method is that of vision and symbolic representation. Daniel is the only book of this kind in the Old Testament; the New Testament canon closes, as you know, with a similar book. I shall not undertake to interpret to you these visions of the Book of Daniel; they are confessedly obscure and mysterious. But there is one portion of the book, the eleventh chapter, which is admitted to be a minute and realistic description of the coalitions and the conflicts between the Graeco-Syrian and the Graeco-Egyptian kings, events which took place about the middle of the second century before Christ. These personages are not named, but they are vividly described, and the intrigues and vicissitudes of that portion of Jewish history in which they are the chief actors are fully told. Moreover the recital is put in the future tense; "There shall stand up yet three kings in Persia; and the fourth shall be richer than they all; and when he is waxed strong through his riches, he shall stir up all against the realm of Greece." If, now, the Book of Daniel was written in the early days of the Exile, this was a very circumstantial prediction of what happened in the second century,—a prediction uttered three hundred years before the event. And respecting these predictions, if such they are, we must say this, that we have no others like them. The other prophets never undertake to tell the particulars of what is coming to pass; they give out, in terms very large and general, the nature of the events which are to come. No such carefully elaborated programme as this is found in any other predictive utterance.

But there are those—and they include the vast majority of the leading Christian scholars of the present day—who say that these words were not written in the early days of the Exile; that they must have been written about the middle of the second century; that they were therefore an account of what was going on, by an onlooker, couched in these phrases of vision and prophecy. The people of Israel were passing through a terrible ordeal; they needed to be heartened and nerved for resistance and endurance. Their heroic leader, Judas Maccabeus, was urging them on to prodigies of valor in their conflict with the vile Antiochus; such a ringing manifesto as this, put forth in the progress of the conflict, might have a powerful influence in reinforcing their patriotism and confirming their faith. It might also have appeared at some stage of the conflict when it would have been imprudent and perhaps impossible to secure currency for the book if the reference to existing rulers had been explicit; such a device as the author adopted may have been perfectly understood by the readers; although slightly veiled in the form of its deliverance, it was, perhaps, for this very reason, all the better fitted for its purpose.

It might, then, have been written when the Ptolemies and the Seleucidae were wasting the fields of Palestine with their conflicts. But was it written then? How do we know that it was not a circumstantial prediction made three hundred years before? We do not know, with absolute certainty, when it was written; but there are strong reasons for believing that the later date is the true date.

1. The book is not in the Hebrew collection of the Prophets. That collection was made at least a hundred years after the time at which Daniel is here said to have lived; if so great a prophecy had been existing then, it is strange that it should not have been gathered with the other prophets into Nehemiah's collection. It is found, instead, among the Ketubim,—the later and supplementary writings of the Hebrew Bible.

2. It is strange also, as I have intimated, that no mention of Daniel or of his book is found in the histories of the Exile and the return, or in any of the prophecies uttered in Israel after the return. That there should be no allusion in any of these books to so distinguished a personage can hardly be explained.

3. Jesus, the son of Sirach, one of the writers of the Apocrypha, who lived about 200 B.C., gives a full catalogue of all the great worthies of Israel; he has a list of the prophets; he names all the other prophets; he does not name Daniel.

4. The nature of this prediction, if it be a prediction, is unaccountable. Daniel is said to have lived in the Babylonian period, and looked forward from that day. His people were in exile, but there is not a vision of his that has any reference to their return from the captivity, to the rebuilding of the temple, or to any of the events of their history belonging to the two centuries following. It is strange that if, standing at that point of time, he was inspired to predict the future of the Jewish people, he should not have had some message respecting those great events in their history which were to happen within the next century. Instead of this, his visions, so far as his own people are concerned, overleap three centuries and land in the days of Antiochus Epiphanes. Here they begin at once to be very specific; they tell all the particulars of this period, but beyond this period they give no particulars at all; the vision of the Messianic triumph which follows is vague and general like the rest of the prophecies. These circumstances strongly support the theory of the later date.

5. Words appear in this writing which almost certainly fix it at a later date than the Babylonian period. There are certainly nine undoubted Persian words in this book; there are no Persian words in Ezekiel, who lived at the time when Daniel is placed at the Babylonian court, nor in Haggai, Zechariah, or Malachi. There are several Greek words, names of musical instruments, and it is almost

certain that no Greek words were in use in Babylonia at that early day. This philological argument may seem very dubious and far-fetched, but it is really one of the most conclusive tests of the date of a document. There is no witness so competent as the written word. Let me give you a homely illustration. Suppose you find in some late history of the United States a quoted letter said to have been written by President Zachary Taylor, who died in 1850, respecting a certain political contest. The letter contains the following paragraph:—

"On receiving this intelligence, I called up the Secretary of State by telephone, and asked him how he explained the defeat. He told me that, in his opinion, boodle was at the bottom of it. I determined to make an investigation, and after wiring to the member of Congress in that district, I ordered my servant to engage me a section in a Pullman car, and started the same night for the scene of the contest."

Now of course you know that this paragraph could not have been written by President Taylor, nor during the period of his administration. The telephone was not then in existence; there were no Pullman cars; the words "boodle" and "wire," in the sense here used, had never been heard. In precisely the same way the trained philologist can often determine with great certainty the date of a writing. He knows the biography of words or word-forms; and he may know that some of the words or the word-forms contained in a certain writing were not yet in the language at the date when it is said to have been written. It is by evidence of this nature that the critics fix the date of the Book of Daniel at a period long after the close of the Babylonian empire.

This verdict reduces, somewhat, the element of the marvelous contained in the book; it does not in any wise reduce the moral and spiritual value of it. The age of the Maccabees, when this book appeared, was one of the great ages of Jewish history. Judas Maccabeus is one of the first of the Israelitish heroes; and the struggle, in which he was the leader, against the dissolute Syrian Greeks brought out some of the strongest qualities of the Hebrew character. The genuine humility, the fervid consecration, the dauntless faith of the Jews of this generation put to shame the conduct of their countrymen in many ages more celebrated. And it cannot be doubted that this book was both the effect and the cause of this lofty national purpose. "Rarely," says Ewald, "does it happen that a book appears as this did, in the very crisis of the times, and in a form most suited to such an age, artificially reserved, close and severe, and yet shedding so clear a light through obscurity, and so marvelously captivating. It was natural that it should soon achieve a success entirely corresponding to its inner truth and glory. And so, for the last time in the literature of the Old Testament, we have in this book an example of a work which, having sprung from the deepest necessities of the noblest impulses of the age, can render to that age the purest service; and which, by the development of events immediately after, receives with such power the stamp of Divine witness that it subsequently attains imperishable sanctity."[5]

5. Quoted by Stanley, *History of the Jewish Church*, iii. p. 336.

Chapter 7

The Poetical Books

The poetical books of the Old Testament now invite our attention,—"The Lamentations," "Proverbs," "Ecclesiastes," "The Song of Solomon," "Job," and "The Psalms." Ecclesiastes is not in poetical form, but it is a prose poem; the movement of the language is often lyrical, and the thought is all expressed in poetic phrases. The other books are all poetical in form as well as in fact.

Lamentations, called in the Hebrew Bible by the quaint title "Ah How," the first two words of the book, and in the Greek Bible "Threnoi," signifying mourning, is placed in the middle of the latest group of the Hebrew writings. In the English Bible it follows the prophecy of Jeremiah. It is called in our version "The Lamentations of Jeremiah." This title preserves the ancient tradition, and there is no reason to doubt that the tradition embodies the truth. "In favor of this opinion," says Bleek, "we may note the agreement of the songs with Jeremiah's prophecies in their whole character and spirit, in their purport, and in the tone of disposition shown in them, as well as in the language. . . . As regards the occasion and substance of these songs, the two first and the two last relate

153

to the misery which had been sent on the Jewish people, and particularly on Jerusalem; the middle one, however, chiefly refers to the personal sufferings of the author."[1]

These five parts are not the five chapters of a book; they are five distinct poems, each complete in itself, though they are all connected in meaning. You notice the regularity of the structure, which is even exhibited to some extent in the Old Version. The first and second, the fourth and fifth, have each twenty-two verses or stanzas; the third one has sixty-six stanzas. All but the last are acrostical poems. There are twenty-two letters in the Hebrew alphabet; each of these letters, in regular order, begins a verse in four of these songs; in the third lamentation there are three verses for each letter.

The time at which these elegies were written was undoubtedly the year of the capture of Jerusalem by the army of Nebuchadnezzar, 586 B.C. The Chaldean army had been investing the city for more than a year; the walls were finally broken down, and the Chaldeans rushed in; as they gained entrance on one side, the wretched King Zedekiah escaped on the other with a few followers and fled down the Jericho road; he was pursued and overtaken, his sons and princes were slain before his face, then his own eyes were put out, and he was led away in chains to Babylon, where he afterward died in captivity. After a few months' work of this sort, a portion of the Chaldeans under Nebuzar-adan returned to the dismantled and pillaged city and utterly destroyed both the city and the temple. It is supposed that Jeremiah, who was allowed to remain in the city during this bloody interval, wrote these elegies in the midst of the desolation

---

1. Vol. ii. p. 102.

and fear then impending. "Never," says Dean Milman, "was ruined city lamented in language so exquisitely pathetic. Jerusalem is, as it were, personified and bewailed with the passionate sorrow of private and domestic attachment; while the more general pictures of the famine, common misery of every rank and age and sex, all the desolation, the carnage, the violation, the dragging away into captivity, the remembrance of former glories, of the gorgeous ceremonies, and of the glad festivals, the awful sense of the Divine wrath, heightening the present calamities, are successively drawn with all the life and reality of an eye-witness."[2] The ethical and spiritual qualities of the book are pure and high; the writer does not fail to enforce the truth that it is because "Jerusalem hath grievously sinned" that "she is become an unclean thing." And in the midst of all this calamity there is no rebellion against God; it is only the cry of a desolate but trusting soul to a just and faithful Ruler.

The Proverbs, in the Hebrew Bible, is called "Mishle," or sometimes "Mishle Shelomoh." The first word signifies Parables or Proverbs or Sayings; the second word is the supposed name of the author, Solomon. By the later Jews it is sometimes called "Sepher Chokmah,"—the Book of Wisdom,—the same title as that which is borne by one of the apocryphal books.

Here, doubtless, we have again, in the name of the author, what Delitzsch calls a common denominator. On this subject the words of William Aldis Wright, in Smith's "Bible Dictionary," express a conservative judgment:—

"The superscriptions which are affixed to several portions of the Book of Proverbs in i. 1, x. 1, xxv. 1, attribute

---

2. *History of the Jews*, i. 446.

the authorship of those portions to Solomon, the son of David, king of Israel. With the exception of the last two chapters, which are distinctly assigned to other authors, it is probable that the statement of the superscriptions is in the main correct, and that the majority of the proverbs contained in the book were uttered or collected by Solomon. It was natural and quite in accordance with the practice of other nations that the Hebrews should connect Solomon's name with a collection of maxims and precepts which form a part of their literature to which he is known to have contributed most largely (1 Kings, iv. 32). In the same way the Greeks attributed most of their sayings to Pythagoras; the Arabs to Lokman, Abu Obeid, Al Mofaddel, Meidani, and Samakhshari; the Persians to Ferid Attar; and the northern people to Odin.

"But there can be no question that the Hebrews were much more justified in assigning the Proverbs to Solomon than the nations which have just been enumerated were in attributing the collections of national maxims to the traditional authors above mentioned."[3]

This is, undoubtedly, as much as can be truly said respecting the Solomonian authorship of these sayings. Professor Davidson, writing at a later day, is more guarded.

"In the book which now exists we find gathered together the most precious fruits of the wisdom of Israel during many hundreds of years, and undoubtedly the later centuries were richer, or at all events fuller, in their contributions than the earlier. The tradition, however, which connects Solomon with the direction of mind known as 'The Wisdom' cannot be reasonably

---

3. Art. "Book of Proverbs."

set aside. . . . Making allowances for the exaggerations of later times, we should leave history and tradition altogether unexplained if we disallowed the claim of Solomon to have exercised a creative influence upon the wisdom in Israel."[4]

The book is divided into several sections:

1. A general introduction, explaining the character and aim of the book, which occupies the first six verses.

2. A connected discourse upon wisdom, not in the form of maxims, but rather in the manner of a connected essay, fills the first nine chapters.

3. The next thirteen chapters (x.-xxii. 16) contain three hundred and seventy-four miscellaneous proverbs, each consisting of two phrases, the second of which is generally antithetical to the first, as "A wise son maketh a glad father, but a foolish son is a heaviness to his mother." There is only one exception (xix. 7), where the couplet is a triplet. Probably one phrase has been lost. The heading of this section is "The Proverbs of Solomon;" the section ends with the twenty-second chapter.

4. From xxii. 17 to xxiv. 22 is a more connected discussion, though in the proverbial form, of the principles of conduct. This is introduced by a brief exhortation to listen to "the words of the wise."

5. At xxiv. 23, begins another short section which extends through the chapter, under this title: "These also are sayings of the wise."

6. The next five chapters (xxv.-xxix.) have for their caption this sentence: "These also are proverbs of Solomon, which the men of Hezekiah, king of Judah, copied out."

---

4. Art. "Proverbs," *Encyc. Brit.*

7. Chapter xxx. is said to contain "The words of Agur, the son of Jakeh, the oracle." The author is wholly unknown.

8. Chapter xxxi. 1–9, contains "The words of King Lemuel, the prophecy that his mother taught him." He too stands here upon the sacred page but the shadow of a name.

9. The book closes with an acrostical poem—twenty-two verses beginning with the Hebrew letters in the order of the alphabet—upon "The Virtuous Woman." The word "virtue" here is used in the Roman sense; it signifies rather the vigorous woman, the capable woman.

Of these sections it seems probable that the one here numbered 6 is the oldest, and that it contains the largest proportion of Solomonian sayings. Professor Davidson thinks that it cannot have taken its present form earlier than the eighth century.

The character of the teaching of the book is not uniform, but on the whole it is best described as prudential rather than prophetic. It embodies what we are in the habit of calling "good common sense." There is an occasional maxim whose application to our own time may be doubted, and now and then one whose morality has been superseded by the higher standards of the New Testament; but, after making all due deductions, we shall doubtless agree that it is a precious legacy of practical counsel, and shall consent to these words of Professor Conant:—

"The gnomic poetry of the most enlightened of other nations will not bear comparison with it in the depth and certainty of its foundation principles, or in the comprehensiveness and moral grandeur of its conceptions of human duty and responsibility."[5]

Ecclesiastes, or the Preacher, bears in the Hebrew collection the name, "Koheleth," which means the assembler of the people, and therefore, probably, the man who addresses the assembly. Ecclesiastes is the Greek name of the book in the Septuagint; we have simply copied the Greek word in English letters.

The first verse is, "The words of Koheleth (the Preacher), the son of David, King in Jerusalem." The only son of David who was ever king in Jerusalem was Solomon; was Solomon the author of this book? This is the apparent claim; the question is whether we have not here, as in the case of Daniel, a book put forth pseudonymously; whether the author does not personate Solomon, and speak his message through Solomon's lips. That this is the fact modern scholars almost unanimously maintain. Their reasons for their opinion may be briefly stated:

1. In the conclusion of the book the author speaks in his own person, laying aside the thin disguise which he has been wearing. In several other passages the literary veil becomes transparent. Thus (i. 12), "I Koheleth was king over Israel in Jerusalem." This sounds like the voice of one looking backward and trying to put himself in Solomon's place. Again, in this and the following chapter, he says of himself: "I have gotten me great wisdom above all that were before me in Jerusalem;" "I was great, and increased more than all that were before me in Jerusalem," etc.,—"all of which," says Bleek, "does not appear

5. Smith's *Bible Dictionary*, iii. 2616.

very natural as coming from the son of David, who first captured Jerusalem." Nobody had been before him in Jerusalem except his father David.

2. The state of society as described in the book, and particularly the reference to rulers, agree better with the theory that it was written during the Persian period, after the Captivity, when the satraps of the Persian king were ruling with vacillating arbitrariness and fitful violence.

3. The religious condition of the people as here depicted, and the religious ideas of the book represent the period following the Captivity, and do not represent the golden age of Israel.

4. More important and indeed perfectly decisive is the fact that the book is full of Chaldaisms, and that the Hebrew is the later Hebrew, of the days of Ezra, Nehemiah, Daniel, and Esther. It could not have been written by Solomon, any more than the "Idylls of the King" could have been written by Edmund Spenser. There are those, of course, who maintain that the book was written by Solomon; just as there are those who still maintain that the sun revolves around the earth. The reason for this opinion is found in the first sentence of the book itself. The book announces its own author, it is said; and to question the truth of this claim is to deny the veracity of Scripture. On this question we may call, from the array of conservative writers who have given us Smith's "Bible Dictionary," such a witness as Professor Plumptre:—

"The hypothesis that every such statement in a canonical book must be received as literally true is, in fact, an assumption that inspired writers were debarred from forms of composition which were open, without blame, to others. In the literature of every other nation the form of personated authorship, when there is no *animus decipi-endi*, has been recognized as a legitimate channel for the expression of opinions, or the quasi-dramatic representation of character. Why should we venture on the assertion that if adopted by the writers of the Old Testament it would make them guilty of falsehood? . . . There is nothing that need startle us in the thought that an inspired writer might use a liberty which has been granted without hesitation to the teachers of mankind in every age and country."[6]

That such is the character of the book and that it appeared some time during the Persian age are well-ascertained results of scholarship.

The doctrine of the book is not so easily summarized. It is a hard book to interpret. Dr. Ginsberg gives a striking *resume* of the different theories of its teaching which have been promulgated. There is no room here to enter upon the great question. Let it suffice to say that we seem to have in these words the soliloquy of a soul struggling with the problem of evil, sometimes borne down by a dismal skepticism, sometimes asserting his faith in the enduring righteousness. The writer's problem is the one to which Mr. Mallock has given an epigrammatic statement: "Is life worth living?" He greatly doubts, yet he strongly hopes. Much of the time it appears to him that the best thing a man can do is to enjoy the present good and let the world wag. But the outcome of all this struggle is the conviction that there is a life beyond this life and a tribunal at which all wrongs will be righted, and that to fear God and keep his commandments is the whole duty of

---

6. Art. "Ecclesiastes," vol. i. p. 645.

man. There are thus many passages in the book which express a bitter skepticism; to winnow the wheat from the chaff and to find out what we ought to think about life is a serious undertaking. It is only the wise and skillful interpreter who can steer his bark along these tortuous channels of reflection, and not run aground. Yet, properly interpreted, the book is sound for substance of doctrine, and the experience which it delineates, though sad and depressing, is full of instruction for us. Dean Stanley's words about it are as true as they are eloquent; they will throw some light on the path which lies just before us:—

"As the Book of Job is couched in the form of a dramatic argument between the patriarch and his friends, as the Song of Songs is a dramatic dialogue between the Lover and the Loved One, so the Book of Ecclesiastes is a drama of a still more tragic kind. It is an interchange of voices, higher and lower, mournful and joyful, within a single human soul. It is like the struggle between the two principles in the Epistle to the Romans. It is like the question and answer of 'The Two Voices' of our modern poet. . . . Every speculation and thought of the human heart is heard and expressed and recognized in turn. The conflicts, which in other parts of the Bible are confined to a single verse or a single chapter, are here expanded into a whole book." And after quoting a few of the darker and more cynical utterances, this clear-sighted teacher goes on: "Their cry is indeed full of doubt and despair and perplexity; it is such as we often hear from the melancholy, skeptical, inquiring spirits of our own age; such as we often refuse to hear and regard as unworthy even a good man's thought or care, but the admission of such a cry into the Book of Ecclesiastes shows that it is not beneath the notice of the Bible, not beneath the notice of God."[7]

"The Song of Songs" is another of the books ascribed to Solomon. It may have been written in Solomon's time; that it was composed by Solomon himself is not probable.

It has generally been regarded as an allegorical poem; the Jews interpreted it as setting forth the love of Jehovah for Israel; the Christian interpreters have made it the representation of the love of Christ for his Church. These are the two principal theories, but it might be instructive to let Archdeacon Farrar recite to us a short list of the explanations which have been given of the book in the course of the ages:—

"It represents, say the commentators, the love of God for the congregation of Israel; it relates the history of the Jews from the Exodus to the Messiah; it is a consolation to afflicted Israel; it is an occult history; it represents the union of the divine soul with the earthly body, or of the material with the active intellect; it is the conversation of Solomon and Wisdom; it describes the love of Christ to his Church; it is historico-prophetic; it is Solomon's thanksgiving for a happy reign; it is a love-song unworthy of any place in the canon; it treats of man's reconciliation to God; it is a prophecy of the Church from the Crucifixion till after the Reformation; it is an anticipation of the Apocalypse; it is the seven days' epithalamium on the marriage of Solomon with the daughter of Pharaoh; it is a magazine for direction and consolation under every condition; it treats in hieroglyphics of the sepulchre of the Saviour, his death, and the Old Testament saints; it refers

---

7. *History of the Jewish Church,* ii. 283, 284.

to Hezekiah and the Ten Tribes; it is written in glorification of the Virgin Mary. Such were the impossible and diverging interpretations of what many regarded as the very Word of God. A few only, till the beginning of this century, saw the truth,—which is so obvious to all who go to the Bible with the humble desire to know what it says, and not to interpret it into their own baseless fancies,—that it is the exquisite celebration of a pure love in humble life; of a love which no splendor can dazzle and no flattery seduce."

These last sentences of Canon Farrar give the probable clew to the interpretation of the book. It is a dramatic poem, celebrating the story of a beautiful peasant girl, a native of the northern village of Shunem, who was carried away by Solomon's officers and confined in his harem at Jerusalem. But in the midst of all this splendor her heart is true to the peasant lover whom she has left behind, nor can any blandishments of the king disturb her constancy; her honor remains unstained, and she is carried home at length, heart-whole and happy, by the swain who has come to Jerusalem for her rescue. This is the beautiful story. The phrases in which it is told are, indeed, too explicit for Occidental ears; the color and the heat of the tropics is in the poetry, but it is perfectly pure; it celebrates the triumph of maiden modesty and innocence. "The song breathes at the same time," says Ewald, "such deep modesty and chaste innocence of heart, such determined defiance of the over-refinement and degeneracy of the court-life, such stinging scorn of the growing corruption of life in great cities and palaces, that no clearer or stronger testimony can be found of the healthy vigor which, in this century, still characterized the nation at large, than the combination of art and simplicity in the Canticles."[8]

The Book of Job has been the subject of a great amount of critical study. The earliest Jewish tradition is that it was written by Moses; this tradition is preserved in the Talmud, which afterward states that it was composed by an Israelite who returned to Palestine from the Babylonian Captivity. It is almost certain that the first of these traditions is baseless. The theory that it was written after the Captivity is held by many scholars, but it is beset with serious difficulties.

The book contains no allusion whatever to the Levitical law, nor to any of the religious rites and ceremonies of the Jews. The inference has therefore been drawn that it must have been written before the giving of the law, probably in the period between Abraham and Moses. It seems inconceivable that a devout Hebrew should have treated all the great questions discussed in this book without any reference to the religious institutions of his own people. It is equally difficult to understand how the divine interposition for the punishment of the wicked and the rewarding of the righteous could have been so fully considered without a glance at the lessons of the Exodus, if the Exodus had taken place before the book was written. But these arguments for an early origin are quite neutralized by the doctrine of the book. The view of divine providence set forth in it is very unlike that contained in the Pentateuch. It is not necessary to say that there is any contradiction between these two views; but the subject is approached from a very different direction, and

---

8. *History of Israel*, iv. 43.

the whole tone of the book indicates a state of religious thought quite different from that which existed among the Hebrews before the Exodus. "If we are to believe that Moses wrote it," says a late critic, "then we must believe that he held these views as an esoteric philosophy, and omitted from the religion which he gave to his people the truths which had been revealed to him in the desert. The book itself must have been suppressed until long after his day. The ignorant Israelites could not have been trained under the discipline of the Law if they had had at the same time the fiery, cynical, half-skeptical, and enigmatical commentary which the Book of Job furnishes. There is nothing abnormal or contrary to the conception of an inspired revelation in the development of truth by wider views and deeper analysis through successive sacred writers. But it is repulsive to conceive an inspired teacher as first gaining the wider view, and then deliberately hiding it, to utter the truth in cruder and more partial forms."[9] The fact that neither the person nor the Book of Job is mentioned in the historical books of the Jews, and that the first reference to him is in the Book of Ezekiel, would indicate that the date of the book must have been much later than the time of Moses. This argument could not be pressed, however, for we have noted already the silence of the earlier historical books concerning the Mosaic law.

The dilemma of the critics may be summed up as follows:—

1. The absence of allusion to the history of the Exodus and to the Mosaic system shows that it must have been

9. Raymond's *The Book of Job*, p. 18.

written before the Exodus. 2. The absence of all reference to the book in the Hebrew history, and more especially the doctrinal character of the book, shows that it could not have been written before the age of Solomon. The latter conclusion is held much more firmly than the former; and the silence respecting the history and the Law is explained on the theory that the book is a historical drama, the scene of which is laid in the period before Moses, and the historic unities of which have been perfectly observed by the writer. *The people of this drama* lived before the Exodus and the giving of the Law, and their conversations do not, therefore, refer to any of the events which have happened since. The locality of the drama is the "Land of Uz," and the geographers agree that the descriptions of the book apply to the region known in the classical geographies as "Arabia Deserta," southeast of Palestine. It is admitted that the scenery and costume of the book are not Jewish; and they agree more perfectly with what is known of that country than with any other. That Job was a real personage, and that the drama is founded upon historical tradition cannot be doubted. It is probable that it was written after the time of Josiah.

I need not rehearse the story. Job is overtaken by great losses and sufferings; in the midst of his calamities three friends draw near to condole with him, and also to administer to him a little wholesome reproof and admonition. Their theory is that suffering such as he is enduring is a sign of the divine displeasure; that Job must have been a great sinner, or he could not be such a sufferer. This argument Job indignantly repels. He does not claim to be perfect, but he knows that he has been an upright man, and he knows that bad men round about him are prospering, while he is scourged and overwhelmed with trouble; he sees this happening all over the earth,—the good afflicted, the evil exalted; and he knows, therefore, that the doctrine of his miserable comforters cannot be true. Sin does bring suffering, that he admits; but that all suffering is the result of sin he denies. He cannot understand it; his heart is bitter when he reflects upon it; and the insistence of his visitors awakes in him a fierce indignation, and leads him to charge God with injustice and cruelty. They are shocked and scandalized at his almost blasphemous outcries against God; but he maintains his righteousness, and drives his critics and censors from the field. Finally Jehovah himself is represented as answering Job out of the whirlwind, in one of the most sublime passages in all literature,—silencing the arguments of his friends, sweeping away all the reasonings which have preceded, explaining nothing, but only affirming his own infinite power and wisdom. Before this august manifestation Job bows with submission; the mystery of evil is not explained; he is only convinced that it cannot be explained, and is content to be silent and wait. The teaching of the book is well summarized in these words of Dr. Raymond:—

"The current notion that calamity is always the punishment of crime and prosperity always the reward of piety is not true. Neither is it true that the distress of a righteous man is an indication of God's anger. There are other purposes in the Divine mind of which we know nothing. For instance, a good man may be afflicted, by permission of God, and through the agency of Satan, to prove the genuine character of his goodness. But whether this or some other reason, involved in the administration of the universe, underlies the dispensation of temporal blessings and afflictions, one thing is certain: the plans of God are not, will not be, cannot be revealed; and the resignation of faith, not of fatalism, is the only wisdom of man."[10]

I have reserved for the last the most precious of all the Hebrew writings, the *Book of Psalms*. The Hebrews called it "Tehillim," praise-book or hymn-book, and the title exactly describes it; in the form in which we have it, it was a hymn-book prepared for the service of the later temple.

If the question "Who wrote the Psalms?" were to be propounded in any meeting of Sunday-school teachers, nine tenths of them would unhesitatingly answer, "David." If the same question were put to an assembly of modern Biblical scholars some would answer that David wrote very few and perhaps not any of the psalms; that they were written during the Maccabean dynasty, only one or two hundred years before Christ. Both these views are extreme. We may believe that David did write several of the psalms, but it is more than probable that the great majority of them are from other writers.

Seventy-three psalms of the book seem to be ascribed to David in their titles. "A Psalm of David," "Maschil of David," "Michtam of David," or something similar is written over seventy-three different psalms. Concerning these titles there has been much discussion. It has been maintained that they are found in the ancient Hebrew text as constituent parts of the Psalms, and are therefore entitled to full credit. But this theory does not seem to be held by the majority of modern scholars. "The variations

---

10. *The Book of Job*, p. 49.

of the inscriptions," says a late conservative writer, "in the Septuagint and the other versions sufficiently prove that they were not regarded as fixed portions of the canon, and that they were open to conjectural emendations."[11] Dr. Moll, the learned author of the monograph on the Psalms in Lange's "Commentary," says in his introduction: "The assumption that all the inscriptions originated with the authors of the Psalms, and are therefore inseparable from the text, cannot be consistently maintained. It can at most be held only of a few. . . . There is now a disposition to admit that some of them may have originated with the authors themselves."

The probability is that most of these inscriptions were added by editors and transcribers of the Psalms. You open your hymn-book, and find over one hymn the name of Watts, and over another the name of Wesley, and over another the name of Montgomery. Who inserted these names? Not the authors, of course, but the editor or compiler of the collection. Compilers in these days are careful and accurate, but they do make mistakes, and you find the same hymn ascribed to different authors in different books, while hymns that are anonymous in one book are credited in another, rightly or wrongly, to the name of some author. The men who collected the hymn-book of the Jews made similar mistakes, and the old copies do not agree in all their titles.

But while the inscriptions over the psalms do not, generally, belong to the psalms themselves, and are not in all cases accurate, most of them were, no doubt, suffixed to the psalms at a very early day. "On the whole," says Dr.

---

11. *Speaker's Commentary,* iv. 151.

Moll, "an opinion favorable to the antiquity and value of these superscriptions has again been wrought out, which ascribes them for the most part to tradition, and indeed a very ancient one."

Even if the titles were rightly translated, then, they would not give us conclusive proof of the authorship of the Psalms. But some of the best scholars assert that they are not rightly translated. The late Professor Murray of Johns Hopkins University, whose little book on the Psalms is vouched for as one of the most admirable productions of Biblical scholarship which has yet appeared in this country, says that "whenever we have an inscription in our version stating that the psalm is 'of David' it is almost invariably a mistranslation of the original." It should be written "to David," and it signifies that the compilers ascribed the psalm to a more ancient collection to which the name of David had been appended, not because he wrote all the poems in it, but because he originated the collection and wrote many of its songs. This older collection was called "The Psalms of David" something as a popular hymn-book of these times is called Robinson's "Laudes Domini," because Dr. Robinson compiled the book, and wrote some of the hymns. This old Davidic collection is not in existence, but many of the psalms in our book were taken from it, and the titles in our version are attempts to credit to this old book such of them as were thus borrowed.

This method of crediting is not altogether unknown in this critical age. In the various eclectic commentaries on the Sunday-school lessons I often find sentences and paragraphs credited to "William Smith" which were taken from Dr. Smith's "Bible Dictionary," the articles from which they are taken being signed in all cases by the initials of the men who wrote them. I find, also, quotations from the "Speaker's Commentary," of which Canon Cook is the editor, ascribed to "F. C. Cook," or to "Cook," though the table of contents in the volume from which the quotation was taken bears in capital letters the name of the writer of the commentary on this particular book. In like manner "Lange" gets the credit of all that is written in his famous "Bibelwerk," though he wrote very little of it himself. The power to distinguish between editorship and authorship was not, probably, possessed by ancient compilers in any greater degree than by modern ones; and the inscriptions over the psalms must be estimated with this fact in view.

I have spoken of the present collection of the Psalms as one book, but it is in reality five books. It is so divided in the Revised Version. The concluding verse of the Forty-first Psalm is as follows: "Blessed be the Lord God of Israel, from everlasting to everlasting. Amen and amen." This doxology marks the close of the first hymn-book prepared by the Jews for the worship of the second temple. It was probably formed soon after the first return from the Exile. All the Psalms except the first, the tenth, and the thirty-third are credited to the old Davidic Psalm Book. The title of the thirty-third has probably been omitted by some copyist; the ninth and tenth in some old Hebrew copies are written as one psalm, and there is an acrostical arrangement which shows that they really belong together. The psalm may have been divided for liturgical purposes, or by accident in copying. The title of the ninth, therefore, covers the tenth. The first and second are, then, the only psalms that are not ascribed to the old book of which this book was simply an abridgment.

At the end of the Seventy-second Psalm is the doxology which marks the close of the second of these hymn-books. After a while the psalms of the first book grew stale and familiar, and a new book was wanted. "Gospel Hymns No. 1," of the Moody and Sankey psalmody, had to be followed after a year or two by "Gospel Hymns No. 2," and then by "No. 3" and "No. 4" and "No. 5," and finally they were all bound up together. I may be pardoned for associating things sacred with things not very sacred, and poetry with something that is not always poetry, but the illustration, familiar to all, shows exactly how these five hymn-books of the Jews first came to be, and how they were at length combined in one.

The last verse of the Seventy-second Psalm has puzzled many readers: "The prayers of David the son of Jesse are ended." After this you find in our collection several psalms ascribed to David, some of which he undoubtedly wrote. The probable explanation is that the Seventy-second Psalm was the last psalm of the old Davidic hymn-book; the compiler made it the last one of this second book, and carelessly copied into this psalm the inscription with which the old book ended.

The second of these hymn-books begins, therefore, with Psalm xlii., and ends with Psalm lxxii., a collection of thirty-one songs of praise.

Number three of the temple-service contains eighteen psalms, and ends with Psalm lxxxix; this book, as well as the one that precedes it, is ascribed by a probable tradition to Nehemiah as its compiler.

The last verse of Psalm cvi. indicates the close of the fourth book. It contains but seventeen psalms, and is the shortest book of the five. The fifth book includes the remaining forty-four psalms, among them the "Songs of David," or Pilgrim Songs, sung by the people on their journeys to Jerusalem to keep the solemn feasts. It is probable that this fifth book was compiled by the authorities in charge of the temple worship, and that they at the same time collected the other four books and put them all together, completing in this way the greater book of sacred lyrics which has been so precious to many generations not only of Jews, but also of Christians.

Various unsuccessful attempts have been made to classify these books according to their subject-matter. It is plain that the first two are composed chiefly of the oldest psalms and of those adapted to the general purposes of worship; the third book reflects the grief of the nation in the Captivity; the fourth, the joy of the returning exiles; the fifth contains a more miscellaneous collection. The Jewish scholars recognize and sometimes attempt to explain this arrangement of the Psalms into five books. The Hebrew Midrash on Psalm i. I., says: "Moses gave the five books of the law to the Israelites, and as a counterpart of them, David gave the Psalms consisting of five books." This is, of course, erroneous; the present collection of Psalms was made long after the time of David; but it is not unlikely that some notion of a symmetrical arrangement of the Psalms, to correspond to the five-fold division of the Law, influenced the compilers of this Praise Book.

Of the contents of this book, of the peculiar structure of Hebrew poetry, and of the historic references in many of the psalms, much might be said, but this investigation would lead us somewhat aside from our present purpose.

It may, however, be well to add a word or two respecting some of the inscriptions and notations borne by the Psalms in our translation. Many of them are composed of Hebrew words, transliterated into English,—spelled out with English letters. King James' translators did not know what they meant, so they reproduced them in this way. There has been much discussion as to the meaning of several of them, and the scholars are by no means agreed; the interpretations which follow are mainly those given by Professor Murray:—

First is the famous "Selah," which we used to hear pronounced with great solemnity when the Psalms were read. It is a musical term, meaning, perhaps, something like our "Da Capo" or, possibly, "Forte"—a mark of expression like those Italian words which you find over the staff on your sheet music.

"Michtam" and "Maschil" are also musical notes, indicating the time of the melody,—metronome-marks, so to speak; and "Gittith" and "Shiggaion" are marks that indicate the kind of melody to which the psalm is to be sung.

"Negiloth" means stringed instruments; it indicates the kind of accompaniment with which the psalm was to be sung. "Nehiloth" signifies pipes or flutes, perhaps wind instruments in general.

The inscription "To the Chief Musician" means, probably, "For the Leader of the Choir," and indicates that the original copy of the psalm thus inserted in the book was one that had belonged to the chorister in the old temple. "Upon Shemimith" means "set for bass voices;" "Upon

Alamoth," "set for female voices." "Upon Muthlabben," a curious transliteration, means "arranged for training the soprano voices." Professor Murray supposes that this particular psalm was used for rehearsal by the women singers.

Some of these inscriptions designate the airs to which the psalms were set, part of which seem to be sacred, and part secular. Such is "Shushan Eduth," over Psalm lx., meaning "Fair as lilies is thy law," apparently the name of a popular religious air. Another, probably secular, is over Psalm xxii., "Aijeleth Shahar," "The stag at dawn," and another, over Psalm 1vi., "Jonathelem Rechokim," which is, being interpreted, "O silent dove, what bringest thou us from out the distance?"

These inscriptions and many other features of this ancient Hebrew poetry have furnished puzzles for the unlearned and problems for the scholars, but the meaning of the psalms themselves is for the most part clear enough. The humble disciple pauses with some bewilderment over "Neginoth" or "Michtam;" he classes them perhaps among the mysteries which the angels desire to look into; but when he reads a little farther on, "The Lord is my shepherd; I shall not want;" or "God is our refuge and strength, a very present help in trouble;" or "Create in me a clean heart, O God, and renew a right spirit within me," he knows full well what these words mean. There is no life so lofty that these psalms do not lift up a standard before it; there is no life so lowly that it does not find in them words that utter its deepest humility and its faintest trust. Wherever we are these psalms find us; they search the deep things of our hearts; they bring to us the great things of God. Of how many heroic characters have these old temple songs been the inspiration! Jewish saints and patriots chanted them in the synagogue and on the battle-field; apostles and evangelists sung them among perils of the wilderness, as they traversed the rugged paths of Syria and Galatia and Macedonia; martyrs in Rome softly hummed them when the lions near at hand were crouching for their prey: in German forests, in Highland glens, Lutherans and Covenanters breathed their lives out through their cadences; in every land penitent souls have found in them words to tell the story of their sorrow, and victorious souls the voices of their triumph; mothers watching their babes by night have cheered the vigil by singing them; mourners walking in lonely ways have been lighted by the great hopes that shine through them, and pilgrims going down into the valley of the shadow of death have found in their firm assurances a strong staff to lean upon. Lyrics like these, into which so much of the divine truth was breathed when they were written, and which a hundred generations of the children of men have saturated with tears and praises, with battle shouts and sobs of pain, with all the highest and deepest experiences of the human soul, will live as long as joy lives and long after sorrow ceases; will live beyond this life, and be sung by pure voices in that land from which the silent dove, coming from afar, brings us now and then upon her shining wings some glimpses of a glory that eye hath never seen.

Note: The reference on page 173 to the Gospel Hymns is not strictly accurate. "Number Five" has not been bound up with the other numbers.

Chapter 8

The Earlier New Testament Writings

The books of the New Testament are now before us. Our task is not without its difficulties; questions will confront us which have never yet been answered, and probably will never be; nevertheless, compared with the Old Testament writings, the books of the New Testament are well-known documents; we are on firm ground of history when we talk about them; of but few of the famous books of Greek and Latin authors can we speak so confidently as to their date and their authorship as we can concerning most of them.

We have in the New Testament a collection of twenty-seven books, by nine different authors. Of these books thirteen are ascribed to the Apostle Paul; five to John the son of Zebedee; two to Peter; two to Luke; one each to Matthew, Mark, James, and Jude, and the authorship of one is unknown.

Of these books it must be first remarked that they were not only written separately but that there is no trace in any of them of the consciousness on the part of the author that he was contributing to a collection of sacred writings. Of the various epistles it is especially evident that they were written on special occasions, with a certain audience immediately in view; the thought that they were to be preserved and gathered into a book, which was to be handed down through the coming centuries as an inspired volume, does not appear to have entered the mind of the writer. But this fact need not detract from their value; often the highest truth to which a man gives utterance is truth of whose value he is imperfectly aware.

It must also be remembered that these books of the New Testament were nearly all written by apostles. The only clear exceptions are the Gospel of Mark, the Gospel of Luke, the Acts of the Apostles, and the Epistle to the Hebrews; and the authors of these books, though not apostles, were undoubtedly in the closest relations with apostolic men, and reflected their thought. These apostolic men had received a special training and a definite commission to bear witness of their Master, to tell the story of his life and death, and to build up his kingdom in the world.

We must admit that they possessed unusual qualifications for this work. Those who had been for three years in constant and loving intercourse with Jesus Christ ought to have been inspired men. And he promised them, before he parted from them, that the Spirit of truth should come to them and abide with them to lead them into all truth.

Now although we may find it difficult to give a satisfactory definition of inspiration; though we may be utterly unable to express, in any formularies of our own, the influence of the Infinite Spirit upon human minds, yet we can easily believe that these apostolic men were exceptionally qualified to teach religious truth. No prophet of the olden time had any such preparation for his mission as that which was vouchsafed to them. No school of the prophets, from the days of Samuel downward, could be compared to that sacred college of apostles,—that group of divine peripatetics, who followed their master through Galilee and Perea, and sat down with him day by day, for three memorable years, on the mountain top and by the lake side, to listen to the words of life from the lips of One who spake as never man spake.

To say that this training made them infallible is to speak beyond the record. There is no promise of infallibility, and the history makes it plain enough that no such gift was bestowed. The Spirit of all truth was promised; but it was promised for their guidance in all their work, in their preaching, their administration, their daily conduct of life. There is no hint anywhere that any special illumination or protection would be given to them when they took the pen into their hands to write; they were then inspired just as much as they were when they stood up to speak, or sat down to plan their missionary campaigns,—just as much and no more.

Now it is certain that the inspiration vouchsafed them did not make them infallible in their ordinary teaching, or in their administration of the church. They made mistakes of a very serious nature. It is beyond question that the majority of the apostles took at the beginning an erroneous view of the relation of the Gentiles to the Christian church. They insisted that Gentiles must first become Jews before they could become Christians; that the only way into the Christian church was through the synagogue and the temple. It was a grievous and radical error; it struck at the foundations of Christian faith. And this error was entertained by these inspired apostles after the day of Pentecost; it influenced their teaching; it led them to proclaim a defective gospel. This is not the assertion of a skeptic, it is the clear testimony of the Apostle Paul. If you will read the second chapter of his Epistle to the Galatians you will learn from the mouth of an unimpeachable witness that the very leaders of the apostolic band, Peter and James and John, were greatly in error with respect to a most important subject of the Christian teaching. In his account of that famous council at Antioch, Paul says that Peter and James and John were wholly in the wrong, and that Peter, for his part, had been acting disingenuously:—

"But when Cephas came to Antioch, I resisted him to the face, because he stood condemned. For before that certain came from James, he did eat with the Gentiles: but when they came, he drew back and separated himself, fearing them that were of the circumcision. And the rest of the Jews [the Jewish Christians] dissembled likewise with him; insomuch that even Barnabas was carried away with their dissimulation. But when I saw that they walked not uprightly according to the truth of the gospel, I said unto Cephas before them all, If thou, being a Jew, livest as do the Gentiles, and not as do the Jews, how compellest thou the Gentiles to live as do the Jews?"

Now it is evident that one or the other of these opposing parties in the apostolic college must have been in error, if not greatly at fault, with respect to this most vital question of Christian faith and doctrine. When one apostle resists another to the face because he stands condemned, and tells him that he walks not uprightly, according to the truth of the gospel, it must be that one or the other of them has, for the time being, ceased to be infallible in his administration of the truth of the gospel. And if these apostolic men, sitting in their councils, teaching in their congregations, can make such mistakes as these, how can we be sure that they never make a mistake when they sit down to write, that then their words are always the very word of God? We can have no such assurance. Indeed we are expressly told that their words are not, in some cases, the very word of God; for the Apostle Paul plainly tells us over and over, in his epistles to the Corinthians (1 Cor. vii.; 2 Cor. xi.), that upon certain questions he is giving his own opinion,—that he has no commandment of the Lord. With respect to one matter he says that he is speaking after his own judgment, but that he "thinks" he has the Spirit of the Lord; two or three times he distinctly declares that it is he, Paul, and not the Lord, that is speaking.

All of these facts, and others of the same nature clearly brought before us by the New Testament itself, must be held firmly in our minds when we make up our theory of what these writings are. That these books were written by inspired men is, indeed, indubitable; that these men possessed a degree of inspiration far exceeding that vouchsafed to any other religious teachers who have lived on the earth is to my mind plain; that this degree of inspiration enabled them to bear witness clearly to the great facts of the gospel of Christ, and to present to us with sufficient fullness and with substantial verity the doctrines of the kingdom of heaven I am very sure; but that they were absolutely protected against error, not one word in the record affirms, and they themselves have taken the utmost pains to disabuse our minds of any such impression. That is a theory about them which men made up out of their own heads hundreds of years after they were dead. We shall certainly find that they were not infallible; but we shall also find that, in all the great matters which pertain to Christian faith and practice, when their final testimony is collected and digested, it is clear, harmonious, consistent, convincing; that they have been guided by the Spirit of the Lord to tell us the truth which we need to know respecting the life that now is and that which is to come.

Furthermore, it is a matter of rejoicing when we take up these books of the New Testament to find their substantial integrity unimpeached. There is no reason to suspect that any important changes have been made in any of these books since they came from the hands of their writers. Whatever may be said about the first three Gospels (and we shall come to that question in our next chapter), the remaining books of the New Testament have come down to us, unaltered, from the men who first wrote them. There is none of that process of redaction, and accretion, and reconstruction whose traces we have found in many of the Old Testament books. There may be, here and there, a word or two or a verse or two which has been interpolated by some officious copyist, but these alterations are very slight. The books in our hands are the very same books which were in the hands of the contemporaries and successors of the apostles.

I shall not attempt any elaborate discussion of these twenty-seven books. I only propose to go rapidly over them, indicating, with the utmost brevity, the salient facts, so far as we know them, respecting their authorship, the date and the place at which they were written, and the circumstances which attended the production of them.

From the fact that the Gospels stand first in the New Testament collection it is generally assumed that they are the earliest of the New Testament books, but this is an error. Several of the Epistles were certainly written before any of the Gospels; and one of the Gospels, that of John, was written later than any of the Epistles, except the three brief ones by the same author.

The first of these New Testament books that saw the light was, as is generally supposed, the First Epistle to the Thessalonians. It was in the year 48 of our era that St. Paul set out on his first missionary journey from Antioch through Cyprus and Eastern Asia Minor, a journey which occupied about a year. Two years afterward, his second journey took him through the eastern part of Asia Minor and across the Aegean Sea to Europe, where he preached in Troas, Philippi, Thessalonica, Athens, and Corinth. His stay in Thessalonica was interrupted, as you will remember, by the hostility of the Jews, and he remained but a short time in that place; long enough, however, to gather a vigorous church. Afterward, while he was in Corinth, he learned from one of his helpers that the people of Thessalonica had misunderstood portions of his teaching, and were in painful doubt on certain important subjects. To set them right on these matters he wrote his first epistle, which was forwarded to them from Corinth, probably about the year 52.

This explanation was also misunderstood by the Thessalonians, and it became necessary during the next year to write to them again. These two letters are in all probability the first of the Christian writings that we possess. They contain instruction and counsel of which the Christians of Thessalonica were just then in need. The question which had most disturbed them had relation to the second coming of Christ. They expected him to return very soon; they were impatient of delay; they thought that those who died before his coming would miss the glorious spectacle; and therefore they deplored the hard fate of some of their number who had been snatched away by death before this sublime event. In his first epistle the apostle assures them that the dead in Christ would be raised to participate in their rejoicing. "We who are alive when the Lord returns," he says, "will have no advantage over those who have been called to their reward before us; for they will be raised from their graves to take part with us in this great triumph." It is manifest that Paul, when he wrote this, expected that Christ would return to earth while he was alive. Alford and other conservative commentators say that he here definitely expresses that expectation; others deny that these words can be so interpreted, but concede that he did entertain some such expectation. "It does not seem improper to admit," says Bishop Ellicott, "that in their ignorance of the day of the Lord the apostles might have imagined that he who was coming would come speedily."[1] "It is unmistakably clear from this," says Olshausen, "that Paul deemed it possible that he and his contemporaries might live to see the coming again of Christ." "The early church, and even the apostles themselves," say Conybeare and Howson, "expected their Lord to come again in that very generation.

---

1. *Com. in loc.*

St. Paul himself shared in that expectation, but being under the guidance of the Spirit of truth, he did not deduce any erroneous conclusions from this mistaken premise."[2] It is evident, then, that St. Paul and the rest of the apostles were mistaken on this point; this is one of the evidences which they themselves have taken pains to point out to us of the fact that though they were inspired men they were not infallible.

Paul's first letter to the Christians at Thessalonica was interpreted by them, very naturally, as teaching that the return of the Lord was imminent; and they began to neglect their daily duties and to behave in the same foolish way that men have behaved in all the later ages, when they have got their heads full of this notion. His second letter was written chiefly to rebuke this fanaticism, and to bid them go right on with their work making ready for the Lord's coming by a faithful discharge of the duties of the present hour. St. Paul might have been mistaken in his theories about the return of his Master, but his practical wisdom was not at fault; it was his spirit that survived in Abraham Davenport, the Connecticut legislator, who, in the "dark day" of 1780 when his colleagues thought that the end of the world had come, refused to vote for the adjournment of the House, but insisted on calling up the next bill; saying as Whittier has phrased it:—

"'This well may be
The Day of Judgment which the world awaits;
But be it so or not, I only know
My present duty, and my Lord's command

2. *Life and Epistles of St. Paul*, i. 401.

To occupy till he come. So at the post
Where he hath set me in his providence,
I choose, for one, to meet him face to face,—
No faithless servant frightened from my task,
But ready when the Lord of the harvest calls;
And therefore, with all reverence, I would say,
Let God do his work, we will see to ours.
Bring in the candles.' And they brought them in."

These two letters are, then, the earliest of the New Testament writings. Like most of the other Epistles of Paul they begin with a salutation. The common salutation with which the Greeks began their letters was "Live well!" that of the Roman was "Health to you!" But Paul almost always began with a Christian greeting, "Grace, mercy, and peace to you." In these letters he associates with himself in this greeting his two companions, Timothy and Silas.

The last words of his epistles are almost always personal messages to individuals known to him in the several churches,—to men and women who had "labored with him in the gospel,"—casual yet significant words, which "show a heart within blood-tinctured, of a veined humanity." The letters were written by an amanuensis,—all save these concluding words which Paul added in his own chirography. He seems to desire to put more of himself into these personal messages than into the didactic and doctrinal parts of his epistles. At the end of the second of the letters to the Thessalonians we find these words: "The salutation of me Paul with mine own hand, which is the token in every epistle: so I write;" better, perhaps, "This is my handwriting." This signature and this concluding greeting are to be proof to them of the genuineness of the letter. It appears from other references in the same epistle (ch. ii. 2) that some busybody had been writing a letter to the Thessalonians, which purported to be a message from Paul; he puts them on their guard against these supposititious documents. At the end of the letter to the Galatians you find in the old version: "Ye see how large a letter I have written unto you with my own hand;" but the right rendering is in the new version: "See with how large letters [what a bold chirography] I have written unto you with my own hand." "These last coarse characters are my own handwriting." It is almost universally assumed that Paul was a sufferer from some affection of the eyes; the large letters are thus explained. Mr. Conybeare, in a foot-note on this passage, speaks of receiving a letter from the venerable Neander a few months before his death, which illustrates this point in a striking manner: "His letter," says Mr. Conybeare, "is written in the fair and flowing hand of an amanuensis, but it ends with a few irregular lines in large and rugged characters, written by himself and explaining the cause of his needing the services of an amanuensis, namely the weakness of his eyes (probably the very malady of St. Paul). It was impossible to read this autograph without thinking of the present passage, and observing that he might have expressed himself in the very words of St. Paul: 'Behold the size of the characters in which I have written to you with my own hand.'"[3]

There is another touching sentence at the end of Paul's letter to the Colossians which was written from Rome

---

3. *Life and Epistles of St. Paul,* ii. 149.

when he was prisoner there: "The salutation of me Paul with mine own hand. Remember my bonds. Grace be with you. Amen." This seems to say: "There is a manacle, you remember, on my wrist. I cannot write very well. Grace be with you." I will only add that the subscriptions which follow the epistles in the old version are no part of the epistles, and in several cases they are erroneous. They embody conjectures of later copyists, or traditions which are without foundation. These letters to the Thessalonians, for example, are said to have been written from Athens; but we know that they were written from Corinth. For Paul expressly says (iii. 6) that the letter was written immediately after the return of Timothy from Thessalonica, and we are told, in Acts xviii. 5, that Silas and Timothy joined him at Corinth after he had left Athens and had gone to Corinth. Besides, he associates Silas and Timothy with himself in his greetings, and they were not with him at Athens. The evidence is therefore conclusive, that the subscription is incorrect. You will not find any of these subscriptions in the new version. Some of them are undoubtedly correct, but some of them are not; and in no case is the subscription an integral part of the epistle. The excision of these traditional addenda was one of the first results of what is called the "Higher Criticism," and admirably illustrates the uses of this kind of criticism, which, to some of our devout brethren, is such a frightful thing. Why should it be regarded as a dangerous, almost a diabolical proceeding, to let the Bible tell its own story about its origin, instead of trusting to rabbinical traditions and mediaeval guesses and *a priori* theories of seventeenth century theologians?

These two letters were, no doubt, read in the assemblies of the Thessalonian Christians more than once, and were sacredly treasured by them. They were the only Christian documents possessed by them; and there was, at this time, no other church so rich as they were. The Gospels, as we have them now, were not then in the possession of any Christian church. The story of the gospel had been repeated to them by Paul and Silas and Timothy, and had been diligently impressed upon their memories; but it was only an oral gospel that had been delivered to them; the written record of Christ's life and sayings was not in their hands. They remembered, therefore, the things which had been told them concerning the life and death of Jesus Christ; they repeated them over one to another, and they explained and supplemented these remembered words by the two letters which they had received from the great apostle.

The next year after Paul wrote these letters to the Thessalonians from Corinth, he returned to Jerusalem and Antioch (Acts xviii. 18–23), and the year following, probably 54, he set out on his third missionary journey, which took him through Galatia and Phrygia in Asia Minor to Ephesus, where his home was for two or three years. While there, perhaps in the year 57, he wrote the first of his letters to the Christians in Corinth. Shortly after writing it he went on to Macedonia, whence the second of his letters to the Corinthians was written; presently he followed his letters to Corinth, and while there, probably in 58, he wrote his letter to the Galatians. Galatia was a province rather than a city; there may have been several churches, which had been established by Paul, in the province; and this may have been a circular letter, to be handed about among them, copies of it to be made, perhaps, for the use of each of the churches. It was in the spring of the next year, while he was still in Corinth, that he wrote his letter to the Romans, the longest, and from some points of view, the most important of his epistles. He had never, at the time of this writing, been in Rome (ch. i. 13), but he had met Roman Christians in many of the cities of the East where he had lived and taught; and, doubtless, since all roads led to Rome, and the metropolis of the world was constantly drawing to itself men of every nation and province, many of Paul's converts in Asia and Macedonia and Achaia had made their way to the Eternal City, and had joined themselves there to the Christian community. The long list of personal greetings with which the epistle closes shows how large was his acquaintance in the Roman church, and, doubtless, by his correspondence, he had become fully informed concerning the needs of these disciples. He tells the Romans, in this letter, that he hopes to visit them by and by; he did not, however, at that time, expect to appear among them as a prisoner. This was the fate awaiting him. Shortly after writing this epistle he returned from Corinth to Jerusalem, bearing a collection which had been gathered in Europe for the poor Christians of the mother church; at Jerusalem he was arrested; in that city and in Caesarea he was for a long time imprisoned; finally, probably in the spring of 61, he was sent as a prisoner to Rome, because he had appealed to the imperial court; and here, for at least two years, he dwelt a prisoner, in lodgings of his own, chained by day and night to a Roman soldier. During this imprisonment, probably in 62, he wrote the letters to the Colossians, the Ephesians, the Philippians, and Philemon. From the first imprisonment he seems to have been released; and to have gone westward as far as Spain, and eastward as far as Asia Minor, preaching the gospel. During this journey he is supposed to have written the first letter to Timothy and the letter to Titus. At length he was re-arrested, and brought to Rome where, in the spring of 68, just before his death, he wrote the second letter to Timothy, the last of his thirteen epistles.

Much of this account of the late years of Paul's life, following the close of his first two years at Rome, where the narrative in the Acts of the Apostles abruptly leaves him, is traditional and conjectural; I do not give it to you as indubitable history; it furnishes the most reasonable explanation that has been suggested of that productive activity of his which finds its chief expression in the letters that bear his name.

Of these letters it is impossible to give any adequate account in this place. Let it suffice to say that the principal theme of the two epistles to the Thessalonians is the expected return of Christ to earth; that those to the Corinthians are largely occupied with questions of Christian casuistry; that those to the Galatians and the Romans are the great doctrinal epistles unfolding the relation of Christianity to Judaism, and discussing the philosophy of the new creed; that the Epistle to the Philippians is a luminous exposition of Christianity as a personal experience; that those to the Colossians and the Ephesians are the defense of Christianity against the insidious errors of the Gnostics, and a wonderful revelation of the immanent Christ; that the Epistle to Philemon is a letter of personal friendship, embodying a great principle of practical religion; and that the letters to Timothy and

Titus are the counsel of an aged apostle to younger men in the ministry.

"May we go farther," with Archdeacon Farrar, "and attempt, in one or two words, a description of each separate epistle, necessarily imperfect from the very brevity, and yet perhaps expressive of some one main characteristic. If so we might perhaps say that the First Epistle to the Thessalonians is the epistle of consolation in the hope of Christ's return; and the second of the immediate hindrances to that return, and our duties with regard to it. The First Epistle to the Corinthians is the solution of practical problems in the light of eternal principles; the second, an impassioned defense of the apostle's impugned authority, his *Apologia pro vita sua.* The Epistle to the Galatians is the epistle of freedom from the bondage of the law; that to the Romans of justification by faith. The Epistle to the Philippians is the epistle of Christian gratitude and of Christian joy in sorrow; that to the Colossians the epistle of Christ the universal Lord; that to the Ephesians, so rich and many-sided, is the epistle of the 'heavenlies,' the epistle of grace, the epistle of ascension with the ascended Christ, the epistle of Christ in his one and universal church; that to Philemon the Magna Charta of Emancipation. The First Epistle to Timothy and that to Titus are the manuals of a Christian pastor; the Second Epistle to Timothy is the last message of a Christian ere his death."[4]

The genuineness of several of these books has been assailed by modern criticism. The authorship of Paul has been disputed in the cases of nine out of the thirteen

---

4. *The Life and Work of St. Paul,* chap. xlvi.

epistles. The Epistle to the Galatians, that to the Romans, and the two to the Corinthians are undisputed; all the rest have been spoken against. I have attended to these criticisms; but the reasons urged for denying the Pauline authorship of these epistles seem to me in many cases far-fetched and fanciful in the extreme. Respecting the pastoral epistles, those to Timothy and Titus, it may be admitted that there are some difficulties. It is not easy for us to understand how there could have been developed in the churches at that early day so much of an ecclesiasticism as these letters assume; and there is force in the suggestion that the peculiar errors against which some of these counsels are directed belong to a later day rather than to the apostolic age. To this it may be replied that ecclesiasticism is a weed which grows rapidly when once it has taken root, and that the germs of Gnosticism were in the church from the earliest day. And although the vocabulary of these epistles differs in rather a striking way, as Dr. Harnack has pointed out,[5] from that of Paul's other epistles, I can easily imagine that in familiar letters to his pupils he would drop into a different style from that in which he wrote his more elaborate theological treatises. One could find in the letters of Macaulay or Charles Kingsley many words that he would not find in the history of the one or the sermons of the other. Putting all these objections together, I do not find in them any adequate reason for denying that these epistles were written by St. Paul. Indeed, it seems to me incredible that the Second Epistle of Timothy should have been written by any other hand than that which wrote the undoubted letters to the Corinthians and the Romans.

---

5. *Encyc. Brit.*, art. "Pastoral Epistles."

When we come to the other disputed epistles, those to the Thessalonians, the Ephesians, the Philippians, and the Colossians, I confess that the doubts of their genuineness seem to me the outcome of a willful dogmatism. What Archdeacon Farrar says of the cavils respecting the epistles to the Philippians applies to much of this theoretic criticism: "The Tubingen school, in its earlier stages, attacked it with the monotonous arguments of their credulous skepticism. With those critics, if an epistle touches on points which make it accord with the narrative of the Acts it was forged to suit them; if it seems to disagree with them the discrepancy shows that it is spurious. If the diction is Pauline it stands forth as a proved imitation; if it is un-Pauline it could not have proceeded from the apostle."[6] One grows weary with this reckless and carping skepticism, much of which springs from a theory of a permanent schism in the early church,—a theory which was mainly evolved from the inner consciousness of some mystical German philosopher, and which has been utterly exploded.

We may, then, receive as genuine the thirteen epistles ascribed to St. Paul; and we have good reason for believing that we have them in their integrity, substantially as he wrote them.

The title of one of these epistles, that to the Ephesians, is, however, undoubtedly erroneous. As Mr. Conybeare says, the least disputable fact about the letter is that it was not addressed to the Ephesians. For it is incredible that Paul should have described a church in whose fellowship he had lived and labored for two years as one of whose

---

6. *Life and Work of St. Paul,* chap, xlvi

religious life he knew only by report (ch. i. 15); and it is strange that he should not have a single word of greeting to any of these Ephesian Christians. Several of the early Christian fathers testify that the words "at Ephesus" are omitted from the first verse of the manuscript known to them. The two oldest manuscripts now in existence, that of the Vatican and that known as the Sinaitic manuscript, both omit these words. The destination of the epistle is not indicated. The place filled by the words "at Ephesus" is left blank. Thus it reads: "Paul, an apostle of Christ Jesus through the will of God, to the saints which are and the faithful in Christ Jesus." Some of the old fathers expatiate on this title, drawing distinctions between the saints which *are* and the saints which *seem to be*,—an amusing example of exegetical thoroughness. Undoubtedly the letter was designed as a circular letter to several churches in Western Asia,—Laodicea among the number; and a blank was left in each copy made, in which the name of the church to which it was delivered might be entered. Some knowing copyist at a later day wrote the words "at Ephesus" into one of these copies; and it is from this that the manuscript descended from which our translation was made.

That these letters of Paul were highly prized and carefully preserved by the churches to which they were written we cannot doubt; and as from time to time messengers passed back and forth between the churches, copies were made of the letters for exchange. The church at Thessalonica would send a copy of its letter to the church at Philippi and to the church at Corinth and to the church at Ephesus, and would receive in return copies of their letters; and thus the writings of Paul early obtained a con-

siderable distribution. We have an illustration of these exchanges in the closing words of the Epistle to the Colossians (iv. 16): "And when this epistle hath been read
among you, cause that it be read also in the church of
the Laodiceans; and that you also read the epistle from
Laodicea." It is probable that the last-named epistle was
the one of which we have just been speaking, called in
our version, the Epistle to the Ephesians.

The Epistle to the Hebrews is ascribed in its title to
"Paul the Apostle." But the title was added at a late date;
the Greek Testaments contain only the brief title "To the
Hebrews," leaving the question of authorship unsettled.
Of all the other epistles ascribed to Paul his name is the
first word; this epistle does not announce its author. In
the early church there was much controversy about it; the
Eastern Christians generally ascribed it to Paul, while the
Western church, until the fourth century, refused to recognize his authorship. One sentence in the epistle (ch. ii. 3)
is supposed to signify that the writer was of the number
of those who had received the gospel at second hand, and
this was an admission that Paul always refused to make;
he steadily contended that his knowledge of the gospel
was as direct and immediate and copious as that of any
of the apostles. For these and other reasons it has been
contended that the letter was written by some one not an
apostle, but an associate and pupil of apostolic men; the
most plausible conjecture ascribes it to Apollos. The date
of it is not easily fixed; it was probably written before the
destruction of Jerusalem; such an elaborate discussion of
the Jewish ritual would scarcely have been made after the
temple was destroyed, without any reference to the fact
of its destruction.

Following the letter to the Hebrews in our New Testament are seven epistles ascribed to four different authors, James, Peter, John, and Jude. These are commonly called the "Catholic Epistles,"—catholic meaning general or universal,—since they are not addressed to any one congregation, but to the whole church, to Christians in general. Two of them, however, the Second and Third of John, hardly deserve the designation, for they are addressed to individuals.

The author of the Epistle of James is not easily identified. There are numerous Jameses in the New Testament history; we do not readily distinguish them. It was not James the son of Zebedee, for he was put to death by Herod only six or seven years after the death of our Lord (Acts xii. 2). Probably this was the one named James the Lord's brother, who was a near relative of Jesus, brother or cousin, and who was the leading man—perhaps they called him bishop—of the church at Jerusalem. He may, also, be identical with that James the son of Alpheus, who was one of the apostles. The letter was issued at an early day, probably before the year 60. It was addressed to the "twelve tribes which are of the Dispersion,"—that was the name by which the Jews scattered through Asia and Europe were generally known. To Christians who had been Jews, therefore, this letter was written; in this respect it is to be classed with the letter to the Hebrews; but in the tenor of its teaching it is wholly unlike that letter; instead of putting emphasis on the ritual and symbolical elements of religion, it leaves these wholly on one side, and makes the ethical contents of the Christian teaching the matter of supreme concern. There is more of applied Christianity in this than in any other of the epistles; and both in style and in substance we are reminded by it of the teaching of our Lord more strongly than by any other portion of the New Testament.

The First Epistle of Peter is addressed to the same class of persons,—to "the elect who are sojourners of the Dispersion" in various provinces of Asia Minor. The only intimation of tha locality of the writing is contained in one of the concluding verses: "She that is in Babylon, elect together with you, saluteth you." What Babylon is this? Is it the famous capital of the Euphrates? So some have supposed, for there is a tradition that Peter journeyed to the distant East and founded Christian churches among the Jews, who, in large numbers, were dwelling there. Others take it to be the mystical Babylon,—Rome upon her seven hills. This theory helps to support the contention, for which there is small evidence, that Peter was the first bishop of Rome. The first conjecture has a firmer basis. But who is "she" that sends her salutations to these Asian saints? Was it the church or the wife of the apostle? Either interpretation is difficult; I cannot choose between them. Of the origin of this letter we know little; but there is nothing in it inconsistent with the unbroken tradition which ascribes it to the impetuous leader of the apostolic band. Like the Epistle of James it is full of a strenuous morality; while it does not disregard the essentials of Christian doctrine it puts the emphasis on Christian conduct.

The Second Epistle of Peter is the one book of the New Testament concerning whose genuineness there is most doubt. From the earliest days the canonicity of this book has been disputed. It is not mentioned by any early Christian writer before the third century; and Origen, who is the first to allude to the book, testifies that its genuineness has been doubted. The early versions do not contain it; Eusebius marks it doubtful; Erasmus and Calvin, in later times, regarded it as a dubious document. It seems almost incredible, with such witnesses against it, that the book should be genuine; but if it is not the work of St. Peter it is a fraudulent writing, for it openly announces him as its author and refers to his first epistle. There is a remarkable similarity between this letter and the short Epistle of Jude; it would appear that this must be an imitation and enlargement of that, or that a condensation of this. There are some passages in this book with which we could ill afford to part,—with which, indeed, we never shall part; for whether they were written by Peter or by another they express clear and indubitable verities; and even though the author, like that Balaam whom he quotes, may have been no true prophet, he was constrained, even as Balaam was, to utter some wholesome and stimulating truth.

The three epistles of John are the last words of the disciple that Jesus loved. The evidence of their genuineness, particularly of the first of them, is abundant and convincing; Polycarp, who was John's pupil and friend, quotes from this book, and there is an unbroken chain of testimony from the early fathers respecting it. Of course those who have determined, for dogmatic reasons, to reject the Fourth Gospel, are bound to reject these epistles also; but that procedure is wholly unwarranted, as we shall see in the next chapter. These epistles were probably written from Ephesus during the last years of the first century. The first is a meditation on the great fact of the incarnation and its mystic relation to the life of men; it sounds the very depths of that wonderful revelation which was made to the world in the person and work of Jesus Christ. The other two are personal letters, wherein the fragrance of a gracious friendship still lingers, and in which we see how the spirit of Christ was beginning, even then, to transfigure with its benignant gentleness the courtesies of life.

The Book of Jude, the last of the epistles, is one of whose author we have little knowledge. He styles himself "the brother of James," but that, as we have seen, is a vague description. Of the close relation between this letter and Second Peter I have spoken. It is not in the early Syriac version; Eusebius and Origen question it, and Chrysostom does not mention it; we may fairly doubt whether it came from the hand of any apostolic witness. One feature of this short letter deserves mention; the writer quotes from one of the old apocryphal books, the Book of Enoch, treating it as Scripture. If a New Testament citation authenticates an ancient writing, Enoch must be regarded as an inspired book. We must either reject Jude or accept Enoch, or abandon the rule that makes a New Testament citation the proof of Old Testament canonicity. The abandonment of the rule is the simplest and the most rational solution of the difficulty.

I have now run rapidly over the history of twenty-one of the twenty-seven books of the New Testament,—all of the Epistles of the inspired book. The end of the first century found these books scattered through Europe and Asia, each probably in possession of the church to which it had been sent; those addressed to individuals probably in the hands of their children or children's children. Some exchanges, such as I have suggested, had taken place; and some churches might have possessed several of these apostolic letters, but there was yet no collection of them. Of the beginning of this collection of the New Testament writings I shall speak in the chapter upon the canon.

I said at the beginning that these writers probably had no thought when they composed these letters that they were contributing to a volume that would outlast empires, and be a manual of study and a guide of conduct in lands to the world then unknown, and in generations farther from them than they were from Abraham. But each of them uttered in sincerity the word that to him seemed the word of the hour; and God who gives life to the seed gave vitality to these true words, so that they are as full of divine energy to-day as ever they were. It is easy to cavil at a sentence here and there, or to pick flaws in their logic; but the question always returns, What kind of fruit have they borne? "By their fruits ye shall know them." One of the most precious gifts of God to men is contained in these twenty-one brief letters. It is not in equal measure in all of them, but there is none among them that does not contain some portion of it. The treasure is in earthen vessels; it was so when the apostles were alive and speaking; it is so now; it always was and always will be so; but the treasure is there, and he who with open mind and reverent spirit seeks for it will find it there, and will know that the excellency of the power is of God, and not of men.

Chapter 9

The Origin of the Gospels

We have arrived in our study of the Sacred Scriptures at the threshold of the most interesting and the most momentous topic which is presented to the student of the Biblical literature,—the question of the origin of the Gospels. These Gospels contain the record of the life and the death of Jesus Christ, that marvelous Personality in whom the histories, the prophecies, the liturgies of the Old Testament are fulfilled, and from whom the growing light and freedom and happiness of eighteen Christian centuries are seen to flow. Most certain it is that the history of the most enlightened lands of earth during these Christian centuries could not be understood without constant reference to the power which came into the world when Jesus Christ was born. Some tremendous social force made its appearance just then by which the whole life of mankind has been affected ever since that day. The most powerful institutions, the most benign influences which are at work in the world to-day, can be followed back to that period as surely as any great river can be followed up to the springs from which it takes its rise. If we had not these four Gospels we should be compelled to seek for an explanation of the chief phenomena of modern history. "We trace," says Mr. Horton, "this astonishing influence back to that life, and if we knew nothing at all about it, but had to construct it out of the creative imagination, we should have to figure to ourselves facts, sayings, and impressions which would account for what has flowed from it. Thus, if the place where this biography comes were actually a blank, we should be able to surmise something of what ought to be there, just as astronomers surmised the existence of a new planet, and knew in what quarter of the heavens to look for it by observing and registering the influences which retarded or deflected the movements of the other planets."[1]

That place is not a blank; it is filled with the fourfold record of the Life from which all these mighty influences have flowed. Must not this record prove to be the most inspiring theme open to human investigation? Is it any wonder that more study has been expended upon this theme than upon any other which has ever claimed the attention of men?

What do we know of the origin of this four-fold record? Origin it must have had like every other book, an origin in time and space. That there are divine elements in it the most of us believe; but the form in which we have it is a purely human form, and it would be worthless to us if it were not in purely human form. The sentences of which it is composed were constructed by human minds, and were written down by human hands on parchment or papyrus leaves. When, and where, and by whom? These are the questions now before us.

---

1. *Inspiration and the Bible*, p. 65.

Let us go back to the last half of the second century and see what traces of these books we can find.

Irenaeus, Bishop of Lyons, in France, who died about 200, speaks distinctly of these four Gospels, which, he declares, are equal in authority to the Old Testament Scriptures, and which he ascribes to the four authors whose names they now bear. With the fanciful reasoning then common among Christian writers, he finds a reason in the four quarters of the globe why there should have been four Gospels and no more.

Clement of Alexandria was living at the same time. He also quotes liberally in his writings from all these four books, of which he speaks as "the four Gospels that have been handed down to us."

Tertullian, who was born in Carthage about 160, also quotes all these Gospels as authoritative Christian writings.

It is clear, therefore, that in the West, the East, and the South,—in all quarters where Christianity was then established,—the four Gospels were recognized and read in the churches in the latter half of the second century. Let us go back a little farther.

Justin Martyr was born at Rome about the year 100, and was writing most abundantly from his fortieth to his forty-fifth year. In one of the books which he has left us, in describing the customs of the Christians, he uses the following language: "On the day which is called Sunday there is an assembly in the same place of all who live in cities or in country districts, and the records of the apostles or the writings of the prophets are read as long as we have time. Then the reader concludes, and the president verbally instructs and exhorts us to the imitation of these excellent things. Then we all rise up together and offer our prayers." In another place he speaks of something commanded by "the apostles in the records which they made, and which are called Gospels." Justin does not say how many of these Gospels the church in his day possessed, but we find in his writings unmistakable quotations from at least three of them. Dr. Edwin Abbott, of London, whom Mrs. Humphry Ward refers to as master of all the German learning on this subject, says that it would be possible "to reconstruct from his (Justin's) quotations a fairly connected narrative of the incarnation, birth, teaching, crucifixion, resurrection, and ascension of the Lord;" that this narrative is all found in the three Synoptic Gospels, and that Justin quotes no words of Christ and refers to no incidents that are not found in these Gospels.[2]

We may fully accept Dr. Abbott's testimony so far as the quotations of Justin from the first three Gospels are concerned; but his arguments, which are intended to prove that there is no certain reference to the fourth Gospel in Justin's works, appear to me inconclusive. When Justin says: "For indeed Christ also said, 'except ye be born again, ye shall not enter into the kingdom of heaven,' but that it is impossible for those who were once born to enter into their mother's womb is plain to all," he is quoting words that are found in the fourth Gospel, and not in any of the other three. The attempt to show that he found these and similar citations in the same sources from which the author of the fourth Gospel derived them is not successful.

---

2. *Encyc. Brit.*, vol. x. p. 817.

Several indirect lines of evidence tend to confirm the belief that Justin possessed all four of our Gospels. This, then, carries us back to the first half of the second century. Between 100 and 150 Papias of Hierapolis, Clement of Rome, and Polycarp of Smyrna were writing. Papias, who wrote about 130–140 A.D., composed five books or commentaries on what he calls "The Oracles of the Lord." He gives us some account of the origin of at least two of these Gospels. "Mark," he says, "was the interpreter of Peter;" "Matthew wrote his scriptures (*logia*) in Hebrew, and each man interpreted them as best he could." "Interpreted" here evidently means translated. Elsewhere he repeats a tradition of "the elder," by which word he apparently means the Apostle John, whom he may have known, in these words: "Mark, having become Peter's interpreter, wrote down accurately all that he remembered,—not, however, in order,—both the words and the deeds of Christ. For he never heard the Lord, nor attached himself to him, but later on, as I said, attached himself to Peter, who used to adapt his lessons to the needs of the occasion, but not as though he was composing a connected treatise of the discourses of our Lord; so that Mark committed no error in writing down some matters just as he remembered them. For one object was in his thoughts, to make no omissions and no false statements in what he heard."[3] This is a perfect description of the Gospel of Mark as we have it in our hands today. And the testimony of Papias to its authorship, and to the spirit and purpose of the author, is significant and memorable. Evidence of this nature would be regarded as decisive in any other case of literary criticism.

---

3. Quoted by Abbott, as above.

Polycarp, who was the friend and pupil of John the Apostle, was born about the year 69, and suffered martyrdom about 155. In his writings we find no express mention of the Gospels, but we do find verbally accurate quotations from them. It is clear that he was acquainted with the books. Polycarp was the teacher of Irenaeus of Lyons whom I first quoted, and he was the pupil and friend of St. John and the other apostles; and Irenaeus, who quotes all these Gospels so freely, bears this testimony respecting Polycarp, in a letter which he wrote to Florinus.

"I saw you, when I was yet a boy, in Lower Asia with Polycarp. . . . I could even point out now the place where the blessed Polycarp sat and spoke, and describe his going out and coming in, his manner of life, his personal appearance, the addresses he delivered to the multitude, how he spoke of his intercourse with John, and with the others who had seen the Lord, and how he recalled their words, and everything that he had heard about the Lord, about his miracles and his teaching. Polycarp told us, as one who had received it from those who had seen the Word of Life with their own eyes, and all this in complete harmony with the Scriptures. To this I then listened, through the mercy of God vouchsafed to me, with all eagerness, and wrote it not on paper, but in my heart, and still by the grace of God I ever bring it into fresh remembrance."

These living witnesses give us solid ground for our statement that the Gospels—the first three of them at any rate—were in existence during the last years of the first century. Indeed, not to prolong this search for the origin of the books, it is now freely admitted, by many of the most radical critics, that the first three Gospels were written before the year 80, and that Mark must have been written before 70.

It is interesting to contrast the course of New Testament criticism with that engaged upon the Old Testament. In the study of the origin of the Pentateuch the gravitation of opinion has been steadily downward, toward a later date, so that the great majority of scholars are now certain that the books must have been put into their present form long after the time of Moses. In the study of the origin of the Gospels the date has been steadily pushed upward, to the very age of the apostles. The earlier critics, Strauss and Baur, insisted that they must have appeared much later, far on in the second century; but the more recent and more scientific criticism has demolished or badly discredited their theories, and has carried the Gospels back to the last part of the first century.

Are we entitled, then, to say that these Gospels were written by Matthew, Mark, Luke, and John? We should be cautious, no doubt, in making such a statement. The Gospels themselves are not so explicit on this point as we could desire. Their titles do not warrant this assertion. It is not "The Gospel of St. Matthew" or "The Gospel of St. Mark;" it is the "Gospel according to St. Matthew" or St. Mark. The import of the title would be fully satisfied with the explanation that this is the story as Matthew or Mark was wont to tell it, put into form by some person or friend of his, in his last days, or even after his death. But the testimony of Papias, to which I have referred, is to my own mind good evidence that these Gospels were written by the men who bear their names. In the case of Luke, as we shall presently see, the evidence is much stronger. And after going over the evidence as carefully as I am able, the theory that the four Gospels were written by the men whose names they bear, all of whom were the contemporaries of our Lord, and two of whom were his apostles, seems to me, on the whole, the best supported by the whole volume of evidence. The case is not absolutely clear; perhaps it was left somewhat obscure for the very purpose of stimulating study. At all events, the study which has been given to the subject has confirmed rather than weakened the belief that the Gospels are contemporary records of the life of Christ. Mr. Norton, a distinguished Unitarian scholar, sums up the evidence as follows: "It consists in the indisputable fact that throughout a community of millions of individuals, scattered over Europe, Asia, and Africa, the Gospels were regarded with the highest reverence, as the works of those to whom they are ascribed, at so early a period that there could be no difficulty in determining whether they were genuine or not, and when every intelligent Christian must have been deeply interested to ascertain the truth. . . . This fact is itself a phenomenon admitting of no explanation except that the four Gospels had all been handed down as genuine from the apostolic age, and had everywhere accompanied our religion as it spread throughout the world."

When we turn from the external or historical evidence for the genuineness of the Gospels to study their internal structure and their relations to one another, we come upon some curious facts. These Gospels, in the form in which we possess them, are written in the Greek language. But the Greek language was not the vernacular of the Jews in Palestine when our Lord was on the earth; the language which was then spoken by them, as I have before explained, was the Aramaic. It is true that Palestine was, to some extent, a bilingual country,—like Wales, one writer suggests, where the English and the Welsh languages are now freely spoken,—that Aramaic and Greek were used indifferently. I can hardly imagine that a people as tenacious of their own institutions as the Jews could have adopted Greek as generally as the Welsh have adopted the English tongue. Even in Wales, if a Welshman were speaking to a congregation of his countrymen on any important topic, he would be likely to speak the Welsh language. And much more probable does it seem to me that the discourses and the common conversation of Jesus must have been spoken in the vernacular. The discourses and sayings of our Lord, as reported for us in these Gospels, are not therefore given us in the words that he used. We have a translation of his words from the Aramaic into the Greek, made either by the writers of the Gospels, or by some one in their day. We have quoted the testimony of Papias, that the Gospel of Matthew was originally written in Hebrew (by which he undoubtedly means Aramaic), and that each one interpreted it as best he could; and if this be true, then that copy first made by Matthew did contain many of our Lord's very words. But that Aramaic copy has never been seen since that day; we have no manuscript of any New Testament book except in the Greek language. There are a few cases in which the writers of the Gospels have preserved for us the very words used by Christ. Thus in the healing of the deaf man in the neighborhood of Decapolis, of which Mark tells us (vii. 34), Jesus touched his ears, and said unto him, "Ephphatha," that is, "Be opened." The Evangelist gives us the Aramaic word which Jesus used, and translates it for his readers into Greek. Likewise in the healing of the ruler's daughter (Mark v. 41) he took her by the hand, and said unto her, "Talitha cumi, which is, being interpreted," the Evangelist explains, "Damsel, I say unto thee, Arise." Doubtless most readers get the impression that our Lord used here some cabalistic words in a foreign tongue; the fact is that these are the words of the common speech of the people; only the Evangelist seems to have thought them especially memorable, and he has given us not merely, as he generally does, a translation into the Greek of our Lord's words, but the Aramaic words themselves, with their meaning appended in a Greek phrase. The same is true of our Lord's words on the cross: "Eli, Eli, lama sabachthani?" These are Aramaic words, the very words that Jesus uttered. The Roman soldiers who stood near might not know what he meant; but every Jew who distinctly heard him must have understood him, for he was speaking in no foreign tongue, but in the language of his own people.

When we speak, therefore, of the Greek as the original language of the Gospels, we do not speak with entire accuracy. The Greek does not give us our Lord's original words. These we have not, except in the cases I have named, and a few others less important. No man on earth knows or ever will know what were the precise words that our Lord used in his Sermon on the Mount, in his conversation with the woman at the well, in his last discourses with his disciples. We have every reason to believe that the substance of what he said is faithfully preserved for us; the fourfold record, so marvelously accordant in its report of his teachings, makes this perfectly clear. But his very words we have not, and this fact itself is the most convincing dis-proof of the dogma of verbal inspiration. If our Lord had thought it important that we should have his very words he would have seen to it that his very words were preserved and recorded for us, instead of that Greek translation of his words, made by his followers, which we now possess. These evangelists could have written Aramaic, doubtless did write Aramaic; and they would certainly have kept our Lord's discourses and sayings in the Aramaic original if they had been instructed to do so. The fact that they were not instructed to do so, but were permitted to give his teachings to the world in other words than those in which they were spoken, shows how little there was of modern literalism in Christ's conception of the work of revelation.

The first three of these Gospels exhibit many striking similarities; they appear to give, from somewhat different standpoints, a condensed and complete synopsis of the events of our Lord's life; therefore they are called the Synoptic Gospels. The fourth Gospel differs widely from them in matter and form. It will be more convenient, therefore, to speak first of the Synoptic Gospels, Matthew, Mark, and Luke.

The singular fact respecting these Gospels is the combination in them of likeness and difference. A considerable portion of each one of them is to be found, word for word, in one or both of the others; other considerable portions of each are not found in either of the others; some passages are nearly alike, but slightly different in two or in all of them. Did these three authors write independently each of the other? If so, how does it happen that their phraseology is so often identical? Did they copy one from another? If so, why did they copy so little? Why, for example, did each one of them omit so much that the others had written? And why are there so many slight differences in passages that are nearly identical? If we accepted the theory of verbal inspiration, we might offer some sort of explanation of this phenomenon. We might say that the Holy Ghost dictated these words, and that that is the end of it; since no explanation can be offered of the reason why the Holy Ghost chose one form of expression rather than another. But the Gospels themselves contain abundant proof that the Holy Ghost did not dictate the words employed by these writers.

The two genealogies of our Lord, one in Matthew and the other in Luke, are widely different. From Abraham to David they substantially agree; from David to Christ, Matthew makes twenty-eight generations, and Luke thirty-eight; only two of the intermediate names in the one table are found in the other; the one list makes Jacob the father of Joseph, and the other declares that the name of Joseph's father was Heli. All sorts of explanations, some plausible and others preposterous, have been offered of this difficulty; the one explanation that cannot be allowed is that these words were dictated by Omniscience. In the story of the healing of the blind near Jericho, Matthew and Mark expressly say that the healing took place as Christ was departing from the city; Luke that it was before he entered it. Matthew says that there were two blind men; Mark and Luke that there was but one. About these details of the transaction there is some mistake,—that is the only thing to be said about it. The various explanations offered are weak and inadmissible. But what difference does it make to anybody whether the healing took place before or after Jesus entered the city, or whether there was one man healed or two? The moral and spiritual lessons of the story are just as distinct in the one case as in the other; and it is these moral and spiritual values only that inspiration is intended to secure.

Similarly, Luke (iv. 38–39) expressly tells us that the healing of Peter's wife's mother took place before the calling of Simon and Andrew; while Matthew and Mark tell us with equal explicitness that the calling took place before the healing. No reconciliation is possible here; either Luke or Matthew and Mark must have misplaced these events.

So in Matthew xxvii. 9, certain words are said to have been spoken by Jeremiah the prophet. These words are not in Jeremiah; they are in Zechariah xi. 13. It is simply a slip of the Evangelist's memory.

So in the record of the inscription on the cross when Jesus was crucified. Each of the four Evangelists copies it for us in a different form. The meaning is the same in all the cases, but the copy was not exactly made by some of them, perhaps not by any of them. If the Holy Ghost had dictated the words, they must, in a case like this, have been exactly alike in all the Evangelists. The substance is given, but the inexactness of the copy shows that the words could not have been dictated by Omniscience. It is sometimes explained that this inscription was in three languages, Greek, Latin, and Hebrew, and that we may have the exact translations of the different inscriptions. This might account for three of them, but not for four.

From these and many other similar facts, we know that the theory of verbal inspiration is not true; but that these Evangelists were allowed to state each in his own language the facts known by him concerning our Lord, and that nothing like infallible accuracy was so much as attempted. The only inspiration that can be claimed for them is that which brought the important facts to their remembrance, and guarded them against serious errors of history or doctrine.

But now the question returns, if they wrote these Gospels in their own language and independently of one another, how happens it that they use so often the very same words and phrases and sentences? Take, for example, the following verses from parallel narratives in Matthew and in Mark, concerning the calling of the first apostles:—

Matthew iv. 18–22:
And walking by the sea of Galilee, he saw two brethren, Simon who is called Peter, and Andrew his brother, casting a net into the sea; for they were fishers. And he saith unto them, Come ye after me, and I will make you fishers of men. And they straightway left the nets, and followed him. And going on from thence he saw two other brethren, James the son of Zebedee, and John his brother, in the boat with Zebedee their father, mending their nets; and he called them. And they straightway left the boat and their father, and followed him.

Mark i. 16–20:
And passing along by the sea of Galilee, he saw Simon and Andrew the brother of Simon casting a net in the sea: for they were fishers. And Jesus said unto them, Come ye after me, and I will make you to become fishers of men. And straightway they left the nets, and followed him. And going on a little further, he saw James the son of Zebedee, and John his brother, who also were in the boat mending the nets. And straightway he called them:

and they left their father Zebedee in the boat with the hired servants, and went after him.

There are slight verbal variations, but in general the words are the same, and the corresponding sentences are in precisely the same order in both narratives. Now, as Archbishop Thomson says, in Smith's "Bible Dictionary," "The verbal and material agreement of the first three Evangelists is such as does not occur in any other authors who have written independently of each other."

Besides many such passages which are substantially alike but verbally or syntactically different, there are quite a number which are identical, word for word, and phrase for phrase. These verbal agreements occur most frequently, as is natural, in the reports of our Lord's discourses and sayings; but they also occur in the descriptive and narrative portions of the gospel. This is the fact which is so difficult to reconcile with the theory that the books were produced by independent writers.

Suppose three competent and truthful reporters are employed by you to write an exact and unvarnished report of some single transaction which has occurred, and which each of them has witnessed. Each is required to do his work without any conference with the others. When these reports are brought to you, if they are very faithful and accurate for substance, you will not be surprised to find some circumstances mentioned by each that are not mentioned by either of the others, and it will be strange if there are not some important discrepancies. But if on reading them, you find that the reports, taken sentence by sentence, are almost identical,—that there is only an occasional difference in a word or in the order of a phrase,— then you at once say, "These reporters must have been copying from some other reporter's note-book, or else they must have been comparing notes; they could not have written with such verbal agreement if they had written independently." Suppose, for example, that each of the three reports began in just these words: "The first object that attracted my notice on entering the door was a chair." Now it is extremely improbable that all these writers, writing independent reports of a transaction, should begin in the same way by mentioning the first object that attracted the attention of each. And even if they should so begin, it is wholly beyond the range of possibilities that they should all select from all the multitude of the words in the English language the very same words in which to make this statement; and should put these words in the very same order, out of the multitude of different orders into which they could grammatically be put. There is not one chance in a million that such a coincidence would occur. But such coincidences occur very often in the first three Gospels. How can we account for it? We say that they wrote independently, that their words were not dictated to them; how does it happen that there is so much verbal agreement?

We may get some hint of the manner in which these biographies were produced if we turn to the beginning of Luke's Gospel:—

"Forasmuch as many have taken in hand to draw up a narrative concerning those matters which have been fulfilled among us, even as they delivered them unto us, which from the beginning were eyewitnesses and ministers of the word, it seemed good to me also, having traced the course of all things accurately from the first, to write unto thee in order, most excellent Theophilus; that thou mightest know the certainty concerning the things wherein thou wast instructed." The marginal reading of this last phrase is, "which thou wast taught by word of mouth." This is the more exact meaning of the Greek. The passage contains these statements:—

1. Theophilus had been orally taught the Gospels.

2. Many persons, not apostles, had undertaken to write out parts of the gospel story, as they had heard it from eyewitnesses and ministers of the word.

3. Luke also, as one who had full and accurate information, had determined to reduce his knowledge to an orderly written narrative, for the benefit of his friend Theophilus.

It appears from this clear statement that written memoranda of the discourses of our Lord and of the incidents of his life had been made by many persons. Numbers of these had undertaken to combine their memoranda with their recollections in an orderly statement. This fact itself shows how powerful an impression had been made by our Lord's life and death upon the people of Palestine. Everything relating to him was treasured with the utmost care; Luke, for his part, believing that he had gained by careful investigation sufficient knowledge to warrant the undertaking, sets out to collect the facts and present them in a consecutive and intelligible literary form. Yet Luke, in this announcement of his purpose, betrays no consciousness that he is using any different powers from those employed by the many others of whom he speaks. Rather does he most clearly rank himself with them, as one of many gleaners in this fruitful field. He does claim thoroughness and painstaking accuracy; I believe that every honest man will concede his claim.

This, then, was the way in which Luke went to work to write his Gospel. This is not guesswork; it is the explicit statement of the author himself. Have we not good reason for believing that the Gospels of Matthew and Mark were composed in much the same way?

In addition to the written memoranda of Christ's life which were in the hands of the apostles, and of many others, there was another source from which the Evangelists must have drawn. Luke alludes to it when he speaks of the fact that Theophilus had received much of his narrative "by word of mouth." There was, unquestionably, an oral gospel, covering the larger part of the deeds and the words of Jesus, which had been widely circulated in Palestine and in the whole missionary field. When it is said (Acts viii. 1–4; xi. 19) that they which were scattered abroad by the early persecutions went everywhere preaching the word, it must be understood that they went about simply telling the story of Jesus, his birth, his life, his deeds, his words, his death upon the cross. Sometimes, when preaching to Jews, they would show the correspondence between his life and the Old Testament prophecies, to prove that he was the Messiah; but the substance of their preaching was the telling over and over again of the story of Jesus. It was upon this oral gospel that the apostles and the first missionaries mainly relied. What they desired to do was to make known as speedily and as rapidly as possible the words of his lips and the facts of his life. And it is highly probable that before they set out on these missionary tours, they took great pains to rehearse to one another the story which they were going forth to tell. "The apostles," says Professor Westcott, "guided by the promised Spirit of truth, remained together in Jerusalem in close communion for a period long enough to shape a common narrative, and to fix it with requisite surroundings."

It was these concerted recollections and rehearsals that gave to so many passages of the gospel its identity in form. Some of the sentences often and devoutly repeated were remembered by all, word for word; in some of them there were verbal differences and discrepancies, as they were repeated by one and another. The verbal resemblances as well as the verbal differences are thus explained by this theory of an oral gospel, prepared at first for preaching by the apostles, and held only in their memory.

The preservation of so many passages in words and sentences nearly or exactly similar is nothing miraculous. Even in our own time there are, as we are told, secret societies whose ritual has never been written, but has been handed down with nearly verbal accuracy, from generation to generation. For the Hebrews, who were a people at this time greatly disinclined to write, and thoroughly practiced in remembering and repeating the sayings of their wise men, this task would not be difficult.

The apostles and the early evangelists, as Westcott suggests, were preachers, not historians, not pamphleteers. They believed in living witnesses more than in transmitted documents. They did not write out the record at first, partly because they were naturally disinclined to write, and partly, no doubt, because they expected the immediate return of our Lord to earth. Their gospel was therefore for many years a spoken and not a written word. As they went on repeating it, changes would occur in the repetition of the words; to the remembrance of one and another of them the Spirit of truth would bring facts and circumstances that they did not think of at first; words, phrases, gestures of our Lord would reappear in the memory of each, and thus the narrative became varied and shaded with the personal peculiarities of the several writers.

Years passed, and the expected return of the Lord to earth did not take place. The churches were spreading over Asia and Europe, and the apostles were unable personally to instruct those who were preaching the gospel in other lands. Thus the need of a written record began to make itself felt; and the apostles themselves wrote out the story which they had been telling, or it was written for them by their companions and fellow-helpers in the gospel. The oral gospel as it lived in their memories would form, no doubt, the substance of it, and the written memoranda of the discourses and incidents, to which Luke refers, would be drawn upon in completing the biography. The oral gospel thus carefully prepared and transmitted by memory would be substantially the same, yet many differences in arrangement of words and phrases would naturally have crept in; the written memoranda would in many cases be verbally identical. And each Evangelist, gleaning from this wide field, would collect some facts and sayings omitted by the others.

There are other explanations of the origin of the Synoptic Gospels, some of which are ingenious and plausible, but I shall not burden your minds with them, since the theory which I have presented appears to me the simplest, the most natural, and the most comprehensive of them all.

The Fourth Gospel, it is evident, must have had a different origin. Beyond question it is a consecutive narrative, composed by a single writer, and not, like the Synoptics, a compilation of memoranda, oral or written. It appears to be, in part at least, a supplementary narrative, omitting much that is contained in the other Gospels, supplying some omissions, and correcting, possibly, certain unimportant errors. Mr. Horton illustrates the supplementary work of this Evangelist by several instances. "The communion of the Lord's Supper," he says, "was so universally known and observed when he wrote that he actually does not mention its institution, but he records a wonderful discourse concerning the Bread of Life which is an indispensable commentary on the unnamed institution, and by filling in with great detail the circumstances of the last evening, he furnished a framework for the ordinance which is among our most precious possessions. On the other hand, because the common tradition was very vague in its date he gave precision to the event which they had recorded by fixing the time of its occurrence. . . . In Matt. iv. 12 and Mark i. 14, the temptation, immediately following Christ's baptism, is immediately followed by the statement, 'When he heard that John was delivered up, he withdrew into Galilee; and leaving Nazareth he came and dwelt in Capernaum.' But this summary narrative had excluded one of the most interesting features of the early ministry of Jesus. Accordingly the Fourth Gospel enlarges the story and emphasizes the marks of time. After the Baptism, according to this authority, Jesus 'went down to Capernaum, he and his mother and his brethren and his disciples, and there they abode not many days' (ii. 12). Then he went up to the Passover at Jerusalem, where he had the interview with Nicodemus. After that he went into the country districts of Judea, where John was baptizing in Aenon, and then the writer adds, as if his eye were on the condensed and misleading narrative of the common tradition, 'For John was not yet cast into prison.' The two great teachers, the Forerunner, and the Greater-than-he, were actually baptizing side by side, and it was because Jesus saw his reputation overshadowing John's that he voluntarily withdrew into Galilee, passing through Samaria. So that while there had been two journeys to Galilee before John was imprisoned, and that early period of the life was full of unique and wonderful interest, all had been compressed and crushed into the brief statement of Matt. iv. 12 and Mark i. 14. In this case we seem to see the Evangelist deliberately loosening and breaking up the current history in order that he might insert into the cramped and lifeless framework some of the most valuable episodes of the Lord's life. If the fourth Evangelist had treated the triple narrative in the way that many of us have treated it, regarding it as a sin against the Holy Spirit to suggest that there was any incompleteness or any misleading abbreviations in it, we should have lost the wonderful accounts of the conversation with Nicodemus and with the woman at the well."[4]

If such is the relation of the Fourth Gospel to the Synoptics, it follows that it must have been the work of one who was thoroughly familiar with the events recorded. That the narrative bears evidence of having been written by an eyewitness is to my own mind clear. That the writer intends to convey the impression that he is the beloved disciple is also manifest. Either it was written

---

4. *Inspiration and the Bible*, pp. 95–99.

by John the Apostle, or else the writer was a deliberate deceiver. There can be no such explanation of his personation of John as that which satisfies our minds in the case of Daniel and Ecclesiastes; the book is either the work of John, or it is a cunning and conscienceless fraud. And it seems to me that any one who will read the book will find it impossible to believe that it is an imposture. If any book of the ages bears in itself the witness to the truth it is the Fourth Gospel. It shines by its own light. Any of us could tell the difference between the sun in the heavens and a brass disk suspended in the sky reflecting the sun's rays; and in much the same way the fact is apparent that the book is not a counterfeit gospel.

It is true that historical criticism has raised difficulties about it; the battle of the critics has been raging around it for half a century; but one after another of the positions taken by men like Strauss and Baur have been shown to be untenable; and it can truthfully be said, in the words of Professor Ladd, "that the vigorous and determined attacks upon the genuineness of the Fourth Gospel have greatly increased instead of impairing our confidence in the traditional view."[5] And I am ready to go farther with the same brave but reverent scholar, and say, "Having thus grounded in historical and critical researches the genuineness of the Fourth Gospel, we have no hesitation in affirming what position it must take in Sacred Scripture. It is the heart of Jesus Christ with which we here come in contact. Inspiration and reflection uniting upon the choicest and most undoubted material of history, and fusing all the material with the holy characteristics of rev-

---

5. *What is the Bible?* p. 327.

elation, are nowhere else so apparent as in the Gospel of the Apostle John."[6]

Such, then, is the fourfold biography of Jesus the Christ preserved for us in the New Testament. If this study has removed something of the mystery with which the origin of these writings has been shrouded, it has, I trust, at the same time, made them appear more real and more human; and it has shown the providential oversight by which their artless record, many-sided, manifold, yet simple and clear as the daylight, has been preserved for us. Of these four Gospels we are certainly entitled to say as much as this, that whatever verbal discrepancies may be detected in them, and however difficult it may be satisfactorily to explain all the phenomena of their structure and relations, in one thing they marvelously agree, and that is in the picture which they give us of the life and character of Jesus Christ. In this each one of them is self-consistent, and they are all consistent with one another. And this, if we will reflect upon it, is a marvelous, not to say a miraculous fact. That four such men as these Evangelists incontestably were should have succeeded in giving us four portraitures of the Divine Man, without contradicting themselves, and without contradicting one another,—four distinct views of this wonderful Person, which show us different sides of his character, and which we yet instantly recognize as the same person, is a very great wonder. No such task was ever laid on any other human biographer as that which confronted these men; no character so difficult to comprehend and describe ever existed; for one man to preserve all the unities of art in

---

6. *Doctrine of Sacred Scripture*, i. 573.

describing him would be notable; for four men to give us, independently, four narratives, from the simple pages of which the same lineaments shine out, so that no one ever thinks of saying that the Jesus of Matthew is a different person from the Jesus of Mark or Luke or John,—this, I say, is marvelous.

And it is this character, majestic in its simplicity, glorious in its humility, the Ideal of Humanity, the Mystery of Godliness, that these Gospels are meant to show us. If they only bring him clearly before us, make his personality real and familiar and vivid before our eyes, so that we may know him and love him, that is all we want of them. Infallibility in details would be worthless if this were wanting; any small discrepancies are beneath notice if this is here. And this is here. Read for yourselves. From the page of Matthew, illuminated with the words of prophecy that tell of the Messiah's coming; from the vivid and rapid record of Mark, in which the Wonder-worker displays his power; from the tender story of Luke, speaking the word of grace to those that are lowest down and farthest off; from the mystical Gospel of the beloved disciple opening to us the deep things that only love can see, the same divine form appears, the same divine face shines, the same divine voice is speaking. Behold the man!

Chapter 10

New Testament History and Prophecy

The Acts of the Apostles contains the history of the Christian church from the time of the ascension of our Lord to the end of the second year of Paul's first imprisonment at Rome. The period covered by the history is therefore only about thirty years. The principal events recorded in it are the great Pentecostal Revival, the Martyrdom of Stephen, the first persecution of the church and the dispersion of the disciples, the conversion and the missionary work of Paul, with the circumstances of his arrest at Jerusalem, his journey as a prisoner to Rome, and a brief account of his residence in that city. In the first part of the book Peter, the leader of the apostolic band, is the central figure; the last part is occupied with the life and work of Paul.

Who is the writer? Irenaeus, about 182, names Luke as the author of the book, and speaks as though the fact were undisputed. He calls him "a follower and disciple of apostles," and declares that "he was inseparable from Paul and was his fellow-helper in the gospel." This is the earliest distinct reference to the book in any ancient Christian writing. After this, Clement of Alexandria, Tertullian, Origen, and Eusebius bear the same testimony. But these are late witnesses. The earliest of them testified a hundred years after the death of Luke. The direct testimony to the existence of this book in the first two cenuries is not, therefore, altogether satisfactory. The indirect testimony is, however, clear and strong.

That the Acts was written by the author of the Third Gospel is scarcely doubted by any critical scholar. The fact of the identity of authorship is stated with the utmost explicitness in the introduction of the Acts. "The former treatise I made, O Theophilus, concerning all that Jesus began both to do and to teach" (Luke i. 1, 2). The author of the Acts of the Apostles certainly intends to say that he is the writer of the Third Gospel. If he is not the author of the Third Gospel he is an artful and shameless deceiver. But the whole atmosphere of the book forbids the theory that it is a cunning imposition. And the internal evidence that the two books were written by the same author is ample and convincing. The style and the method of the treatment of the two books are unmistakably identical. Every page bears witness to the fact that the author of the Third Gospel and the author of the Acts are one and the same person. Now we know, beyond all reasonable doubt, that the Gospel of Luke was written certainly as early as the year 80 A.D. And there is as good reason, as we have seen already, for accepting the ancient and universal tradition of the church that Luke was its author. If Luke wrote the two books, the date of both of them is carried back to the last part of the first century. But the concluding portion of the Acts of the Apostles seems to fix the date of that book much more precisely. The author, after narrating Paul's journey to Rome, his arrival there, and his first unsatisfactory interview with the Jewish leaders, closes his book with this compendious statement:—

"And he abode two whole years in his own hired dwelling, and received all that went in unto him, preaching the kingdom of God, and teaching all things concerning the Lord Jesus Christ with all boldness, none forbidding him."

This is the last word in the New Testament history respecting the Apostle Paul. Now it is evident that this writer was Paul's friend and traveling companion. It is true that he keeps himself out of sight in the history. We only know when he joined Paul by the fact that the narrative changes from the third person singular to the first person plural; he ceases to say "he," and begins to say "we." Thus we are made aware that he joined Paul at Troas on his second missionary journey, and went with him as far as Philippi; rejoined him at the same place on his third missionary tour, and accompanied him to Jerusalem; was his fellow-voyager on that memorable journey to Rome, and there abode with him for two years. The Epistle to the Colossians and the Epistle to Philemon were written during this imprisonment at Rome, and in both of these Epistles Paul speaks of the fact that Luke is near him. In the second letter to Timothy, which is supposed to have been written during the second imprisonment at Rome, and near the close of his life, he says again, "Only Luke is with me. Take Mark, and bring him unto me, for he is useful to me for ministering." If the common opinion concerning the date of this letter is correct, then

Luke must have remained with Paul at Rome until the close of his life. But the narrative in Luke does not give any account of the closing years of Paul's life. It breaks off abruptly at the end of his two years' residence in Rome. Why is this? Evidently because there is no more to tell at this time. The writer continues the history up to the date of his writing and stops there. If he had been writing after the death of Paul, he would certainly have told us of the circumstances of his death. There is no rational explanation of this abrupt ending, except that the book was written at about the time when the story closes. This was certainly about 63 A.D. And if the Book of Acts was written as early as this, the Gospel of Luke, the "former treatise" by the same author, must have been written earlier than this. Thus the Book of Acts not only furnishes strong evidence of its own early date, but helps to establish the early date of the third Gospel.

These conclusions, to my own mind, are irresistible. No theory which consists with the common honesty of the writer can bring these books down to a later date. And I cannot doubt the honesty of the writer. His writings prove him to be a careful, painstaking, veracious historian. In many slight matters this accuracy appears. The political structure of the Roman Empire at this time was somewhat complicated. The provinces were divided between the Emperor and the Senate; those heads of provinces who were directly responsible to the Emperor and the military authorities were called propraetors; those who were under the jurisdiction of the Senate were called proconsuls. In mentioning these officers Luke never makes a mistake; he gets the precise title every time. Once, indeed, the critics thought they had caught him in an error. Sergius Paulus, the Roman ruler of Cyprus, he calls proconsul. "Wrong!" said the critics, "Cyprus was an imperial province; the title of this officer must have been propraetor." But when the critics studied a little more, they found out that Augustus put this province back under the Senate, so that Luke's title is exactly right. And to clinch the matter, old coins of this very date have been found in Cyprus, giving to the chief magistrate of the island the title of proconsul. Such evidences of the accuracy of the writer are not wanting. It is needless to insist that he never makes a mistake; doubtless he does, in some small matters, and we have learned to take such a view of the inspiration of the Scriptures that the discovery of some small error does not trouble us in the least; but the admission that he is not infallible is perfectly consistent with the belief that he is an honest, competent, faithful witness. This is all that he claims for himself, this is all that we claim for him, but this we do claim. We do not believe that he was a conscienceless impostor. We do not believe that the man who told the story of Ananias and Sapphira was himself a monumental liar. We believe that he meant to tell the truth, and the whole truth, and nothing but the truth. Therefore, we believe that he lived in the times of the apostles, and received from them, as he says that he did, the facts that he recorded in his Gospel; that he was the traveling companion and missionary helper of Paul, as he intimates that he was, and that he has given us a true account of the life and work of that great apostle.

The constant and undesigned coincidences between the Acts of the Apostles and the Epistles of Paul—the many ways in which the personal and historical refer-

ences of the latter support the statements of the former—
are also strong evidence of the genuineness of the Acts.
Putting all these indirect and incidental proofs together
the historical verity of the Acts seems to me very firmly
established. That there are critical difficulties may be admitted; some passages of this ancient writing are not
easily explained; there are discrepancies, for example,
between the story of the resurrection and ascension of
Christ as told in Luke and the same story as related in the
Acts; possibly the writer obtained fuller information in
the interval between the publication of these two books
by which he corrected the earlier narrative. In the different accounts of the conversion of Paul there are also disagreements which we cannot reconcile; nevertheless, in
the words of Dr. Donaldson, "Even these very accounts
contain evidence in them that they were written by the
same writer, and they do not destroy the force of the rest
of the evidence."[1]

The theory of Baur that this book was written in the
last part of the second century by a disciple of St. Paul,
and that it is mainly a work of fiction, intended to bring
about a reconciliation between two bitterly hostile parties
in the church, the Pauline and the Petrine sects, need not
detain us long. Baur contends that the church in the first
two centuries was split in twain, the followers of Peter
insisting that no man could become a Christian without
first becoming a Jew, the followers of Paul maintaining
that the Jewish ritual was abolished, and that the Gentiles
ought to have immediate access to the Christian fellowship. Their antagonism was so radical and far-reaching

---

1. *Encyc. Brit.*, i. 124.

that at the end of the apostolic age the two parties had no dealings with each other. "Then," in the words of Professor Fisher, who is here summarizing the theory of Baur, "followed attempts to reconcile the difference, and to bridge the gulf that separated Gentile from Jewish, Pauline from Petrine Christianity. To this end various irenical and compromising books were written in the name of the apostles and their helpers. The most important monument of this pacifying effort is the Book of Acts, written in the earlier part of the second century by a Pauline Christian who, by making Paul something of a Judaizer, and then representing Peter as agreeing with him in the recognition of the rights of the Gentiles, hoped, not in vain, to produce a mutual friendliness between the respective partisans of the rival apostles. The Acts is a fiction founded on facts, and written for a specific doctrinal purpose. The narrative of the council or conference of the Apostles, for example (Acts xx.), is pronounced a pure invention of the writer, and such a representation of the condition of things as is inconsistent with Paul's own statements, and for this and other reasons plainly false. The same ground is taken in respect to the conversion of Cornelius, and the vision of Peter concerning it."[2]

For this theory there is, of course, some slight historical basis. It is true, as we have seen, that Peter and Paul did have a sharp disagreement on this very question at Antioch. It is also true that both these great apostles behaved quite inconsistently, Peter at Antioch, and Paul afterwards at Jerusalem, when he consented to the propositions of the Judaizers, and burdened himself with certain Jewish observances in a vain attempt to conciliate

---

2. *The Supernatural Origin of Christianity*, pp. 211, 212.

some of the weaker brethren. That the story of the Acts unflinchingly shows us the weaknesses and errors of the great apostles is good evidence of its veracity. But the notion that it is a work of fiction fabricated for such purposes as are outlined above is utterly incredible. Those Epistles of Paul which Baur admits to be genuine contain abundant disproof of his theory. There never was any such schism as he fancies. Paul spends a good part of his time in his last missionary journey in collecting funds for the relief of those poor "saints," for so he calls them, at Jerusalem; and every reference that he makes to them is of the most affectionate character. Paul recognizes in the most emphatic way the authority of the other apostles, and the fellowship of labor and suffering by which he is united to them. All this and much more of the same import we find in those epistles which Baur admits to be the genuine writings of Paul. In short, it may be said that after the thorough discussion to which his theory has been subjected for the last twenty-five years, it has scarcely a sound leg left to stand on. It may be admitted to be one of the most brilliant works of the historical imagination which the century has produced. It is supported by vast learning, and it has thrown much light on certain movements of the early church; but, taken as a whole it is unscientific and contradictory; it raises two difficulties, where it disposes of one, and it ignores more facts than it includes.

We return from this excursion through the fields of destructive criticism with a strong conviction that this narrative of the Acts of the Apostles was written by Luke the Evangelist, the companion and fellow-worker of Paul,

and that it gives us a veracious history of the earliest
years of the Christian church.

The last of the New Testament books does not belong
chronologically at the end of the collection. There was a
tradition, to which Irenaeus gives currency, that it was
written during the reign of Domitian, about 97 or 98 A.D.
But this tradition is now almost universally discredited.
Critics of all classes date the book as early as 75–79 A.D.,
while the best authorities put it nearly ten years earlier,
in the autumn of 68 or the spring of 69. As Archdeacon
Farrar suggests, it would be vastly better if these books
of the New Testament were arranged in true chronological order; they could be more easily understood. The fact
that this weird production stands at the end of the collection has made upon many minds a wrong impression as
to its meaning, and has given it a kind of significance to
which it is not entitled.

The authorship of the book is quite generally ascribed
to John the son of Zebedee, brother of James, and one
of the apostles of our Lord. Even the destructive critics
agree to this; some among them say that there is less
doubt about the date and the authorship of this book
than about almost any other New Testament writing. In
making this concession they intend, however, to discredit
the Johannine authorship of the Fourth Gospel. The more
certain we are that John wrote the Revelation, they ar-
gue, the more certain are we that he did not write the
Gospel which bears his name; for the style of the two
writings is so glaringly contrasted that it is simply impossible that both could have come from the same writer.
This does not seem nearly so clear to me as it does to
some of these learned and perspicacious critics. A great

contrast there is, indeed, between the style of the Revelation and that of the Gospel; but this contrast may be explained. It is said, in the first place, that the Greek of the Apocalypse is very bad Greek, full of ungrammatical sentences, abounding in Hebraisms, while that of the Gospel is good Greek, accurate and rhetorical in its structure. But this is by no means an unaccountable phenomenon. The first book was written by the apostle very soon, probably, after his removal to Ephesus. He had never, I suppose, been accustomed to use the Greek familiarly in his own country; had never written in it at all, and it is not strange that he should express himself awkwardly when he first began to write Greek; that the Aramaic idioms should constantly reproduce themselves in his Greek sentences. After he had been living for twenty-five years in the cultivated Greek city of Ephesus, using the Greek language continually, it is probable that he would write it more elegantly.

But it is said that the rhetorical style of the one book differs radically from that of the other. Doubtless. The one book is an apocalypse, the other is a biography. John may not have been a practiced *litterateur*, but he certainly had literary sense and feeling enough to know how to put a very different color and atmosphere into an apocalyptical writing from that which he would employ in a report of the life and words of Jesus. Without any reflection, indeed, he would instinctively use the apocalyptic imagery; his pages would flare and resound with the lurid symbolism peculiar to the apocalypses. How definite a type of literature this was we shall presently see; no writer, while using it, would clearly manifest his own personality. And if through all this disguise we do discern symptoms of a temper more fervid and a spirit more Judaic than that which finds expression in the Fourth Gospel, let us remember that the ripened wisdom of the old man speaks in the latter, and the intense enthusiasm of conscious strength in the former. This John, let us not forget, was not in his youth a paragon of mildness; it was he and his brother James who earned the sobriquet of Boanerges, "Sons of thunder;" it was they who wanted to call down fire from heaven to consume an inhospitable Samaritan village. Moreover, we shall see as we go on that the times in which this apocalypse was written were times in which the mildest, mannered men would be apt to forget their decorum, and speak with unwonted intensity. A man with any blood in him, who undertook to write in the year 68 of the themes with which the soul of this apostle was then on fire, would be likely to show, no matter in what vehicle of speech his thought might be conveyed, some sign of the tumult then raging within him.

All these circumstances, taken together, enable me to explain the difference between the literary form of the Revelation and that of the Gospel. But when we come to look a little more deeply into the meaning of the two books, we shall find that beneath all this dissimilarity there are some remarkable points of agreement. Quite a number of the leading ideas and conceptions of the one book reappear in the other; the idea of Christ as the *Word* or *Logos* of God, the representation of Christ as the Lamb, as the Good Shepherd, as the Light, are peculiar to John; we find them emphasized in the Gospel and in the Revelation. The unity of the two books in fundamental conceptions has been admirably brought out by Dr. Sears, in his volume entitled "The Heart of Christ." And after weighing the evidence, I find neither historical nor psychological reasons sufficient to overthrow my belief that the Fourth Gospel, as well as the Revelation, was written by John the Apostle.

The Greek name of the book means an uncovering or unveiling, and is fairly interpreted, therefore, by our word Revelation. It belongs to a class of books which were produced in great numbers during the two centuries preceding the birth of Christ and the two centuries following; and no one can understand it or interpret it who does not know something of this species of literature, of the forms of expression peculiar to it, and of the purposes which it was intended to serve.

We have in the Old Testament one Apocalyptic book, that of Daniel, and there are apocalyptical elements in two or three of the prophecies. The fact that the Book of Daniel bears this character is a strong argument for the lateness of its origin; for it was in the last years of the Jewish nationality that this kind of writing became popular. We have six or seven books of this kind, which are written mainly from the standpoint of the old dispensation, part of which appeared just before and part shortly after the beginning of our era; and there are nearly a dozen volumes of Christian apocalypses, all of which employ similar forms of expression, and are directed towards similar ends. Doubtless these are only a few of the great number of apocalyptical books which those ages produced. Their characteristics are well set forth by Dr. Davidson:—

"This branch of later Jewish literature took its rise after the older prophecy had ceased, when Israel suffered sorely from Syrian and Roman oppression. Its object was to encourage and comfort the people by holding forth the speedy restoration of the Davidic Kingdom of Messiah. Attaching itself to the national hope, it proclaimed the impending of a glorious future, in which Israel freed from her enemies should enjoy a peaceful and prosperous life under her long-wished-for deliverer. The old prophets became the vehicle of these utterances. Revelations, sketching the history of Israel and of heathenism, are put into their mouths. The prophecies take the form of symbolical images and marvelous visions. . . . Working in this fashion upon the basis of well-known writings, imitating their style, and artificially reproducing their substance, the authors naturally adopted the anonymous. The difficulty was increased by their having to paint as future, events actually near, and to fit the manifestation of a personal Messiah into the history of the times. Many apocalyptists employed obscure symbols and mysterious pictures, veiling the meaning that it might not be readily seen.[3]

"Every time," says Dr. Harnack, "the political situation culminated in a crisis for the people of God, the apocalypses appeared stirring up the believers; in spirit, form, plan, and execution they closely resembled each other. . . . They all spoke in riddles; that is, by means of images, symbols, mystic numbers, forms of animals, etc., they half concealed what they meant to reveal. The reasons for this procedure are not far to seek: (1.) Clearness and distinctness would have been too profane; only the mysterious appears divine. (2.) It was often dangerous to be too distinct."[4]

---

3. *Encyc. Brit.*, i. 174.
4. *Encyc. Brit.*, xx. 496.

That these writings appeared in troublous times, and that they dealt with affairs of the present and of the immediate future, must always be borne in mind. Certain symbolical conceptions are common to them; earthquakes denote revolutions; stars falling from heaven typify the downfall of kings and dynasties; a beast is often the emblem of a tyrant; the turning of the sun into darkness and the moon into blood signify carnage and destruction upon the earth. We have these symbolisms in several of the Old Testament writings as well as in many of the apocalyptical books which are not in our canon; and the interpretation of such passages is not at all difficult when we understand the usage of the writers.

Of these apocalyptic books one of the most remarkable is the Book of Enoch, which appears to have been written a century or two before Christ. It purports to be a revelation made to and through the patriarch Enoch; it contains an account of the fall of the angels, and of a progeny of giants that sprung from the union of these exiled celestials with the daughters of men; it takes Enoch on a tour of observation through heaven and earth under the guidance of angels, who explain to him many things supernal and mundane; it deals in astronomical and meteorological mysteries of various sorts, and in a series of symbolical visions seeks to disclose the events of the future. It is a grotesque production; one does not find much spiritual nutriment in it, but Jude makes a quotation from it, in his epistle, as if he considered it Holy Scripture.

"The Fourth Book of Esdras" is another Jewish book of the same kind, which may have been written about the hundredth year of our era. It purports to be the work of Ezra, whom it misplaces, chronologically, putting him in the thirtieth year of the Captivity. The problem of the writer is the restoration of the nation, destroyed and scattered by the Roman power. He makes the ancient scribe and law-giver of Israel his mouthpiece, but he is dealing with the events of his own time. Nevertheless, his allusions are veiled and obscure; he speaks in riddles, yet he speaks to a people who understand his riddles, and know how to take his symbolic visions. This book is in our English Apocrypha, under the title 2 Esdras.

"The Book of Jubilees," which assumes to be a revelation made to Moses on Mount Sinai, "The Ascension of Moses," "The Apocalypse of Moses," and the "Apocalypse of Baruch," are other similar books of the Jewish literature.

Of apocalyptical Christian writings, I may mention "The Sibylline Books," "The Apocalypse of Paul," "The Apocalypse of Peter," "The Revelation of Bartholomew," and "The Ascension of Isaiah," and there is also another "Apocalypse of John," a feeble imitation of the one with which our canon closes. These books appeared in the second, third, and fourth centuries of our era; they generally look forward to the second coming of Christ, and set forth in various figures and symbols the conflicts and persecutions which his saints must encounter, the destruction of his foes, and the establishment of his kingdom.

It will be seen, therefore, that the Revelation of St. John is not unique; and the inference will not be rash that much light may be thrown upon its dark sayings by a careful study of kindred books.

It may be answered that the writer of this book is inspired, and that nothing can be learned of the meaning of an inspired book by studying uninspired books.

I reply that no inspired book can be understood at all without a careful study of uninspired books. The Greek grammar and the Greek lexicon are uninspired books, and no man can understand a single one of the books of the New Testament without carefully studying both of them, or else availing himself of the labor of some one else who has diligently studied them. An inspired writer uses language,—the same language that uninspired writers use; the meaning of language is fixed not by inspiration, but by usage; you must study the grammar and the lexicon to learn about the usage. And the case is precisely similar when an inspired writer uses a peculiar form of literature like the apocalyptical writings. He knows when he uses symbolisms of this class that they will be interpreted according to the common usage; he expects and desires that they shall be so understood; and, therefore, in order to understand them, we must know what the usage is.

When our Lord, speaking of the calamities which were about to fall upon the Jewish people, said, "Immediately after the tribulation of those days, the sun shall be darkened, and the moon shall not give her light, and the stars shall fall from heaven, and the powers of the heavens shall be shaken," he was speaking to people who were perfectly familiar with language of this sort, because the same expressions occur over and over again in their prophets, and are there distinctly declared to mean great political overturnings. He used the apocalyptic phraseology, and he expected them to give it the apocalyptic signification. If we wish to understand the Scripture, we must understand the language of Scripture, and this means not only the grammatical forms, but also the symbolic usages of the language.

We have seen that the apocalypses are apt to appear in times of great calamity, and we have accepted the verdict of later scholarship, that this Apocalypse of St. John appeared about 68 or 69 A.D. Was this a time of trouble in that Eastern world? Verily it was; the most appalling hour perhaps in the world's history. The unspeakable Nero was either still upon the throne of the Roman Empire, or had just reeled from that eminence to the doom of a craven suicide. The last years of his life were gorged with horror. The murder of his brother, the burning of Rome, probably by his connivance, if not by his command, in order that he might sate his appetite for sensations upon this horrid spectacle; following this the fiendish scheme to charge this incendiarism upon the Christians, and slaughter them by tens of thousands in all the cities of the Empire,—these are only instances of a career which words are too feeble to portray. Those who succeeded him in this supreme power were not much less ferocious; the very name of pity seemed to have been blotted from the Roman speech; the whole Empire reeked with cruelty and perfidy. While such men ruled at Rome it could not be supposed that the imperial representatives in the provinces would be temperate and just. Some of them, at any rate, had learned the lesson of the hour, and were as perfidious, as truculent, as base as their master could have wished. Such a one was that Gessius Floras who was the procurator of Judea, and who seemed to have exhausted the ingenuity of a malignant nature in stirring up the Jews to insurrection. By every species of indignity and cruelty he finally stung the long-suffering people into a perfect fury, and the rebellion which broke out in Palestine in the year 66 was one of the most fearful eruptions of human nature that the world has ever seen. Florus had raised the demon; now the legions of Rome must be called in to exorcise it. It was a terrible struggle. All the energies of Jewish fanaticisms were enlisted; the Zealots, the fiercest party among them, not content with slaughtering their Roman enemies, turned their hands against every man of their own nation who ventured to question the wisdom of their desperate resistance. In Jerusalem itself a reign of terror raged which makes the French Revolution seem in comparison a calm and orderly procedure.

At the beginning of the outbreak Nero had sent one of his trusted generals, Vespasian, and Vespasian's son Titus, to put down the insurrection. Neither of these soldiers was a sentimentalist; both believed as heartily as did Wentworth in later years that the word of the hour was Thorough. They started with their armies from Antioch in March, 67, resolved on sweeping Palestine with the besom of destruction. Cities and villages, one by one, were besieged, captured, destroyed; men, women, and children were indiscriminately massacred. The Jewish army fought every inch of the ground like tigers; but they were overpowered and beaten in detail, and steadily forced southward. Blackened walls, pools of blood, and putrefying corpses were all that the Romans left in their rear; ruthlessly they drove the doomed people before them toward their stronghold of Jerusalem. In the autumn of that year Vespasian withdrew his army into winter-quarters, and left the Zealots in Jerusalem to their orgy of brigandage and butchery. He could well afford to rest and let them do his deadly work.

In the spring of the following year, the siege of Jerusalem began. The Christians of the city had fled to Pella, east of the Jordan; the remnant of the Jews held their sacred heights with the courage of despair.

It is at this very juncture that this book of the Revelation was written. John testifies that it was written on Patmos, a desolate islet of the Aegean Sea, west of Asia Minor, to which he had either been banished by some tool of Nero, or else had betaken himself for solitude and reflection. To him, in this retreat, the awful tidings had come of the scourge that had fallen on the land of his fathers; added to this, the conflagration at Rome, the Neronian persecution, all the horrors of the past decade were fresh in his memory. May we not say that the time was ripe for an apocalyptic message?

It is in these events, then, that we must find the explanation of much of this symbolical language. Such is the law of the apocalypse, and this apocalypse may be expected to conform to the law. St. John is instructed by the angel to write "the things which thou sawest, and the things which are, and the things which shall come to pass hereafter,"—"the things which must *shortly* come to pass," the first verse more explicitly states. It is the past which he has seen, the present, and the immediate future with which his visions are concerned. It is not any attempt to outline the whole course of human history; it is the picture, in mystic symbols, of the present crisis and of the deliverance which is to follow it. There is no room here for a commentary on the Apocalypse; I will only indicate, in a rapid glance, the outline of the book.

The first three chapters are occupied with the epistles to the seven churches which are in Asia, administering reproof, exhortation, comfort, and counsel to the Christians in these churches,—faithful, stirring, persuasive appeals, whose meaning can be easily understood, and whose truth is often sorely needed by the churches of our own time.

Then begins the proper Apocalypse, with the first vision of the throne in heaven, and sitting thereon the Lamb that was slain, who is also the Lion of the tribe of Judah. The book sealed with seven seals is given to him to open, and the opening of each seal discloses a new vision. The first seal opened shows a white horse bearing a rider who carries a bow and wears a crown, and who goes forth conquering and to conquer. This is the emblem of the Messiah whose conquest of the world is represented as beginning. But the Messiah once said, "I came not to bring peace, but a sword," and the consequences of his coming must often be strife and sorrow because of the malignity of men. And therefore the three seals which are opened next disclose a fiery horse, the symbol of War, a black horse, whose rider is Famine, a pale horse in whose saddle is Death. The opening of the fifth seal shows the martyred multitude before the throne of God. The sixth discloses the desolation and the ruin taking place upon the earth. Thus the mighty panorama passes constantly before our eyes; the confusion, the devastation, the woes, the scourges of mankind through which Messiah's Kingdom is advancing to its triumph. The seals, the trumpets, the vials bring before us representations of the retributions and calamities which are falling upon mankind. Sometimes we seem to be able to fix upon a historical event which the vision clearly symbolizes; sometimes the meaning to us is vague; perhaps if we had lived in that day the allusion would have been more intelligible.

There is, however, one great central group of these visions round about which the others seem to be arrayed as scenic accessories, whose interpretation the writer has taken great pains to indicate. These are the visions found in chapters xii., xiii., xvi., and xvii. The woman, sun-clad, with the moon under her feet and a crown of twelve stars upon her head (chap, xii.), is beyond all question the ancient Jewish church; the child which is born to the woman is the Christian church; the great red dragon that seeks to devour the child is the Satanic power, the Prince of this world. The Dragon is here on the earth because he has been expelled from heaven. The war of the Dragon against the woman indicates the persecutions of the church; the flight of the woman to the wilderness may symbolize the recent escape of the mother church from Jerusalem to Pella.

The next vision shows a Beast, coming up out of the sea, with seven heads and ten horns, and on his horns ten diadems, and on his heads names of blasphemy. Here we have an instance of that confounding of symbols, the merging of one in another, which is very common in the apocalyptic writings. The beast is, primarily, Nero, or the Roman Empire, as represented by—Nero. The ten horns are the ten chief provinces; the seven heads are seven emperors. "It is a symbol," says Dr. Farrar, "interchangeably of the Roman Empire and of the Emperor. In fact, to a greater degree than at any period of history, the two were one. Roman history had dwindled down into a personal drama. The Roman Emperor could say with literal truth,

'L'Etat c'est moi.' And a wild beast was a Jew's natural symbol either for a Pagan Kingdom or for its autocrat."[5] I can do no better than to repeat to you a small part of Dr. Farrar's further comment upon this vision.

"This wild beast of Heathen Rome has ten horns, which represent the ten main provinces of Imperial Rome. It has the power of the Dragon, that is, it possesses the Satanic dominion of the 'Prince of the power of the air.'

"On each of its heads is the name of blasphemy. Every one of the seven Kings, however counted, had borne the (to Jewish ears) blasphemous surname of Augustus (Sebastos, one to be adored); had received apotheosis, and been spoken of as *Divine* after his death; had been crowned with statues, adorned with divine attributes, had been saluted with divine titles, and, in some instances, had been absolutely worshiped, and that in his lifetime. . . .

"The diadems are on the horns, because the Roman *Proconsuls*, as delegates of the Emperor, enjoy no little share of the Caesarean autocracy and splendor, but the name of blasphemy is only on the heads, because the Emperor alone receives divine honors and alone bears the daring title of Augustus."[6]

One of the heads of this Beast was wounded to death, but the deadly wound was healed. It was the universal belief among Pagans and Christians that the world had not yet seen the last of Nero. Either his suicide was feigned and ineffectual, and he was in hiding, or else he would come to life and resume his savage splendors and

5. *The Early Days of Christianity*, p. 463.
6. *Ibid.*, p. 464.

his gilded villainies. To make it certain that the writer here refers to this expectation, we find, in chapter xvii., another reference to the Beast, which seems at first a riddle, but which is easily interpreted. "The five are fallen, the one is, the other is not yet come"; "The Beast that thou sawest was and is not, and is about to come out of the abyss." "The Beast that was and is not, even he is an eighth, and is of the seven." The head and the Beast are here identified. The meaning is that five Roman Emperors are dead, Augustus, Tiberius, Caligula, Claudius, Nero; "one is,"—Galba is now reigning; "the other" (Otho) "is not yet come;" but he must come soon for Galba is an old man and cannot long survive, and "the Beast that was and is not,"—Nero,—who is "about to come out of the abyss,"—to return to life,—"even he is an eighth, and is of the seven." He is one of the seven, for he was the fifth, and he will be the eighth. It was the universal Christian belief that Nero, raised from the dead, would be the future Antichrist, and it is this belief which the vision reflects. To make the case still clearer the writer gives us, by the current Hebrew Kabbalistic method, the number of the Beast, that is to say, the numerical value of his name. Each letter of the old alphabets has a numerical value. Thus the writer of the Sibyllines points out the Greek name of Jesus—[Greek: Iota-eta-sigma-omicron-upsilon-sigma],—by saying that its whole number is equivalent to eight units, eight tens, and eight hundreds. This is the exact numerical value of the six Greek letters composing the Saviour's name, $10+8+200+70+400+200=888$. Precisely so John here tells us what is the numerical value of the letters in the name of the Beast. If we tried the Latin or the Greek names of

Nero the clue would not be found; but John was writing mainly for Hebrews, and the Hebrew letters of *Kesar Neron*, the name by which every Jew knew this Emperor, amount to exactly 666.

Many other of the features of this veiled description tally perfectly with the character of this infamous ruler; and when the evidence is all brought together it seems as though the apostle could scarcely have made his meaning more obvious if he had written Nero's name in capital letters.

This is the central vision of the Apocalypse, as I have said; round about this the whole cyclorama revolves; and it has been the standing enigma of the interpreters in all the ages. The early church generally divined its meaning; but in later years the high-soaring exegesis which has spread this Apocalypse all over the centuries and found in it prophetic symbols of almost all the events that have happened in mediaeval and modern history, has identified the Beast with countless characters, among them Genseric, King of the Vandals, Benedict, Trajan, Paul V., Calvin, Luther, Mohammed, Napoleon. All this wild guessing arises from ignorance of the essential character and purpose of the apocalyptical writings.

I can follow this enticing theme no further. Let it suffice to call the attention of all who desire to reach some sober conclusions upon the meaning of the book to Archdeacon Farrar's "Early Days of Christianity," in which the whole subject is treated with the amplest learning and the soundest literary judgment.

The Book of Revelation has been, as I have intimated, the favorite tramping ground of all the hosts of theological visionaries; men who possessed not the slightest knowledge of the history or the nature of apocalyptic literature, and whose appetite for the mysterious and the monstrous was insatiable, have expatiated here with boundless license. To find in these visions descriptions of events now passing and characters now upon the stage is a sore temptation. To use these hard words, the Beast, the Dragon, the False Prophet, as missiles wherewith to assail those who belong to a school or a party with which you are at variance, is a chance that no properly constituted partisan could willingly fore-go. Thus we have seen this book dragged into the controversies and applied to the events of all the centuries, and the history of its interpretation is, as one of its interpreters confesses, the opprobrium of exegesis. But if one ceases to look among these symbols for a predictive outline of modern history, "a sort of anticipated Gibbon," and begins to read it in the light of the apocalyptic method, it may have rich and large meanings for him. He will not be able, indeed, to explain it all; to some of these riddles the clue has been lost; but, in the words of Dr. Farrar, "he will find that the Apocalypse is what it professes to be,—an inspired outline of contemporary history, and of the events to which the sixth decade of the first century gave immediate rise. He will read in it the tremendous manifesto of a Christian seer against the blood-stained triumph of imperial heathenism; a paean and a prophecy over the ashes of the martyrs; the thundering reverberations of a mighty spirit struck by the fierce plectrum of the Neronian persecution, and answering in impassioned music which, like many of David's Psalms, dies away into the language of rapturous hope."[7]

---

7. *Early Days of Christianity*, p. 429.

For we must not forget that this is a song of triumph. This seer is no pessimist. The strife is hot, the carnage is fearful, they that rise up against our Lord and his Messiah are many and mighty, but there is no misgiving as to the event. For all these woes there is solace, after all these conflicts peace. Even in the midst of the raging wars and persecutions, the door is opened now and again into the upper realm of endless joy and unfading light. And he "whose name is called The Word of God," upon whose garment and whose thigh the name is written, "King of Kings and Lord of Lords," will prevail at last over all his foes. The Beast and the Dragon, and the False Prophet and the Scarlet Woman (the harlot city upon her seven hills whose mystic name is Babylon) will all be cast into the lake of fire; then to the purified earth the New Jerusalem shall come down out of heaven from God. This is the emblem and the prophecy, not of the city beyond the stars, but of the purified society which shall yet exist upon the earth,—the fruition of his work who came, not to judge the world, but to save the world. It is on these plains, along these rivers, by these fair shores that the New Jerusalem is to stand; it is not heaven; it is a city that comes down out of heaven from God. No statement could be more explicit. The glorious visions which fill the last chapters of this wonderful book are the promise of that "All hail Hereafter," for which every Christian patriot, every lover of mankind, is always looking and longing and fighting and waiting. And he who, by the mouth of this seer, testifieth the words of the prophecy of this book saith, "Yea, I come quickly. Even so, come, Lord Jesus."

Chapter 11

The Canon

We have studied with what care we were able tee historical problem of the origin and authorship of the several
books of the Old and New Testament; we now come to a
deeply interesting question,—the question of the canon.

This word, as used in this connection, means simply
an authoritative list or catalogue. The canon of the Bible
is the determined and official table of contents. The settlement of the canon is the process of determining what
and how many books the Bible shall contain. In the Old
Testament are thirty-nine books, in the New Testament
twenty-seven; and it is a fixed principle with Protestants
that these books and no others constitute the Sacred
Scriptures,—that no more can be added and none taken
away.

The popular belief respecting this matter has been
largely founded upon the words with which the Book of
Revelation concludes:—

"For I testify unto every man that heareth the words
of the prophecy of this book, If any man shall add unto
them, God shall add unto him the plagues which are written in this book: and if any man shall take away from

257

the words of the book of this prophecy, God shall take away his part from the tree of life, and out of the holy city, which are written in this book."

The common notion is that the "book" here referred to is the Bible; and that these sentences, therefore, are the divine authorization of the present contents of the Bible, a solemn testimony from the Lord himself to the integrity of the canon. But this is a misapprehension. The book referred to is the Revelation of St. John,—not the Bible, not even the New Testament. When these words were written, says Dr. Barnes in his "Commentary," "the books that now constitute what we call the Bible were not collected into a single volume. That passage, therefore, should not be adduced as referring to the whole of the Sacred Scriptures." In fact, when these words of the Revelation were written, several of the books of the New Testament were not yet in existence; for this is by no means the last of the New Testament writings, though it stands at the end of the collection. The Gospel and the Epistles of John were added after this; and we may trust that no plagues were "added" to the beloved disciple for writing them.

Nevertheless, as I said, it is assumed that the contents of the Bible are fixed; that the collection is and for a long time has been complete and perfect; that it admits neither of subtractions nor of additions; that nothing is in the book which ought not to be there, and that there is nothing outside of its covers which ought to be within them; that the canon is settled, inflexibly and infallibly and finally.

The questions now to be considered are these: Who settled it? When was it settled? On what grounds was it determined? Was any question ever raised concerning

the sacredness or authority of any of the books now included in the canon? Did any other books, not now included in the canon, ever claim a place in it? If so, why
were these rejected and those retained?

This is, as will be seen, a simple question of history.
We can trace with tolerable certainty the steps by which
this collection of sacred writings was made; we know
pretty well who did it, and when and how it was done.
And there is nothing profane or irreverent in this inquiry, for the work of collecting these writings and fixing
this canon has been done mainly, if not wholly, by men
who were not inspired and did not claim to be. There
is nothing mysterious or miraculous about their doings
any more than there is about the acts of the framers of
the Westminster Confession, or the American Constitu-
tion. They were dealing with sacred matters, no doubt,
when they were trying to determine what books should
be received and used as Scriptures, but they were dealing
with them in exactly the same way that we do, by using
the best lights they had.

As we have learned in previous chapters, the beginning of our canon was made by Ezra the scribe, who, in
the fifth century before Christ, newly published and con-
secrated the Pentateuch, or Five Books of Moses, as the
Holy Book of the Jewish people.

After Ezra came Nehemiah, to whom the beginning
of the second collection of Jewish Scriptures, called the
Prophets, is ascribed in one of the apocryphal books. But
this collection was not apparently finished and closed by
Nehemiah. The histories of Joshua and Judges, of Samuel
and Kings, and the principal books of the Prophets were

undoubtedly gathered by him; but it would seem that the collection was left open for future prophecies.

About the same time the third group of the Old Testament Scriptures, "The Hagiographa," or "Writings," began to be collected. No book of the Bible contains any information concerning the making of these two later collections, the Prophets and the Hagiographa; and we are obliged to rely wholly upon Jewish tradition, and upon references which we find in Jewish writers. Professor Westcott, who is one of the most conservative of Biblical scholars, says that "the combined evidence of tradition and of the general course of Jewish history leads to the conclusion that the canon in its present shape was formed gradually during a lengthened interval, beginning with Ezra and extending through a part, or even the whole of the Persian period," or from B.C. 458 to 332. Without adopting this conclusion, we may remark that this last date, 332, was nearly a century after Nehemiah and Malachi, the last of the prophets; so that if the canon was closed at a date so late as this, it must have been closed by men who were certainly not known to have been inspired. If it was forming, through all this period, then it must have been formed in part by men in behalf of whom no claim of inspiration has ever been set up.

According to Jewish tradition the work of collecting, editing, and authorizing the sacred writings was done by a certain "Great Synagogue," founded by Ezra, presided over by Nehemiah, after him, and continuing in existence down to about the year 200 B.C. This is wholly a tradition, and has been proved to be baseless. There never was such a synagogue; the Scriptures know nothing about it; the apocryphal writers, so numerous and widely dispersed, have never heard of it; Philo and Josephus are ignorant concerning it. None of the Jewish authors of the period who freely discuss the Scriptures and their authority makes mention of this Great Synagogue. The story of its existence is first heard from some Jewish rabbin hundreds of years after Christ.

We have proof enough in the New Testament that the Jews had certain Sacred Scriptures; the New Testament writers often quote them and refer to them; but there is no conclusive proof that they had been gathered at this time into a complete collection. Jesus tells the Jews that they search the Scriptures, but he does not say how many of these Scriptures there were in his day; Paul reminds Timothy that from a child he had known the Holy Scriptures, but he gives no list of their titles. If we found all the books of the Old Testament quoted or referred to by the New Testament writers, then we should know that they possessed the same books that we have. Most of these books are thus referred to; but there are seven Old Testament books whose names the New Testament never quotes, and at least five to which it makes no reference whatever: Ecclesiastes, Song of Solomon, Esther, Ezra, and Nehemiah. To Judges, Chronicles, and Ezekiel it refers only in the same way that it refers to a number of the apocryphal books. Some of these omissions appear to be significant. The New Testament gives us therefore no definite information by which we can determine whether the Old Testament canon was closed at the time of Christ, nor does it tell us of what books it was composed.

We have seen already that two different collections of Old Testament writings were in existence, one in Hebrew, and the other a translation into the Greek, made by Jews in Alexandria, and called the Septuagint. The latter collection was the one most used by our Lord and the apostles; much the greater number of quotations from the Old Testament found in the Gospels and the Epistles are taken from the Septuagint. This Greek Bible contained quite a number of books which are not in the Hebrew Bible: they were later in their origin than any of the Old Testament books; most of them were originally written in Greek; and while they were regarded by some of the more conservative of the Jews in Egypt as inferior to the Law and the Prophets, they were generally ranked with the books of the Hagiographa as sacred writings. This is evident from the fact that they were mingled indiscriminately with these books of the older Scriptures. You know that I am speaking now of the apocryphal books which you find in some of your old Bibles, between the Old and New Testaments. These were the later books contained in the Septuagint, and not in the Hebrew Bible. But they were not sorted out by themselves in the Septuagint; they were interspersed through the other books, as of equal value. Thus in the Vatican Bible, of which we shall learn more by and by, Esdras First and Second succeed the Chronicles; Tobit and Judith are between Nehemiah and Esther; the Wisdom of Solomon and Sirach follow Solomon's Song; Baruch is next to Jeremiah; Daniel is followed by Susanna and Bel and the Dragon, and the collection closes with the three books of Maccabees.

All the old manuscripts of the Bible which we possess—those which are regarded as above all others sacred and authoritative—contain these apocryphal writings thus intermingled with the books of our own canon. It is clear, therefore, that to the Alexandrian Jews these later books were Sacred Scriptures; and it is certain also that our Lord and his apostles used the collection which contained these books. It is said that they do not refer to them, and it is true that they do not mention them by name; but they do use them occasionally. Let me read you a few passages which will illustrate their familiarity with the apocryphal books.

James i.19: "Let every man be swift to hear, slow to speak." Sirach v. 11; iv. 29: "Be swift to hear." "Be not hasty in thy tongue."

Hebrews i. 3: "Who being the effulgence of his glory, and the very image of his substance, and upholding all things by the word of his power." Wisdom vii. 26: "For she (Wisdom) is the brightness of the everlasting light, the unspotted mirror of the power of God, and the image of his goodness."

Rom. ix. 21: "Hath not the potter a right over the clay, from the same lump to make one part a vessel unto honor, and another unto dishonor?" Wisdom xv. 7: "For the potter, tempering soft earth, fashioneth every vessel with much labor for our service; yea, of the same clay he maketh both the vessels that serve for clean uses, and likewise also such as serve to the contrary: but what is the use of either sort, the potter himself is the judge."

I Cor. ii. 10, 11: "The Spirit searcheth all things, yea, the deep things of God. For who among men knoweth the things of a man, save the spirit of the man, which is in him? even so the things of God none knoweth save the Spirit of God." Judith viii. 14: "For ye cannot find the depth of the heart of man, neither can ye perceive the things that he thinketh: then how can ye search out God, that hath made all these things, and know his mind, or comprehend his purpose?"

Several similar indications of the familiarity of the New Testament writers with these apocryphal books might be pointed out. These are not express citations, but they are clear appropriations of the thought and the language of the apocryphal writers. We have, then, the most indubitable proof that the apocryphal books were in the hands of the New Testament writers; and so far as New Testament use authenticates an Old Testament writing, several of the apocryphal books stand on much better footing than do five of our Old Testament books.

It is true that the Hebrew or Palestinian canon differed from the Greek or Alexandrian canon; the books which were written in Greek had never been translated into the Hebrew, and could not, of course, be incorporated into the Hebrew canon; and there was undoubtedly a strong feeling among the stricter Jews against recognizing any of these later books as Sacred Scriptures; nevertheless, the Greek Bible, with all its additions, had large currency among the Jews even in Palestine, and the assertion that our Lord and his apostles measured the Alexandrian Bible by the Palestinian canon, and accepted all the books of the latter while declining to recognize any of the additions of the former, is sheer assumption, for which there is not a particle of evidence, and against which the facts already adduced bear convincingly. Paul, in his letter to Timothy, refers to the "Scriptures" as having been in the hands of Timothy from his childhood; and we have every reason to believe that the Scriptures to which he refers was this Greek collection containing the Apocrypha. Whatever Paul says about the inspiration of the

Scriptures must be interpreted with this fact in mind. To find in these words of Paul the guarantee of the inspiration and infallibility of the books of the collection which are translated from the Hebrew, and not those which are written in Greek, is a freak of exegesis not more violent than fantastic. We know that Paul read and used some of these apocryphal books, and there are several of the books in our Hebrew Bible that he never quotes or refers to in the remotest way. The attempt which is often made to show that the New Testament writers have established, by their testimony, the Old Testament canon, as containing just those books which are in our Old Testament, and no more, is a most unwarrantable distortion of the facts.

It is true that at the time of Christ the Palestinian Jews had not, for a century or so, added any new books to their collection, and were not inclined to add any more. Their canon was practically closed to this extent, that no new books were likely to get in. But it was not yet settled that some later books, which had been trying to maintain a footing in the canon, should not be put out. Esther, Ecclesiastes, and Solomon's Song were regarded by some of the Palestinian Jews as sacred books, but their right to this distinction was hotly disputed by others. This question was not settled at the time of our Lord.

"The canon," says Davidson, "was not considered to be closed in the first century before and the first after Christ. There were doubts about some portions. The Book of Ezekiel gave offense, because some of its statements seemed to contradict the Law. Doubts about some of the others were of a more serious nature—about Ecclesiastes, the Canticles, Esther, and the Proverbs. The first was impugned because it had contradictory passages and a heretical tendency; the second because of its worldly and sensual tone; Esther for its want of religiousness; and Proverbs on account of inconsistencies. This skepticism went far to procure the exclusion of the suspected works from the canon and their relegation to the class of the *genuzim*. But it did not prevail. Hananiah, son of Hezekiah, son of Garon, about 32 B.C., is said to have reconciled the contradictions and allayed the doubts. But these traces of resistance to the fixity of the canon were not the last. They reappeared about 65 A.D., as we learn from the Talmud, when the controversy turned mainly upon the canonicity of Ecclesiastes, which the school of Schammai, which had the majority, opposed; so that that book was probably excluded. The question emerged again at a later synod in Jabneh or Jamnia, when R. Eleaser ben Asaria was chosen patriarch, and Gamaliel the Second, deposed. Here it was decided, not unanimously, however, but by a majority of Hillelites, that Ecclesiastes and the Song of Songs 'pollute the hands,' *i. e.*, belong properly to the Hagiographa. This was about 90 A.D. Thus the question of the canonicity of certain books was discussed by two synods."[1]

By such a plain tale do we put down the fiction, so widely disseminated, that the canon of the Old Testament was "fixed" long before the time of Christ, and, presumably, by inspired men. It was not "fixed," even in Palestine, until sixty years after our Lord's death; several of the books were in dispute during the whole apostolic period, and these are the very books which are not referred to in the New Testament. Whether the men who

---

1. *Encyc. Brit., v. 3.*

finally "fixed" it were exceptionally qualified to judge of the ethical and spiritual values of the writings in question may be doubted. They were the kind of men who slew our Lord and persecuted his followers. When we are asked what are our historical reasons for believing that Esther and Ecclesiastes and Solomon's Song are sacred books and ought to be in the Old Testament canon, let us answer: It is not because any prophet or inspired person adjudged them to be sacred, for no such person had anything to say about them; it is not because our Lord and his apostles indorsed them, for they do not even mention them; it is not because they held a place in a collection of Sacred Scriptures used by our Lord and his apostles, for their position in that collection was in dispute at that time; it is because the chief priests and scribes who rejected Christ pronounced them sacred. The external authority for these books reduces to exactly this. Those who insist that all parts of the Old Testament are of equal value and authority, and that a questioning of the sacredness of one book casts doubts upon the whole collection, ought to look these facts in the face and see on what a slender thread they suspend the Bible which they so highly value. These later books, says one, "have been delivered to us; they have their use and value, which is to be ascertained by a frank and reverent study of the texts themselves; but those who insist on placing them on the same footing of undisputed authority with the Law, the Prophets, and the Psalms, to which our Lord bears direct testimony, and so make the whole doctrine of the canon depend on its weakest part, sacrifice the true strength of the evidence on which the Old Testament is received by Christians."[2]

Such, then, is the statement with respect to the Old Testament canon in the apostolic age. The Palestinian canon, which was identical with our Old Testament, was practically settled at the synod of Jamnia about 90 A.D., though doubts were still entertained by devout Jews concerning Esther. The Alexandrian collection, containing our apocryphal books, was, however, widely circulated; and as it was the Greek version which had been most used by the apostles, so it was the Greek version which the early Christian fathers universally studied and quoted. Very few if any of these Christian fathers of the first two centuries understood the Hebrew; they could not, therefore, use the Palestinian manuscripts; the Greek Bible was their only treasury of inspired truth, and the Greek Bible contained the Apocrypha. Accordingly we find them quoting freely as Sacred Scripture all the apocryphal books. Westcott gives us a table, in Smith's "Bible Dictionary," of citations made from these apocryphal books by fifteen of the Greek fathers, beginning with Clement of Rome and ending with Chrysostom, and by eight Latin writers, beginning with Tertullian and ending with Augustine. Every one of these apocryphal books is thus quoted with some such formula as "The Scripture saith," or "It is written," by one or more of these writers; the Book of Wisdom is quoted by all of them except Polycarp and Cyril; Baruch and the Additions to Daniel are quoted by the great majority of them; Origen quotes them all, Clement of Alexandria all but one, Cyprian all but

---

2. *The Old Testament in the Jewish Church*, p. 175.

two. It will therefore be seen that these books must have had wide acceptance as Sacred Scriptures during the first centuries of the Christian church. In the face of these facts, which may be found in sources as unassailable as Smith's "Bible Dictionary," we have such statements as the following, put forth by teachers of the people, and indorsed by eminent theological professors:—

"We may say of the apocryphal books of the Old Testament that, while some who were not Jews and who were unacquainted with Hebrew used them to some extent, yet they never gained wide acceptance, and soon dropped out altogether."

"Certain apocryphal writings have since been bound up with the Septuagint, but *there is no reason to think that they made any part of it in the days of our Saviour*"!

"These books were not received as canonical by the Christian fathers, but were expressly declared to be apocryphal"!

The last statements are copied from a volume on the Bible, prepared for popular circulation by the president of a theological seminary!

It is true that some of the most inquisitive and critical of the Christian fathers entertained doubts about these apocryphal books; Melito of Sardis traveled to Palestine on purpose to inquire into the matter, and came back, of course, with the Palestinian canon to which, however, he did not adhere. Origen made a similar investigation, and seems to have been convinced that the later books ought to be regarded as uncanonical; nevertheless, he keeps on quoting them; Jerome was the first strenuously to challenge the canonicity of these later Greek books and to maintain a tolerably consistent opposition to them.

While, therefore, several of these early fathers were led by their investigations in Palestine to believe that the narrower canon was the more correct one, their opinions had but little weight with the people at large; and even these fathers themselves freely and constantly quoted as Sacred Scripture the questionable writings.

In 393 the African bishops held a council at Hippo, in which the canon was discussed. The list agreed upon includes all the Old Testament Scriptures of our canon, and, in addition to them, Wisdom, Ecclesiasticus, Tobit, Judith, and the two books of Maccabees. In 397 another council at Carthage reaffirmed the list of its predecessor. Augustine was the leader of both councils.

In spite of the protests of Jerome and of other scholars in all the centuries, this list, for substance, was regarded as authoritative, until the Council of Trent, in 1546, when the long debate was finally settled, so far as the Roman Catholic Church is concerned, by the adoption of the Augustinian canon, embracing the apocryphal books, the list concluding with the following anathema. "If any one will not receive as sacred and authoritative the whole books with all their parts, let him be accursed." This determines the matter for all good Catholics. Since 1546, they have known exactly how many books their Bible contains. And if usage and tradition are and ought to be authoritative, they have the strongest reasons for receiving as sacred the books of their Bible; for it is beyond question that the books which they accept and which we reject have been received and used as Sacred Scriptures in all the ages of the church. Most of us who do not accept usage and tradition as authoritative will continue, no doubt, to think our own thoughts about the matter.

The Council of Trent marks the definite separation of the Roman Catholic Church from the Protestant reformers. Up to this time there had been among the reformers some differences of opinion respecting the Old Testament books; when they were excluded from the Holy Church and were compelled to fall back upon the authority of the Bible, the present limits of the canon at once became an important question. They did not settle it all at once. Luther, in making his German version of the Bible, translated Judith, Wisdom, Tobit, Sirach, Baruch, 1 and 2 Maccabees, the Greek additions to Esther and Daniel, with the Prayer of Manasseh. Each of these books he prefaces with comments of his own. First Maccabees he regards as almost equal to the other books of Holy Scripture, and not unworthy to be reckoned among them. He had doubted long whether Wisdom should not be admitted to the canon, and he truly says of Sirach that it is a right good book, the work of a wise man. Baruch and 2 Maccabees he finds fault with; but of none of these apocryphal books does he speak so severely as of Esther, which he is more than willing to cast out of the canon. The fact that Luther translated these apocryphal books is good evidence that he thought them of value to the church; nevertheless, he considered the books of the Hebrew canon, with the exception of Esther, as occupying a higher plane than those of the Apocrypha. Gradually this opinion gained acceptance among the Protestants; the apocryphal books were separated from the rest, and although by some of the Reformed churches, as by the Anglican church, they were commended to be read "for example of life and instruction of manners," they ceased to be regarded as authoritative sources of Christian doctrine. Since the sixteenth century, there has been little question among Protestants as to the extent of the canon. The books which now compose our Old Testament, and no others, have been found in the Bible of the Protestants for the past three hundred years. The apocryphal books have sometimes been printed between the Old and the New Testaments, but they have not been used in the churches,[3] nor have they been regarded as part of the Sacred Scripture.

The history of the New Testament canon is much less obscure, and may be more briefly treated. The Bible of the early Christians was the Old Testament. They relied wholly upon this for religious instruction; they had no thought of any other Sacred Scripture.

I have explained in a former chapter how the Epistles and the Gospels originated; but when these writings first came into the hands of the disciples there was not, it is probable, any conception in their minds that these were sacred writings, to be ranked along with the books of the Old Testament. They read them for instruction and suggestion; they did not at first think of them as holy. But their conviction of the value and sacredness of these writings soon began to strengthen; we find them quoting Gospels and Epistles with the same formula that they apply to the Old Testament books; and thus they began to feel the need of making a collection of this apostolic literature for use in the churches. It is not until the second half of the second century that any such collection comes into view. It consisted at first of two parts, The Gospel and The Apostle; the first part contained the four Gospels, and the second the Acts, thirteen Epistles of Paul, one of

---

3. The English Church uses some portions of them.

Peter, one of John, and the Revelation. It will be seen that this twofold Testament omitted several of our books,—the Epistle to the Hebrews, two of John's Epistles, one of Peter's, and the Epistles of James and Jude.

About this time there was also in circulation certain writings which are not now in our canon, but which were sometimes included by the authorities of that time among the apostolic writings, and were quoted as Scripture by the early fathers. There was a book called "The Gospel according to the Egyptians," and another entitled "The Preaching of Peter," and another called "The Acts of Paul," and another called "The Shepherd of Hermas," and an epistle attributed to Barnabas, and several others, all claiming to be sacred and apostolic writings. It became, therefore, a delicate and important question for these early Christians to decide which of these writings were sacred, and which were not; and they began to make lists of those which they regarded as canonical. The earliest of these lists is a fragmentary anonymous canon, which was made about 170. It mentions all the books in our New Testament but four,—Hebrews, First and Second Peter, and James.

Irenaeus, who died about 200, had a canon which included all the books of our New Testament except Hebrews, Jude, James, Second Peter, and Third John. First Peter, Second John, and "The Shepherd of Hermas" he put by themselves in a second class of writings, which he thought excellent but not inspired.

Clement of Alexandria (180) puts into his list most of our canonical books, but regards several of them as of inferior value, among them Hebrews, Second John, and Jude. In the same list of inferior writings he includes "The

Shepherd of Hermas," the "Epistle of Barnabas," and the "Apocalypse of Peter."

Tertullian (200) omits entirely James, Second Peter, and Third John, but includes among useful though not inspired books, Hebrews, Jude, "The Shepherd of Hermas," Second John, and Second Peter.

These are the greatest authorities of the first two centuries. No Christian teachers of that day were better informed or more trustworthy than these, and it will be seen that they were far from agreeing with one another or with our canon; that each one of them received as sacred some books which we do not possess, and rejected some which we receive.

Coming down into the third century, we find Origen (250), one of the great scholars, wrestling with the problem. He seems to have made three classes of the New Testament writings, the authentic, the non-authentic, and the doubtful. The authentic books are the Gospels, the Acts, the thirteen Epistles of Paul, and the Apocalypse; the non-authentic ones are "The Shepherd of Hermas," "The Epistle of Barnabas," and several other books not in our canon; and the doubtful ones are James, Jude, Second and Third John, and Second Peter. It will be seen that Origen admits none that are not in our collection, but that he is in doubt respecting some that are in it.

Facts like these are writ large over every page of the history of the early church. And yet we have eminent theological professors asserting that the canon of the New Testament was finally settled "during the first half of the second century, within fifty years after the death of the Apostle John." A more baseless statement could not be fabricated. It is from teachers of this class that we hear the most vehement outcries against the "Higher Criticism."

Eusebius, who died in 340, has a list agreeing substantially with that of Origen.

Cyril of Jerusalem (386) includes all of our books except the Apocalypse, and no others.

Athanasius (365) and Augustine (430) have lists identical with ours. This indicates a steady progress toward unanimity, and when the two great councils of Hippo and Carthage confirmed this judgment of the two great fathers last named, the question of the New Testament canon was practically settled.[4] Nevertheless, considerable independent judgment on the subject still seems to have been tolerated, and writings which we do not now receive were long included in the New Testament collection. The three oldest manuscripts of the Bible now in existence are the Sinaitic, the Vatican, and the Alexandrian Bibles, dating from the fourth and the fifth centuries. Of these the Sinaitic and the Alexandrian Bibles both include some of these doubtful books in the New Testament collection; the Sinai Bible has "The Epistle of Barnabas" and "The Shepherd of Hermas;" the Alexandrian Bible the Epistle of Clement and one of Athanasius. These old Bibles are clear witnesses to the fact that the contents of the New Testament were not clearly defined even so late as the fifth century. Indeed, there was always some freedom of opinion concerning this matter until the

---

4. It is noted, however, that the reception of the doubtful books into the canon does not imply a recognition of their equality with the other books. The distinct admission of their inferiority was made by all the ecclesiastical authorities of that period. None of the early fathers believed that all these writings were equally inspired and equally authoritative.

Reformation era. Then, of course, the Council of Trent fixed the canon of the New Testament as well as of the Old for all good Catholics; and the New Testament of the Catholics, unlike their Old Testament, is identical with our own.

The Protestants of that time were still in doubt about certain of the New Testament books. Luther, as every one knows, was inclined to reject the Epistle of James; he called it "a right strawy epistle." The letter to the Hebrews was a good book, but not apostolic; he put it in a subordinate class. Jude was a poor transcript of Second Peter, and he assigned that also to a lower place. "The Apocalypse," says Davidson, "he considered neither apostolic nor prophetic, but put it almost on a level with the Fourth Book of Esdras, which he spoke elsewhere of tossing into the Elbe." Luther's principle of judgment in many of these cases was quite too subjective; he carried the Protestant principle of private judgment to an extreme; I only quote his opinions to show with what freedom the strong men of the Reformation handled these questions of Biblical criticism.

Zwingli rejected the Apocalypse. Oecolampadius placed James, Jude, Second Peter, Second and Third John and the Apocalypse along with the Apocryphal books, on a lower level than the other New Testament Scriptures.

The great majority of the Reformers, however, speedily fixed upon that canon which we now receive, and their decision has not been seriously called in question since the sixteenth century.

I have now answered most of the questions proposed at the beginning of this chapter. We have seen that while the great majority of the books in both Testaments have been universally received, questions have been raised at various times concerning the canonicity of several of the books in either Testament; that many good men, from the second century before Christ until the sixteenth century after Christ, have disputed the authority of some of these books. We have seen also that quite a number of other books have at one time and another been regarded as sacred and numbered among the Holy Scriptures; we have seen that the final judgment respecting these doubtful books is different in different branches of the church, the Roman Catholic Church and the Greek Catholic Church admitting into their canons several books that the Reformed churches exclude from theirs.

We have seen that the decision which has been reached by the several branches of the church respecting this matter has been reached as the result of discussion and argument; that the canonicity of the disputed books was freely canvassed by the church fathers in their writings, by the church councils in their assemblies, by the Reformers in their inquiries; that no supernatural methods have been employed to determine the canonicity of these several books; but that the enlightened reason of the church has been the arbiter of the whole matter.

The grounds upon which the Jews acted in admitting or rejecting books into their Scriptures it might be difficult for us to determine. In some cases we know that they were fanciful and absurd. But the grounds on which the Christians proceeded in making up their canon we know pretty well.

The first question respecting each one of the Christian writings seems to have been: "Was it written by an apostle?" If this question could be answered in the affirmative, the book was admitted. And in deciding this question, the Christians of later times made appeal to the opinions of those of earlier times; authority and tradition had much to do in determining it. "Was it the general opinion of the early church that this book was written by an apostle?" they asked. And if this seemed to be the case, they were inclined to admit it. Besides, they compared Scripture with Scripture: certain books were unquestionably written by Paul or Luke or John; other books which were doubted were also ascribed to them; if they found the language of the disputed book corresponding to that of the undisputed book, in style and in forms of expression, they judged that it must have been written by the same man. Upon such grounds of external and internal evidence, it finally came to be believed that all of the New Testament books except four were written by apostles, and that these four, Mark, Luke, The Acts of the Apostles, and the Epistle to the Hebrews, were written by men under the immediate direction of apostles.

But, it may be said, there have been great differences of opinion on this matter through all the ages, down to the sixteenth century; how do we know but that those good and holy men, like Ignatius and Clement and Tertullian and Origen in the early church, and Luther and Zwingli and Oecolampadius in the Reformed church, were right in rejecting some books that we receive and in receiving some that we reject?

If you were a good Catholic, that question would not trouble you. For the fundamental article of your creed would then be, The Holy Catholic Church, when she is represented by her bishops in a general council, can never make a mistake. And the Holy Catholic Church in a general council at Trent, in 1546, said that such and such books belonged to the Bible, and that no others do; and the council of the Vatican, in 1870, said the same thing over again, making it doubly sure; so, that, as a good Catholic, you would have no right to any doubts or questions about it.

But, being a Protestant, you cannot help knowing that all general councils have made grave and terrible mistakes; that no one of them ever was infallible; and so you could not rest satisfied with the decisions of Trent and the Vatican, even if they gave you the same Bible that you now possess, which, of course, they do not. What certainty has the Protestant, then, that his canon is the correct one? He has no absolute certainty. There is no such thing as absolute certainty with respect to historical religious truth. But this discussion has made one or two things plain to the dullest apprehension.

The first is that the books of this Bible are not all of equal rank and sacredness. If there is one truth which all the ages, with all their voices, join to declare, it is that the Bible is made up of many different kinds of books, with very different degrees of sacredness and authority. For one, I do not wish to part with any of them; I find instruction in all of them, though in some of them, as in Esther and Ecclesiastes, it is rather as records of savagery and of skepticism, from which every Christian ought to recoil, that I can see any value in them. As powerful delineations of the kind of sentiments that the Christian ought not to cherish, and the kind of doubts that he cannot entertain without imperilling his soul, they may be useful. It is not, therefore, at all desirable that these ancient records should be torn asunder and portions of them flung away. That process of mutilation none of us is wise enough to attempt. Let the Bible stand; there are good uses for every part of it. But let us remember the lesson which this survey has brought home to us, that these books are not all alike, and that the message of divine wisdom is spoken to us in some of them far more clearly than in others,

Richard Baxter is an authority in religion for whose opinion all conservative people ought to entertain respect. He cannot be suspected of being a "New Departure" man; he was a stanch Presbyterian, and he passed to the "Saints' Rest" nearly two hundred years ago. With a few words of his upon the question now before us, this chapter may fitly close:—

"And here I must tell you a great and needful truth, which Christians, fearing to confess, by overdoing, tempt men to infidelity. The Scripture is like a man's body, where some parts are but for the preservation of the rest, and may be maimed without death. The sense is the soul of the Scripture, and the letters but the body or vehicle. The doctrine of the Creed, Lord's Prayer and Decalogue, Baptism and the Lord's Supper, is the vital part and Christianity itself. The Old Testament letter (written as we have it about Ezra's time) is that vehicle which is as imperfect as the revelation of those times was. But as, after Christ's incarnation and ascension, the Spirit was more abundantly given, and the revelation more perfect and sealed, so the doctrine is more full, and the vehicle or body, that is the words, are less imperfect and more sure to us; so that he which doubteth of the truth of some words in the Old Testament or of some circumstances in the New, hath no reason therefore to doubt of the Christian religion of which these writings are but the vehicle or body, sufficient to ascertain us of the truth of the History and Doctrine."[5]

---

5. *The Catechizing of Christian Families*, p. 36.

Chapter 12

How the Books Were Written

The books of the Old Testament were originally written upon skins of some sort. The Talmud provided that the law might be inscribed on the skins of clean animals, tame or wild, or even of clean birds. These skins were usually cut into strips, the ends of which were neatly joined together, making a continuous belt of parchment or vellum which was rolled upon two sticks and fastened by a thread. They were commonly written on one side only, with an iron pen which was dipped in ink composed of lampblack dissolved in gall juice.

The Hebrew is a language quite unlike our own in form and appearance. Not only do we read it from right to left, instead of from left to right, but the consonants only of the several words are written in distinct characters on the line; the vowels being little dots or dashes standing under the consonants, or within their curves. These vowel points were not used in the original Hebrew; they are a modern invention, originating some centuries after Christ. It is true that it was the belief of the Jews in former times that these vowel points were an original part of the language; their scholars made this claim with great confidence, which shows how little reliance is to be placed on Jewish tradition. The evidence is abundant that the Hebrew was originally written without vowels, precisely as stenographers often write in these days. We know from the testimony of old students and interpreters of the Hebrew that they constantly encountered this difficulty in reading the language. Write a paragraph of our own language without vowels and look at it. Or, better, ask some one else to treat for you in the same way a paragraph with which you are not familiar, and see if you can decipher it. Undoubtedly, you could with some difficulty make out the sense of most passages. It would puzzle you at first, but after you had had some practice in supplying the vowels you would learn to read quite readily. Stenographers, as I have said, have a somewhat similar task. Nevertheless, you would sometimes be in uncertainty as to the words. Suppose you have the three consonants *brd,* how would you know whether the word was bard, or bird, or bread, or board, or brad, or broad, or bride, or braid, or brood, or breed? It might be any one of them. You could usually tell what it was by a glance at the connection, but you could not tell infallibly, for there might be sentences in which more than one of these words would make sense, and it would be impossible to determine which the writer meant to use. Now the old Hebrew as it came from the hands of the original writers was all in this form; while, therefore, the meaning of the writer can generally be gained with sufficient accuracy, you see at a glance that absolute certainty is out of the question; that the Jewish scholars who supplied these vowel points a thousand years or more after the original manuscripts were written may sometimes have got the wrong word.

Jerome gives numerous illustrations of this uncertainty. In Jer. ix. 21, "Death is come up into our windows," he says that we have for the first word the three Hebrew consonants corresponding to our *dbr*; the word may be *dabar*, signifying death, or *deber*, signifying pestilence; it is impossible to tell which it is. In Habakkuk iii. 5, we have the same consonants, and there the word is written pestilence. Either word will made good sense in either place; and we are perfectly helpless in our choice between them. Again, in Isaiah xxvi. 14, we have a prediction concerning the wicked, "Therefore hast thou visited and destroyed them and made all their memory to perish." The Hebrew word here translated "memory" consists of three consonants represented by our English *zkr*; it may be the word *zeker*, which signifies memory, or the word *zakar*, which signifies a male person. And Jerome says that it is believed that Saul was deceived, perhaps willingly, by the difference in these words (I Sam. xv.); having been commanded to cut off every *zeker*—memorial or vestige—of Amaiek, he took the word to be *zakar*, instead of zeker, and contented himself with destroying the males of the army and keeping for himself the spoil. Jerome's conjecture in this case is sufficiently fanciful; nevertheless he illustrates the impossibility of determining the exact meaning of many Hebrew sentences. This impossibility is abundantly demonstrated by the Septuagint, for we find many undoubted errors in that translation from the Hebrew into the Greek, which have arisen from this lack of precision in the Hebrew language.

When, therefore, we know that the Bible was written in such a language—a language without vowels—and that it was not until six hundred years after Christ that the vowel points were invented and the words were written out in full, the theory of the verbal inerrancy of the text as we now have it becomes incredible. Unless the men who supplied the vowel points were gifted with supernatural knowledge they must have made mistakes in spelling out some of these words. I do not believe that these mistakes were serious, or that they affect in any important way the meaning of the Scripture, but the assumption that in this stupendous game of guess-work no wrong guesses were made is in the highest degree gratuitous. The substantial truthfulness of the record is not impeached by this discovery, but the verbal inerrancy of the document can never be maintained by any honest man who knows these facts.

It is unsafe and mischievous to indulge in *a priori* reasonings about inspiration; we have had too much of that; but the following proposition is unassailable: If the Divine Wisdom had proposed to deliver to man an infallible book, he would not have had it recorded in a language whose written words consist only of consonants, leaving readers a thousand years after to fill in the vowels by conjecture. The very fact that such a language was chosen is the conclusive and unanswerable evidence that God never designed to give us an infallible book.

We are familiar with the fact that the Old Testament writings in general use among the early churches were those of the Septuagint. The Christians from the second to the sixteenth centuries knew very little Hebrew. But during all these ages the Palestinian Jews and their successors in other lands were preserving their own Scriptures; it was they who added at a late day—probably as late as the sixth century—the vowel points, which were invented in Syria; and when, at length, under the impulse of Biblical study which led to the Reformation, Christian scholars began to think of going back to the original Hebrew, they were obliged to obtain from the Jews the copies which they studied. It is somewhat remarkable that the Jews, who were the exclusive custodians of the Hebrew writings up to the sixteenth century, had not been careful to preserve their old manuscripts. After the vowel points had been introduced into the text, they seem to have been willing that copies not written in this manner should pass out of existence. Accordingly we have few Hebrew manuscripts that are even supposed to be more than six or seven hundred years old. There is one copy of the Pentateuch which may have been made as early as 580 A.D., but this is extremely doubtful; aside from this I do not know that there are any Hebrew Bibles which claim to be older than the ninth century. Of these Hebrew manuscripts nearly six hundred are now known to be in existence, but the greater part of these are only fragmentary copies of the Pentateuch or of single books. There are two classes of these—synagogue rolls, prepared for reading in the way that I have described, and manuscripts in the book form, some on parchment and some on paper.

The variations in these manuscripts are few. Compared with the Greek manuscripts of the New Testament, the accuracy of these Hebrew codices is remarkable. It is evident that the care of the Scribes to guard their Scriptures against error has been scrupulous and vigilant. Doubtless this intense devotion to the very letter of the sacred books has been exercised for many centuries. We know that in the earliest days this precision was not sought; for the Septuagint translation, made during the second and third centuries before Christ, gives us indubitable proof, when we compare it with the Hebrew text, that changes, some of them radical and sweeping, have been made in the text of the Hebrew books since that translation was finished. But it is evident that the Scribes at an early day, certainly as early as the beginning of the Christian era, determined to have a uniform and an unchangeable text. For this purpose they chose some manuscript copy of the Scriptures, doubtless the one which seemed to them most accurate, and made that the standard; all the copies made since that time have been religiously conformed to that. Consequently, all the Hebrew manuscripts now in existence are remarkably uniform. The Old Testament contains more than three times as many pages as the New Testament; but while we have more than one hundred and fifty thousand "various readings" in the Greek manuscripts and versions of the New Testament, we have less than ten thousand such variations in those of the Old Testament. It must be remembered, however, that this uniformity has its source in some copy chosen to be the standard hundreds of years after most of the Old Testament books were written; and it does not guarantee the close correspondence between this copy and the autographs of the original writers.[1]

---

1. For an interesting discussion of the preservation and transmission of the Hebrew text, the reader is referred to Mr. Robertson Smith's *The Old Testament in the Jewish Church*, Lectures ii. and iii.

Our chief interest centres, however, in the Greek manuscripts of the Bible preserved and transmitted by Christians, and including both Testaments. All the oldest and most precious documents that we possess belong to this class.

The original New Testament writings which came from the hands of the apostles and their amanuenses we do not possess. These were probably written, not on skins, but upon the papyrus paper commonly used at that day, which was a frail and flimsy fabric, and under ordinary circumstances would soon perish. Fragments of this papyrus have come down to us, but only those which were preserved with exceptional care. Jerome tells us of a library in Cassarea that was partly destroyed, owing to the crumbling of its paper, though it was only a hundred years old. Parchment was sometimes used by the apostles; Paul requests Timothy, in his second letter, to bring with him, when he comes, certain parchments that belong to him. But these materials were costly, and it is not likely that the apostles used them to any extent in the preparation of the books of the New Testament. At any rate the autographic copies of these books disappeared at an early date. This seems strange to us. Placing the estimate that we do upon these writings, we should have taken the greatest care to preserve them. It is clear that the Christians into whose hands they fell did not value them as highly as we do. As Westcott says, "They were given as a heritage to man, and it was some time before men felt the full value of the gift."

At the close of the second century there were disputes concerning the correct reading of certain passages, but neither party appeals to the apostolic originals,—

showing that they must before that time have perished. In after years legends were told about the preservation of these originals, but these are contradictory and incredible.

No manuscript is now in existence which was written during the first three centuries. But we have one or two that date back to the fourth century; and from that time through all the ages to the invention of printing many copies were made of the Sacred Scriptures, in whole or in part, which are still in the hands of scholars. It is from these old Greek manuscripts that our received text of the New Testament is derived; by a comparison of them the scholars of the seventeenth century made up a Greek New Testament which they regarded as approximately accurate, and from that our English version was made.

The number of these old manuscripts is large, and the first general division of them is into "uncials" or "cursives," as they are called; the uncial manuscripts being written in capital letters, the cursives in small letters more or less connected, as in our written hand. The uncials are the oldest, as they are the fewest; there are only one hundred and twenty-seven of them in all; while of the cursives there are about fifteen hundred.

Yet most of these manuscripts are fragmentary. Some of them contain only the Gospels or portions of them; some of them contain the Acts and the Catholic Epistles; some of them the Epistles of Paul or a single epistle; some are selections from the Gospels or the Epistles, prepared to be read in church, and called lectionaries.

Professor Ezra Abbot gives us a classification of these manuscripts which will be found instructive.

"For the New Testament, . . . we have manuscripts more or less complete, written in uncial or capital letters, and ranging from the fourth to the tenth century; of the Gospels twenty-seven, besides thirty small fragments; of the Acts and Catholic Epistles ten, besides six small fragments; of the Pauline Epistles eleven, besides nine small fragments, and of the Revelation five. All of these have been most thoroughly collated, and the text of the most important of them has been published. One of these manuscripts, the Sinaitic, containing the whole of the New Testament, and another, the Vatican, containing much the larger part of it, were written probably as early as the middle of the fourth century; two others, the Alexandrian and the Ephraem, belong to about the middle of the fifth, of which date are two more, containing considerable portions of the Gospels. A very remarkable manuscript of the Gospels and Acts—the Cambridge manuscript, or Codex Bezae—belongs to the sixth century. . . . I pass by a number of small but valuable fragments of the fifth and sixth centuries. As to the cursive manuscripts ranging from the tenth century to the sixteenth, we have of the Gospels more than six hundred; of the Acts over two hundred; of the Pauline Epistles nearly three hundred; of the Revelation about one hundred,— not reckoning the lectionaries, or manuscripts containing the lessons from the Gospels, Acts, and Epistles, read in the service of the church, of which there are more than four hundred."[2]

Out of all this vast mass of extant manuscripts, only twenty-seven contain the New Testament entire.

---

2. *Anglo-American Bible Revision*, p. 95.

The three oldest and most valuable manuscripts among those named by Professor Abbot, in the passage above, are the Sinaitic, the Vatican, and the Alexandrian manuscripts.

Of these old Bibles perhaps the oldest is the one in the Vatican Library at Rome. It was enrolled in that library as late as the year 1475; what its history was before that time is unknown. By whose hands or at what place it was written, no one can tell. Some have supposed that it was brought from Constantinople to Rome, in the fifteenth century, by John Bessarion, a learned patriarch; some that it was written in Alexandria, when that city was the metropolis of the world's culture; some that it was produced in Southern Italy when that region was celebrated for its learning. The signs favor the latter theory. The form of the letters is like those found on papyri in Herculaneum; and other manuscripts of the Bible found in southern Italy agree remarkably with this one in many peculiar readings. But this is all guess-work. Nobody knows where the old Bible came from or who brought it to Rome.

Some things, however, the old book plainly tells us about its own history. It bears the unmistakable marks of great antiquity. The scholar who is familiar with old Greek manuscripts can judge by looking at a document something about its probable age. By the form of the letters, by the presence or absence of certain marks of punctuation, by the general style of the manuscript, he can determine within a century or so the date at which it was written.

This old Bible is written in the uncial or capital letters; this would make it tolerably certain that it must be older than the tenth century. We have scarcely any uncial manuscripts later than the tenth century. But other unmistakable marks take it back much farther than this. The words are written continuously, with no breaks or spaces between them; there are no accents, no rough or smooth breathings, no punctuation marks of any sort. These are signs of great age. Another peculiarity is the manner of the division of the books into sections. I cannot stop to describe to you the various methods of division adopted in antiquity. The present separation into chapters and verses was, as you know, a quite modern device. But the divisions of this old Bible follow a method that we know to have been in use at a very early day; and the conclusion of all the scholars is that it must have been written as early as the year 350, possibly as early as 300.

It is not, however, a roll, but a book in form like those we handle every day. Before this date manuscripts were generally prepared in this way. Martial, the Latin poet, who died about 100, mentions as a novelty in his day books with square leaves, bound together at the edges.

The Vatican Bible is a heavy quarto, the covers are red morocco discolored with age, the leaves, of which there are 759, are of fine and delicate vellum. It contains the Septuagint translation of the Old Testament, except the first forty-five chapters in Genesis and a few of the Psalms, which have been torn out and lost. Of the New Testament writings, the last five chapters of Hebrews, First and Second Timothy, Titus, Philemon, and the Apocalypse are wanting. Otherwise both Testaments are complete.

We may recall another fact, to which allusion has been made, that this old Bible contains among the Old Testament books those books which we now call apocryphal, and that these apocryphal books, instead of being divided from the rest in a separate group, are mingled with them, the *order* of the books being quite unlike that of our Bibles or of the Hebrew canon. The apocryphal First Book of Esdras *precedes* our Book of Ezra; while our Book of Ezra is united with Nehemiah, forming the Second Book of Esdras. Judith and Tobit follow Esther, and next comes the twelve minor prophets, and so on.

The same thing is true of all these oldest Bibles; they all contain the apocryphal books, and these books are mingled with the other books, either promiscuously, or by some system of classification which accepts them as equal in value with the other Old Testament writings. There is no indication in these old Bibles that the apocryphal books are any less sacred or authoritative than the others.

Another manuscript Bible, scarcely less venerable and no less precious than the Vatican Bible, is the one known as the Sinaitic manuscript This was discovered by Constantine Tischendorf, a German scholar, in an ancient convent at the base of Mount Sinai. The first journey of Tischendorf to the Sinaitic peninsula was undertaken in 1844, for the express purpose of searching in the old monasteries of this neighborhood for ancient copies of the Scriptures that might be preserved in them. The monks of this old convent admitted him to their ancient library,—a place not greatly frequented by them,—and there in the middle of the room he found a waste basket, filled with leaves and torn pieces of old parchment gathered to be burned. In looking them over he discovered one hundred and twenty leaves of a Bible that seemed to him of great antiquity. He asked for these leaves, but when they found that he wanted them, the monks began to suspect their value, and permitted him to take only forty-three of them. In 1853 he returned again, but this time could not find the rest of the precious manuscript. He feared that it had been destroyed long before, but this was not the case. Stimulated by his desire to possess the loose leaves, the monks had made search for the rest of the volume, and, using as samples the leaves they had refused to give him, they had found them all and secreted them. Upon his second visit they did not show him the book, however, nor reveal to him in any way its existence.

Six years later, in 1859, he returned again, this time fortified with a letter from the Emperor of Russia, the head of the Greek Church; and this mighty document made the monks open their treasures for his inspection. He obtained permission, first, to carry the old Bible to Cairo to be copied, and finally, under the imperial influence, the monks surrendered it, and suffered it to be removed to St. Petersburg, where since 1859 it has been sacredly kept.

"The Sinai Bible," says Dr. F. P. Woodbury, "contains the New Testament, the Epistle of Barnabas, a portion of the Shepherd of Hennas, and twenty-two books of the Old Testament. The whole is written on fine vellum made from antelope skins into the largest pages known in our ancient manuscripts. While most of the oldest manuscripts have only three columns to the page, and the Vatican Bible has three, the Sinai Bible alone shows four. The letters are somewhat larger than those of the Vatican and much more roughly written. The book contains many blunders in copying, and there are a few cases of willful omission. Its remote age is attested by many of the same proofs that have been mentioned in the description of the Vatican Bible."[3]

It is known that the Emperor Constantine, in the year 331, authorized the preparation of fifty costly and beautiful copies of the Holy Scriptures under the care of Eusebius of Caesarea. Tischendorf himself thinks—and his conjecture is accepted by other scholars—that this is one of those fifty Bibles, and that it was sent from Byzantium to the monks of this convent by the Emperor Justinian, who was its founder. At all events, it is incontestably a manuscript of great age, certainly of the fourth century, and probably of the first half of that century.

The other great Bible is the one known as the Alexandrian, which was presented, in 1628, to King Charles I of England by Cyril Lucar, patriarch of Constantinople, who had brought it from Alexandria. It was transferred in 1753 from the king's private library to the British Museum, where it is now preserved. It is bound in four folio volumes, three of which contain the text of the Old and one of the New Testament. The portion which contains the Old Testament is more perfect than that which contains the New, quite a number of leaves having been lost from the latter. "The material of which this volume is composed is thin vellum, the page being about thirteen inches high by ten broad, containing from fifty to fifty-two lines on each page, each line consisting of about twenty letters. The number of pages is 773, of which 640 are occupied with the text of the Old Testament and 133 with the New. The characters are uncial, but larger than

---

3. From an interesting sketch of "Three Old Bibles," in *Sunday Afternoon*, vol. i pp. 65–71.

the Vatican manuscript. There are no accents or breathings, no spaces between the letters or words save at
the end of a paragraph, and the contractions, which are
not numerous, are only such as are found in the oldest
manuscripts. The punctuation consists of a point placed
at the end of a sentence, usually on a level with the top
of the preceding letter."[4] The general verdict of scholars
is that this manuscript belongs to about the middle of the
fifth century.

The contents of this old Bible are curious, and they are
curiously arranged. The first volume contains the Pentateuch, Joshua, Judges, Ruth, the two books of Samuel, the
two books of Kings, and the two books of Chronicles. The
second contains, first, the twelve minor prophets (from
Hosea to Malachi), then Isaiah, Jeremiah, *Baruch,* Lamentations, *The Epistle of Jeremiah,* Ezekiel, Daniel, Esther, *Tobit, Judith, Esdras I.* (the apocryphal Esdras), Esdras II.
(including our Nehemiah and part of our Ezra), and *the
four books of the Maccabees.* The third volume contains An
Epistle of Athanasius to Marcellenus on the Psalms; The
Hypothesis of Eusebius on the Psalms; then the Book of
the Psalms, of which there are one hundred and fifty-
one, and fifteen Hymns; then Job, Proverbs, Ecclesiastes,
Canticles, Wisdom of Solomon, and Ecclesiasticus, or Sirach. The fourth volume contains the four Gospels, the
Acts, the seven Catholic Epistles (one of James, two of
Peter, three of John, and one of Jude), fourteen Epistles of
Paul (including the one to the Hebrews), The Revelation
of John, two Epistles of Clement to the Corinthians, and
eight Psalms of Solomon.

---

4. *Encyc. Brit.,* i. p. 496.

This, it will be admitted, is a generous Bible. It contains most of the apocryphal books, and several others that we do not find in the other collections. It is probable that the works of Athanasius and Eusebius on the Psalms were admitted rather as introduction or commentary than as text; but the rest, judging from the positions in which they stand, must have been regarded as Sacred Scriptures.

These, then, are the three oldest, most complete, and most trustworthy copies of the Sacred Scriptures now in existence. By all scholars they are regarded as precious beyond price; and any reading in which they agree would probably be regarded as the right reading, if all the other manuscripts in the world were against them.

I have suggested that these old manuscripts do not always agree. The fact is that no two of them are exactly alike, and that there are a great many slight differences between those which are most closely assimilated. Of these differences Professor Westcott says that "there cannot be less than 120,000,—though of these a very large proportion consists of differences of spelling and isolated aberrations of scribes." It is not generally difficult for the student on comparing them to tell which is the right reading. A word may be misspelled, for example, in several different ways; the student knows the right way to spell it, and is not in doubt concerning the word. "Probably," says Mr. Westcott, "there are not more than from sixteen hundred to two thousand places in which the true reading is a matter of uncertainty, even if we include in this questions of order, inflection, and orthography; the doubtful readings by which the sense is in any way affected are very much fewer, and those of dogmatic importance can be easily numbered."

The ways in which these errors and variations arose are easily explained. The men who copied these manuscripts were careful men, many of them, but all of them were fallible. Sometimes they would mistake a letter for another letter much like it, and change the form of a word in that way; sometimes there would be two clauses of a sentence ending with the same word, and the eye of the copyist, glancing back to the manuscript after writing the first of these words, would alight upon the second one, and go on from that; so that the clause preceding it would be omitted. Sometimes in copying the continuous writing of the uncial manuscripts, mistakes would be made in dividing words. For example, if a number of English words, written in close order, with no spaces between them, were given you to copy, and you found "infancy," you might make two words of it or one; and if you were a little careless you might write it "in fancy" when it should be "infancy," or *vice versa.* A case might arise in which it would be difficult for you to tell whether it should be "in fancy" or "infancy." Such uncertainties the copyists encountered, and such mistakes they sometimes made.

Mistakes of memory they also made in copying, just as I sometimes do when I undertake to copy a passage from Mr. Westcott or Mr. Davidson into one of these chapters. I look upon the book, and take a sentence in my mind, but perhaps while I am writing it down I will change slightly the order of the words, or it may be put a word of my own in the place of another that much resembles it, as "but" for "though," or "from" for "out of," or "doubtless" for "without doubt." I try to copy very exactly, but there are, unquestionably, now and then such slips as these in my quotations. And such mistakes were made by the copyists of the Old Scriptures.

There are some instances of intentional changes. Sometimes a copyist evidently substituted a word that he thought was plainer for one that was more obscure; a more elegant word for one less elegant; a grammatical construction for one that was not grammatical.

Other differences have arisen from the habit of some of the copyists or owners of manuscripts of writing glosses, or brief explanatory notes, on the margin. Some of these marginalia were copied by subsequent scribes into the text, where, in our version, they still remain. Some of them, however, were removed in the late revision.

The great majority of these errors are, however, as I have said, extremely unimportant; and nearly all of them seem to have arisen in the ways I have suggested—through simple carelessness, and not with any intent of corrupting the text.

The translations of the Bible which were made in early days into other languages than our own must be dismissed with the briefest mention. The most important version of the Old Testament was the Septuagint, of which nothing more needs to be said.

You will remember that the Hebrew was a dead language while our Lord was on the earth, the Jews of Palestine speaking the Aramaic. For their use, translations of the Hebrew into the Aramaic, called Targums, were made. There is a great variety of these, and there are many opinions about their age; but it is not likely that the oldest of them was committed to writing before the second century A.D. They are curious specimens of the translator's work, combining text and commentary in a remarkable manner. Additions and changes are freely made; the simple sentences of the old record are greatly expanded; not only is a spade generally called a useful ligneous and ferruginous agricultural implement, but many things are said concerning the aforesaid spade which Moses or David or Isaiah never dreamed of saying.

For example, in Judges v. 10, the Hebrew is literally translated in our English Bible thus: "Speak, ye that ride on white asses, ye that sit in judgment and walk by the way." The Targum of Jonathan expatiates thereon as follows: "Those who had interrupted their occupations are riding on asses covered with many colored caparisons, and they ride about freely in all the territory of Israel, and congregate to sit in judgment. They walk in their old ways, and are speaking of the power Thou hast shown in the land of Israel," etc. This may be pronounced a remarkably free translation; and the Targums generally evince a similar liberality of sentiment and phraseology.

Besides these, the ancient translations of the Bible, which must be mentioned, are the Old Latin, made in the second century, out of which, by many revisions, grew that Latin Vulgate which is now used in the Catholic ritual; an ancient Syriac version of about the same age; two Egyptian versions, in different dialects, made in the third century; the Peshito-Syriac, the Gothic, and the Ethiopic in the fourth, and the Armenian in the fifth; besides several later translations, including the Arabic and the Slavonic. These ancient translations are all of value to modern scholars in helping them to reach more certain conclusions respecting the nature of the Sacred Scriptures and the right reading in disputed passages.

The ages which we have been traversing in this chapter—when the Bible was a manuscript—were ages of great darkness. The copies of the book were few, and the common people could neither possess them nor read them. It is hard for us who have had the book in our hands from our infancy, who have gone to it so freely for light in darkness, for comfort in sorrow, for wisdom to work with, for weapons to fight with, to understand how men could have lived the life of faith without it; how a godly seed could have been nourished in the earth without the sincere milk of the word for them to feed on.

It was indeed a great privation that they suffered, but we must not suppose that they were left without witness. For there is another and even a clearer revelation than the written word, and that is a godly life. Godly lives there were in all these dark times; and it was at their fires that the torch of gospel truth was kindled and kept burning. There may be reason for a question whether we have not come to trust in these times too much in a word that is written, and to undervalue that other revelation which God is making of his truth and love in the characters of his children. For it is only in the light that Christ is constantly manifesting to the world in the lives of men that we can see any meaning in the words of the book. "The Christian," says Dr. Christlieb, "is the world's Bible." This is the word that is known and read of men. Let it be our care to make it, not an infallible, but a clear, an adequate, and a safe revelation of the truth and love of God to men.

Chapter 13

How Much Is the Bible Worth?

Of the Bible as a book among books, of the human elements which enter into its composition, some account has been given in the preceding chapters. But in these studies the whole story of the Bible has not been told. There is need, therefore, that we should enlarge our view somewhat, and take more directly into account certain elements with which we have not hitherto been chiefly concerned.

Our study has, indeed, made a few things plain. Among them is the certainty that the Bible is not an infallible Book, in the sense in which it is popularly supposed to be infallible. When we study the history of the several books, the history of the canon, the history of the distribution and reproduction of the manuscript copies, and the history of the versions,—when we discover that the "various readings" of the differing manuscripts amount to one hundred and fifty thousand, the impossibility of maintaining the verbal inerrancy of the Bible becomes evident. We see how human ignorance and error have been suffered to mingle with this stream of living water throughout all its course; if our assurance of salvation were made to depend upon our knowledge that every word of the Bible was of divine origin, our hopes of eternal life would be altogether insecure.

The book is not infallible historically. It is a veracious record; we may depend upon the truthfulness of the outline which it gives us of the history of the Jewish people; but the discrepancies and contradictions which appear here and there upon its pages show that its writers were not miraculously protected from mistakes in dates and numbers and the order of events.

It is not infallible scientifically. It is idle to try to force the narrative of Genesis into an exact correspondence with geological science. It is a hymn of creation, wonderfully beautiful and pure; the central truths of monotheistic religion and of modern science are involved in it; but it is not intended to give us the scientific history of creation, and the attempt to make it bear this construction is highly injudicious.

It is not infallible morally. By this I mean that portions of this revelation involve an imperfect morality. Many things are here commanded which it would be wrong for us to do. This is not saying that these commands were not divinely wise for the people to whom they were given; nor is it denying that the morality of the New Testament, which is the fulfillment and consummation of the moral progress which the book records, is a perfect morality; it is simply asserting that the stages of this progress from a lower to a higher morality are here clearly marked; that the standards of the earlier time are therefore inadequate and misleading in these later times; and that any man who accepts the Bible as a code of moral rules, all of which are equally binding, will be led into the gravest errors. It is no more true that the ceremonial legislation of the Old Testament is obsolete than that large portions of the moral legislation are obsolete. The notions of the writers of these books concerning their duties to God were dim and imperfect; so were their notions concerning their duties to man. All the truth that they could receive was given to them; but there were many truths which they could not receive, which to us are as plain as the daylight.

Not to recognize the partialness and imperfection of this record in all these respects is to be guilty of a grave disloyalty to the kingdom of the truth. With all these facts staring him in the face, the attempt of any intelligent man to maintain the theoretical and ideal infallibility of all parts of these writings is a criminal blunder. Nor is there any use in loudly asserting the inerrancy of these books, with vehement denunciations of all who call it in question, and then in a breath admitting that there may be some errors and discrepancies and interpolations. Perfection is perfection. To stoutly affirm that a thing is perfect, and then admit that it may be in some respects imperfect, is an insensate procedure. Infallibility is infallibility. The Scriptures are, or they are not, infallible. The admission that there may be a few errors gives every man the right, nay it lays upon him the duty, of finding what those errors are. Our friends who so sturdily assert the traditional theory can hardly be aware of the extent to which they stultify themselves when their sweeping and reiterated assertion that the Bible can *never* contain a mistake is followed, as it always must be, by their timid and deprecatory, "hardly ever." The old rabbinical theory, as adopted and extended by some of the post-Reformation theologians, that the Bible was verbally dictated by God and is absolutely accurate in every word, letter, and vowel-point, and that it is therefore blasphemy to raise a question concerning any part of it, is a consistent theory. Between this and a free but reverent inquiry into the Bible itself, to discover what human elements it contains and how it is affected by them, there is no middle ground. That it is useless and mischievous to make for the Bible claims that it nowhere makes for itself,—to hold and teach a theory concerning it which at once breaks down when an intelligent man begins to study it with open mind—is beginning to be very plain. The quibbling, the concealment, the disingenuousness which this method of using the Bible involves are not conducive to Christian integrity. This kind of "lying for God" has driven hundreds of thousands already into irreconcilable alienation from the Christian church. It is time to stop it.

How did this theory of the infallibility of the Bible arise? Those who have followed these discussions to this point know that it has not always been held by the Christian church. The history of the canon, told with any measure of truthfulness, will make this plain. The history of the variations between the Septuagint and the Hebrew shows, beyond the shadow of a doubt, that this theory of the unchangeable and absolute divinity of the words of the Scripture had no practical hold upon transcribers and copyists in the early Jewish church. The New Testament writers could not have consistently held such a theory respecting the Old Testament books, else they would not have quoted them, as they did, with small care for verbal accuracy. They believed them to be substantially true, and therefore they give the substance of them in their quotations; but there is no such slavish attention to the letter as there must have been if they had regarded them as verbally dictated by God himself. The Christian Fathers were inclined, no doubt, to accept the rabbinical theories of inspiration respecting the Old Testament; but they sometimes avoid the difficulties growing out of manifest errors in the text by a theory of an inner sense which is faultless, frankly admitting that the natural meaning cannot always be defended. As to the early Reformers, we have seen how freely they handled the Sacred Writings, submitting them to a scrutiny which they would not have ventured upon if they had believed concerning them what we have been taught. It was not until the period succeeding the Reformation that this dogma of Biblical Infallibility was clearly formulated and imposed upon the Protestant churches. As taught by Quenstedt and Voetius and Calovius, the dogma asserts that "not only the substance of truth and the views proposed in their minutest detail, but even the identical words, all and in particular, were supplied and dictated by the Holy Ghost. Not a word is contained in the Holy Scriptures which is not in the strictest sense inspired, the very interpunctuation not excepted. . . . Errors of any sort whatever, even verbal or grammatical, as well as all inelegancies of style, are to be denied as unworthy of the Divine Spirit who is throughout the primary author of the Bible."[1] This view was long maintained with all strictness, and many a man has been made a heretic for denying it. Within the last century the form of the doctrine has been somewhat modified by theologians, yet the substance of it is still regarded as essential orthodoxy. Dr. Charles Hodge, in his

1. *The Doctrine of Sacred Scripture*, ii. p. 209.

"Theology," vol. i. p. 152, says, "Protestants hold that the Scriptures of the Old and New Testaments are the word of God, written under the inspiration of God the Holy Ghost, and are therefore infallible, and consequently free from all error, whether of doctrine, of fact, or of precept." And again (p. 163), "All the books of Scripture are equally inspired. All alike are infallible in what they teach." Such is the doctrine now held by the great majority of Christians. Intelligent pastors do not hold it, but the body of the laity have no other conception.

Whence is it derived? Where do the teachers quoted above get their authority for their affirmations?

Not, as we have seen, from any statements of the Bible itself. There is not one word in the Bible which affirms or implies that this character of inerrancy attaches to the entire collection of writings, or to any one of them.

The doctrine arose, as I have said, in the seventeenth century, and it was in part, no doubt, a reflection of the teaching of the later rabbins, whose fantastic notions about the origin of their sacred books I have before alluded to. It was also developed, as a polemical necessity, in the exigencies of that conflict with the Roman Catholic theologians which followed the Reformation. The eminent German scholar and saint, Professor Tholuck, gives the following account of its origin:

"In proportion as controversy, sharpened by Jesuitism, made the Protestant party sensible of an externally fortified ground of combat, in that same proportion did Protestantism seek, by the exaltation of the outward authoritative character of the Sacred Writings, to recover that infallible authority which it had lost through its rejection of infallible councils and the infallible authority of the Pope. In this manner arose, *not earlier than the seventeenth century*, those sentiments which regarded the Holy Scripture as the infallible production of the Divine Spirit—in its entire contents and its very form—so that not only the sense but also the words, the letters, the Hebrew vowel points, and the very punctuation were regarded as proceeding from the Spirit of God."[2] The fact that the doctrine had this origin is itself suspicious. A theory which is framed in the heat of a great controversy, by one party in the church, is apt to be somewhat extreme.

The strength of the doctrine lies, however, in the fact that it is a theological inference from the doctrine of God. "God is the author of the Bible," men have said; "God is omniscient; he can make no mistakes; therefore the Book must be infallible. To deny that it is infallible is to deny that it is God's book; if it is not his book it is worthless." Or, putting it in another form, they have said, "The Bible is an inspired book. God is the source of inspiration. He cannot inspire men to write error. Therefore every word of the inspired book must be true." This is what the logicians call an *a priori* argument. The view of what inspiration is, and of what the Bible is, are deduced from our theory of God. It amounts to just this: If God is what we think him to be, he must do what seems wise to us. This is hardly a safe argument. Doubtless we would have said beforehand that if God, who is all-wise and all-powerful, should create a world, he would make one free from suffering and every form of evil. We find, however, that he has not made such a world. And it may be wiser for us, instead of making up our minds beforehand what God

---

2. *Theological Essays*, collected by George R. Noyes.

must do, to try and find out what he has done. It might seem to us, doubtless, that if he has given us a revelation, it must be a faultless revelation. But has he? That is the question. We can only know by studying the revelation itself. We have no right to determine beforehand what it must be. We might have said with equal confidence, that if God wished to have his truth taught in the world, he would certainly send infallible teachers. He has not done so. The treasure of his truth is in earthen vessels, to-day. Has it not always been so?

The trouble in this whole matter arises from the fact that men have made up their theories of the Bible out of their ideas about God, and have then gone to work to fit the facts of the Bible to their preconceived theories. This has required a great deal of stretching and twisting and lopping off here and there; the truth has been badly distorted, sometimes mutilated. The changed view of the Bible, which greatly alarms some good people, arises from the fact that certain honest men have determined to go directly to the Bible itself and find out by studying it what manner of book it is. They have discovered that it is not precisely such a book as it has been believed to be, and the answer that they make to those who hold the old theory about it is simply this: "We cannot believe what you have told us about the Bible, because the Bible contradicts you. It is because we believe the Bible itself that we reject your theory. We believe that the Bible is an inspired book, nay, that it is by eminence The Inspired Book; but when you ask us 'What is an inspired book?' instead of making up a definition of inspiration out of our own heads, we only say, 'It is such a book as the Bible is,' and then we proceed to frame our definition of inspiration by the study of the Bible. Therefore, when you say that inspiration must imply infallibility, we answer, No; it does not; for here is The Inspired Book and it is not infallible."

In what sense the book is inspired we may be able, after a little, to see more clearly. For the present I only desire to point out the sources of the traditional doctrine of the Bible, and the sources of the new doctrine. The one is the result of the speculations of men about what the Bible must be; the other is the result of a careful and reverent study of the Bible itself.

What, then, do we find the Bible to be?

I. It is the book of righteousness. No other book in the world fixes our thoughts so steadily upon the great interest of character. Whatever else the Bible may show us or may fail to show us, it does keep always before us the fact that the one great concern of every man is to be right in heart and in life. Righteousness tendeth to life; righteousness is salvation; Jehovah is He who loveth righteousness and hateth iniquity, and in his favor is life; these are the truths which form the very substance of this revelation. It is quite true that in the application of this principle to the affairs of every day, the early records show us much confusion and uncertainty; the definitions of righteousness which sufficed for the people of that time would not suffice for us at all; but the fact remains that the only interest of this Book in the individuals and the races which it brings before us is in their loyalty or disloyalty to that ideal of conduct which it always lifts up before us. Righteousness is life; righteousness is salvation; this is the one message of the Bible to men. There are rites and ceremonies, but these are not the principal thing; "To obey is better than sacrifice, and to hearken than the fat of rams." "He hath showed thee, O man, what is good; and what doth the Lord require of thee, but to do justly, and to love mercy, and to walk humbly with thy God?" This great truth of the Bible has been but imperfectly apprehended, even among modern Christians; there is always a tendency to make the belief in sound dogma, or the performance of decorous rites, or the experience of emotional raptures the principal thing; but the testimony of the Bible to the supremacy of character and conduct is clear and convincing, and the world is coming to understand it.

Now for any man who cares for the right, to whom character is more precious than anything else in the world, this book is worth more than any other book can be. Even the Old Testament narratives, indistinctly as they reveal the real nature of true conduct to us in this day, show us plainly the fact that nothing else in the world is to be compared with it; and the struggles and temptations of the heroes of that old book are full of instruction for us; their failures and follies and sins admonish and warn us; their steadfastness and fidelity inspire and hearten us.

II. The Bible is the record of the development of the kingdom of righteousness in the world. Man knows intuitively that he ought to do right; his notion of what is right is continually being purified and enlarged. The Bible is the record of this moral progress in the one nation of the earth to which morality has been the great concern. We have seen, clearly enough, the imperfection of the ethical standards to which the early Hebrew legislation was made to conform; we have also seen that this legislation was always a little in advance of the popular morality, leading it on to purer conceptions and better practices. The legislation concerning divorce, the legislation regulating blood-vengeance, recognizes the evils with which it deals and accommodates itself to them, but always with the purpose and the result of giving to men a larger thought and a better standard. Laws which conformed to our moral ideal would have been powerless to control such a semi-barbarous people as the Hebrews were when they came out of Egypt. The higher morality must be imparted little by little; one principle after another must be drilled into their apprehension; they could not well be learning more than one or two simple lessons at a time, and while they were learning these, other coarse and cruel and savage practices of theirs must be "winked at," as Paul says. Against any rule more strict at this early time the Hebrews would have revolted; the divine wisdom of this legislation is seen in this method which takes men as they are, and does for them the thing that is feasible, patiently leading them on and up to higher ground. If you would seize a running horse by the rein and stop him, you had better run with him for a little. This homely parable illustrates much of the Old Testament legislation which we find so defective, when judged by our standards.

It is in this larger sense that we see the signs of divinity in this old Book. It is a book of inspiration because it is the record of an inspired or divinely guided development; because the life it shows as unfolding is divine; because the goal to which we see the people steadily conducted in its vivid chapters is the goal which God has marked for human progress; because it gives us the origin and growth of the kingdom of God in the world.

"Whence came," asks one, "and of what manner of spirit is this *anti-historic* power in Israel and the Bible? Some inner principle of development struggles against the outward historical environment, and will not rest until it prevails. What was it which selected Israel, and in one narrow land, while all the surrounding country was sinking, lifted man up in spite of himself? which along the course of one national history carried on a progressive development of religious life and truth, while other peoples, though taught by many wise men and seers, and not without their truths, still can show no one connected and progressive revelation like this?"[3]

What is the power that has wrought all this but the divine Power? If you ask for a proof of the existence of God, I point you to the life of the Jewish people as the Bible records it. *That history is the revelation of God.* In the record of this nation's life, in its privileges and its vicissitudes, its captivities and its restorations, its blessings and its chastenings, its institutions and its laws, its teachers and its legislators, its seers and its lawgivers, in all the forces that combine to make up the great movement of the national life, I see God present all the while, shaping the ends of this nation, no matter how perversely it may rough-hew them, till at last it stands on an elevation far above the other nations, breathing a better atmosphere, thinking worthier and more spiritual thoughts of God, obeying a far purer moral law, holding fast a nobler ideal of righteousness,—polytheism gradually and

3. *Old Faiths in New Light*, p. 81.

finally rooted out of the national consciousness; the family established and honored as in no other nation; woman lifted up to a dignity and purity known nowhere else in the world; the Sabbath of rest sanctified; the principles of the decalogue fastened in the convictions of the people, the sure foundations laid of the kingdom of God in the world.

We are quite too apt unduly to disparage Judaism. Doubtless the formalism that our Lord found in it needed rebuke; its worship and its morality were yet far away from the ideal when Jesus came to earth; nevertheless, compared with all the peoples round about them even then—compared with classic Greeks and noble Romans— the ethical and spiritual development of the Jews had reached a higher stage. It is not extravagant to claim for this race the moral leadership of the world. Hear Ernest Renan, no champion of orthodoxy, as you know: "I am eager, gentlemen,"—I quote from a lecture of his on "The Share of the Semitic People in the History of Civilization,"—"to come at the prime service which the Semitic race has rendered to the world; its peculiar work, its providential mission, if I may so express myself. We owe to the Semitic race neither political life, art, poetry, philosophy, nor science. *We owe to them religion.* The whole world—we except India, China, Japan, and tribes altogether savage—*has adopted the Semitic religions.*" Speaking then of the gradual decay of the various pagan faiths of the Aryan races, Renan continues: "It is precisely at this epoch that the civilized world finds itself face to face with the Jewish faith. Based upon the clear and simple dogma of the divine unity, discarding naturalism and pantheism by the marvelously terse phrase,

'In the beginning God created the heavens and the earth,' possessing a law, a book, the depository of grand moral precepts and of an elevated religious poetry, Judaism had an incontestable superiority, and it might have been foreseen then that some day the world would become Jewish, that is to say, would forsake the old mythology for monotheism."[4]

Here is the testimony of a man who can be suspected of no undue leanings toward the religion of the Bible, to the fact that the world is indebted for its great thoughts of religion to the Semitic races, and chiefly to the Hebrew race; that the religion of Judaism, brought into comparison with the other religions, is incontestably superior. Now any man who believes in religion and in God must believe that the people to whom such a task was committed must have been trained by God to perform it. The history of this nation will then be the history of this training. That is exactly what the Old Testament is. No disputes over the nature of inspiration must be suffered to obscure this great fact. The Old Testament Scriptures do contain in biography and history, in statute and story and song and sermon, the records of the life of the nation to which God at sundry times and in divers manners was revealing himself; which he was preparing to be the bearer of the torch of his own truth into all the world. And now I ask whether anybody needs to be told that these records are precious, precious above all price? Are there any authentic portions of them that any man can afford to despise? Is not every step in the progress of this people out of savagery into a spiritual faith, matter

---

4. *Religious History and Criticism*, pp. 159, 160.

of the profoundest interest to every human soul? Even the dullness and ignorance and crudity of this people,— even the crookedness and blindness of their leaders and teachers, are full of instruction for us; they show us with what materials and what instruments the divine wisdom and patience wrought out this great result. What other book is there that can compare in value with this book, which tells us the way of God with the people whom he chose, as Renan declares, to teach the world religion? And when one has firmly grasped this great fact, that the Bible contains the history of the religious development of the Jewish people under providential care and tuition, how little is he troubled by the small difficulties which grow out of theories of inspiration! "We can listen," says Dr. Newman Smyth, "with incurious complacency while small disputants discuss vehemently the story of the ark or Jonah's strange adventure. . . . After all the work of the critics, the Bible still remains, the great, sublime, enduring work of the Eternal who loves righteousness and hates iniquity."[5]

But what have I been vindicating? The Bible? Nay, I have carefully restricted my argument to the Old Testament. It is in behalf of the Old Testament writings alone that I have sought to establish this exalted claim. What I have shown you is only the pedestal on which the beauty and strength of the Bible rests, the enduring portals which open into the glory that excelleth. The Old Testament shows us the progressive revelation of God to the Jewish people; the New Testament gives us the consummation of that work, the perfect flower of that growth of

5. *Old Faiths in New Light,* pp. 60, 61.

317

centuries. After shadows and hints and refracted lights of prophecy, breaks at last upon the world the Light that lighteth every man! When the fullness of time had come, God sent forth his Son. It was for this that the age-long discipline of this people had been preparing them. True, "He came to his own, and they received him not," but where else in the world would the seed of his kingdom have found any lodgment at all? The multitude rejected him, but there was a remnant who did receive him, and to whom he gave power to become the sons of God. So the word of God, that had been painfully and dimly communicated to the ancient people in laws and ordinances and prophecies, in providential mercies and chastenings, in lives of saints and prophets and martyrs, was now made flesh, and dwelt among men full of grace and truth, and they beheld his glory.

It is here that we find the real meaning of the Bible. "The end," as Canon Mozley has so strongly shown, "is the test of a progressive revelation." Jesus Christ, who is himself the Word, toward whom these laws and prophecies point, and in whom they culminate, is indeed the perfect Revelation of God. From his judgment there is no appeal; at his feet the wisest of us must sit and learn the way of life. With his words all these old Scriptures must be compared; so far as they agree with his teachings we may take them as eternal truth; those portions of them which fall below this standard, we may pass by as a partial revelation upon us no longer binding. He himself has given us, in the Sermon on the Mount, the method by which we are to test the older Scriptures. When we refuse to apply his method and go on to declare every portion of those old records authoritative, we are not honoring him. The mischief and bane of the traditional theory is that it equalizes things which are utterly unlike. When it says that "all the books of the Scripture are equally inspired; all alike are infallible in what they teach," it puts the Gospels on the same level with Deuteronomy and Ecclesiastes and Esther. The effect of this is not to lift the latter up, but to drag the former down. They are not on the same level; it is treason to our Master Christ to say that they are alike; the one is as much higher than the other as the heavens are higher than the earth.

It is here, then, in the simple veracious records that bring before us the life of Christ, that we have the very Word of God. Whatever else the four Gospels may or may not be, they certainly do contain the story of the Life that has been for many centuries the light and the hope of the world. It is the same unique Person who stands before us in every one of these narratives,—

"So meek, forgiving, godlike, high,
So glorious in humility."

What fault has criticism to find with this Life? What word or deed is here ascribed to him that is not worthy of him, that is not like him? Is it any wonder to us when we read this record through, that the guileless Nathanael cried out as he communed with him, "Rabbi, thou art the Son of God, thou art the King of Israel."

If, then, the New Testament gives us the artless record of the life and words of this divine Person, the Son of God and the Saviour of the world; if it brings Him before us and manifests to us, so far as words can do it, his power and his glory; if it shows us how, by bearing

witness to the truth in his life and in his death, he established in the world the kingdom which for long ages had
been preparing; if it makes known to us the messages he
brought of pardon and salvation; if it gives us the record of the planting and training of his church in the early
ages, is there any need that I should go about to praise
and magnify its worth to the children of men? If light is
worth anything to those who sit in darkness, or hope to
those who are oppressed with tormenting doubt; if wisdom is to be desired by those who are in perplexity, and
comfort by those who are in trouble, and peace by those
whose hearts are full of strife, and forgiveness by those
who bear the burden of sin; if strength is a good gift to
the weak, and rest to the weary, and heaven to the dying,
and the eternal life of God to the fainting soul of man,
then the book that tells us of Jesus Christ and his salvation is not to be compared with any other book on earth
for preciousness; it is the one book that every one of us
ought to know by heart.

The value of the Bible, the greatness of the Bible, are in
this Life that it discloses to us. "It is upon Jesus," says a
modern rationalist, "that the whole Bible turns. In this
lies the value, not only of the New Testament, a great
part of which refers to him directly, but of the Old Testament as well." Rationalist though he is, no man could
have stated the truth more clearly. "It is upon Jesus that
the whole Bible turns." The Old Testament shows us the
way preparing by which the swift feet of the messengers
approach that tell us of his coming; the New Testament
lifts the veil and bids us, Behold the man! The Bible is of
value to us, just in proportion as it helps us to see him, to
know him, to trust him. You may have a cast-iron theory

of inspiration with every joint riveted; you may believe in the infallible accuracy of every vowel point and every punctuation mark; but if the Bible does not bring you into a vital union with Jesus Christ, so that you have his mind and follow in his footsteps, it profiteth you nothing. And if, by your study of it, you are brought into this saving fellowship, your theories of inspiration will take care of themselves.

I fear that we do not always comprehend the fact that it is this divine Life shining out of its pages that makes the Bible glorious. We strain our eyes so much in verifying commas, and in trying to prove that the dot of a certain i is not a fly-speck, that we fail to get much impression of the meaning or the beauty of the Saviour's life. See those two critics, with their eyes close to the wonderful "Ecce Homo" of Correggio, disputing whether there is or is not a visible stitch in the garment of Christ that ought to be seamless. How red their faces; how hot their words! Stand back a little, brothers! look away, for a moment, from the garment's seam; let the infinite pain and the infinite pity and the infinite yearning of that Face dawn on you for a moment, and you will cease your quarreling. So, not seldom, do the idolaters of the letter wholly miss the meaning of the sacred book, and remain in mournful ignorance of him who himself is the Word.

There are those to whom the view of the Bible presented in these chapters seems not only inadequate but destructive. "If the Bible is not infallible," they say, "it is no more than any other book; we have no further use for it." In one of the leading church reviews I find these words, the joint utterance of two eminent American theologians: "A proved error in Scripture contradicts not only our doctrine but the Scripture's claims, and therefore its inspiration in making those claims."[6] A proved error in Scripture stamps the book as fraudulent and worthless! Worthless it is then! Proved errors there are, scores of them. It is fatuity, it is imbecility, to deny it. And every man who can find an error in these old writings has the warrant of these teachers for throwing the book away. Tens of thousands of ingenuous and fair-minded men have taken the word of such teachers, and have thrown the book away. May God forgive the folly of these blind guides!

But what stupid reasoning is this! "If the Bible is not infallible, it is worthless." Your watch is not infallible; is it therefore worthless? Your physician is not infallible; are his services therefore worthless? Your father is not infallible; are his counsels worthless? Will you say that the moment you discover in him an error concerning any subject in heaven or on earth, that moment you will refuse to listen to his counsel? The church of God is not infallible, and never was, whatever infatuated ecclesiastics may have claimed for it; are its solemn services and its inspiring labors and its uplifting fellowships worthless?

"A ship on a lee shore," says one, "in the midst of a driving storm, throws up signal rockets or fires a gun for a pilot. A white sail emerges from the mist; it is the pilot boat. A man climbs on board, and the captain gives to him the command of the ship. All his orders are obeyed implicitly. The ship, laden with a precious cargo and hundreds of human lives, is confided to a rough-looking man whom no one ever saw before, who is to guide them

---

6. *Presbyterian Review*, vol. ii. p. 245.

through a narrow channel, where to vary a few fathoms to the right or left will be utter destruction. The pilot is invested with absolute authority as regards bringing the vessel into port."[7] Is this because the man is infallible, because he has never been detected in holding an erroneous opinion? Doubtless any of these intelligent passengers could find out, by half an hour's conversation with him, that his mind was full of crass ignorance and misconception. And nobody supposes that he is infallible, even as a pilot. He may make a mistake. What then? Will these passengers gather around the captain, and demand that he be ordered down from the bridge and thrown overboard if he disobeys? Will they say, "A pilot who is not on all subjects infallible is one whom we will not trust?" No; they believe him to be, not omniscient, but competent and trustworthy, and a great burden is lifted from their hearts when they see him take command of the ship. On all other subjects besides religion, people are able to exercise their common sense; why can they not use a modicum of the same common sense when they come to deal with religious truth?

It is not true, as a matter of fact, that the Bible no longer has any value for those who have ceased to hold the traditional view of it. Not seldom, indeed, those who have been compelled by overwhelming evidence to relinquish the traditional view have been driven by the natural reaction against it to undervalue the Bible, and even to treat it with contempt and bitterness; but even some of these have come back to it again and have found in it, when they studied it with open mind, more truth than they ever

---

7. *Orthodoxy; its Truths and Errors,* by James Freeman Clarke, p. 114.

before had known. Let me cite an extreme case. I could take you to a society of free-thinkers, consisting of people who have long been outspoken in their rejection of all the doctrines of historical Christianity, many of whom formerly flouted the Bible as a book of fables, but who are now studying it diligently week by week, in the most sympathetic spirit. They do not now accept its supernaturalism; but they believe that as a manual of conduct, as a guide to life, it excels all other books. The young people of their Sunday-school are told that the Bible is not like other books; that the men who wrote it knew more about the human soul and its struggles and its aspirations after good than any other men who ever lived; and they are besought to attend, most carefully, to the lessons of life which this ancient book teaches. I should like to take some of our ultra orthodox friends, who are pettishly crying out that the Bible, if not infallible, is good for nothing, and set them down for a Sunday or two in the midst of this free-thinking Sunday-school; they might learn some things about its value that they never knew before.

This incident ought to be of service, also, to those who, having discovered that the Bible contains human elements, have rushed to the conclusion that it is no more than any other book, and who, although they do not cast it from them, hold it off, at arm's length, as it were, and maintain toward it an attitude of critical superiority. Even these free-thinkers treat it more fairly. They are learning to approach it with open mind; they sit down before it with reverent expectancy. The Bible has a right to this sympathetic treatment. It is not just like other books. Do not take my word for this; listen rather to the testimony of one who was known, while he was alive, as the arch-heretic of New England:—

"This collection of books has taken such a hold on the world as no other. The literature of Greece, which goes up like incense from that land of temples and heroic deeds, has not half the influence of this book, from a nation alike despised in ancient and in modern times. It is read of a Sabbath in all the ten thousand pulpits of our land. In all the temples of religion is its voice lifted up week by week. The sun never sets on its gleaming page. It goes equally to the cottage of the plain man and the palace of the king. It is woven into the literature of the scholar, and colors the talk of the street. The bark of the merchant cannot sail the sea without it; no ships of war go to the conflict, but the Bible is there. It enters men's closets; mingles in all their grief and cheerfulness of life. The affianced maiden prays God in Scripture for strength in her new duties; men are married by Scripture. The Bible attends them in their sickness, when the fever of the world is on them. The aching head finds a softer pillow when the Bible lies underneath. The mariner escaping from shipwreck clutches this first of his treasures and keeps it sacred to God. It goes with the peddler in his crowded pack; cheers him at eventide when he sits down dusty and fatigued; brightens the freshness of his morning face. It blesses us when we are born, gives names to half Christendom; rejoices with us; has sympathy for our mourning; tempers our grief to finer issues. It is the better part of our sermons. It lifts man above himself; our best of uttered prayers are in its storied speech, wherewith our fathers and the patriarchs prayed. The timid man, about awaking from this dream of life, looks through the glass of Scripture and his eye grows bright; he does not fear to stand alone, to tread the way unknown and distant, to take the death angel by the hand and bid farewell to wife and babes and home. Men rest on this their dearest hopes; it tells them of God and of his blessed Son, of earthly duties and of heavenly rest."[8]

This is not mere rhetoric; it is simplest truth of human experience. How is it possible for any man to treat this book just as he would any other book? He ought to come to its perusal with the expectation of finding in it wisdom and light and life. He must not stultify his reason and stifle his moral sense when he reads it; he must keep his mind awake and his conscience active; but there is treasure here if he will search for it; search he must, yet the only right attitude before it is one of reverence and trust. Any man of ripe wisdom and high character, who has been known to you all your life, whose judgment you have verified, whose goodness you have witnessed and experienced, commands your respectful attention the moment he begins to speak. You do not believe him to be infallible, but you listen to what he says with trustfulness; you expect to find it true. To say that you listen to him as you do to every other man is not the fact; the posture of your mind in his presence is different from that in which you stand before most other men. It ought to be. He has gained, by his probity, the power to speak to you with authority. The Bible has gained the same power. You do not use it fairly when you use it as you do every other book.

There is the nation's flag proudly flying from the summit of the Capitol. It may be a banner that was

---

8. Theodore Parker, *Discourses on Religion*.

borne upon the battlefield, decorated now with well-mended rents, and with stains of carnage. "Behold it!" cries the idolater. "It is absolutely faultless in perfection and beauty! There is not a blemish on its folds, there is not an imperfection in its web; every thread in warp and woof is flawless; every seam is absolutely straight; every star is geometrically accurate; every proportion is exact; the man who denies it is a traitor!"

"Absurd!" replies the iconoclast. "See the holes and the stains; there is not one straight seam; there is not a star that is in perfect form; ravel it, and you will find no thread in warp or woof that is flawless; nay, you may even discover shreds of shoddy mixed with the fine fibre. Your flag is nothing more than any other old piece of bunting, and if you think it is, you are a fool."

Nay, good friends, you are both wrong. The blemishes are there; it would be fanaticism to deny them; and he who says that no man can be loyal to the nation who will not profess that this banner is immaculate is setting up a fantastic standard of patriotism. But, on the other hand, this flag is something more than any other old piece of bunting, and he who thinks it something more is not a fool. It is the symbol of liberty; it is the emblem of sovereignty; it is the pledge of protection; it is the sign and guarantee of justice and order and peace. What memories cluster round it, of dauntless heroism, and holy sacrifice, and noble consecration! What hopes are gleaming from its stars and fluttering in its shining folds—hopes of a day when wars shall be no more and all mankind shall be one brotherhood! The man to whom the flag of his country is no more than any other piece of weather-beaten bunting is a man without a country.

Is not my parable already interpreted? Are not the idolaters who make it treason to disbelieve a single word of the Bible, and the iconoclasts who treat it as nothing better than any other book, equally far from the truth? Is it not the part of wisdom to use the book rationally, but reverently; to refrain from worshiping the letter, but to rejoice in the gifts of the Spirit which it proffers? The same divine influence which illumines and sanctifies its pages is waiting to enlighten our minds that we may comprehend its words, and to prepare our hearts that we may receive its messages. Some things hard to understand are here, but the Spirit of truth can make plain to us all that we need to know. No man wisely opens the book who does not first lift up his heart for help to find in it the way of life, and to him who studies it in this spirit it will show the salvation of God.

www.ingramcontent.com/pod-product-compliance
Lightning Source LLC
Chambersburg PA
CBHW030911090426

42737CB00007B/157